Gao Xingjian
and
Transcultural
Chinese Theater

Gao Xingjian and Transcultural Chinese Theater

Sy Ren Quah

University of Hawai'i Press
Honolulu

© 2004 University of Hawai'i Press
All rights reserved
Printed in the United States of America
09 08 07 06 05 04   6 5 4 3 2 1

Library of Congress Cataloging-in-Publication Data
Quah, Sy Ren.
  Gao Xingjian and transcultural Chinese theater / Sy Ren Quah.
    p. cm.
  Includes bibliographical references and index.
    ISBN 0-8248-2629-9 (hardcover : alk. paper)
  1. Gao, Xingjian—Criticism and interpretation. 2. Theater.
3. Theater—China. I. Title.
PL2869.O128Z8 2004
895.1'252—dc22

                                    2003026804

University of Hawai'i Press books are printed on acid-free
paper and meet the guidelines for permanence and durability
of the Council on Library Resources.

Designed by the University of Hawai'i Press Production Staff

Printed by The Maple-Vail Book Manufacturing Group

*This book is dedicated
to the memory of my mother
Kao Seng Kow*

Contents

Acknowledgments

This book started as a doctoral dissertation at the University of Cambridge. My deepest gratitude is to Susan Daruvala, a most inspiring and caring teacher whom I am truly privileged to have had as my research supervisor. She not only unwearyingly guided me in intellectual inquiry, but also provided moral support when it was needed. I will always remember my wonderful, idyllic Cambridge days with Susan at the center of the picture.

I am very grateful to Gao Xingjian, who, with immense hospitality and patience, granted me two extended interviews in May 1998 in Paris. He also generously provided me with copies of his recent plays as well as writings on his works, which were not easily available then. Immediately after completing my Ph.D., I visited him again in the winter of 1999. We had long, enjoyable conversations, and I saw a French production of his *Dialogue and Rebuttal* in Bordeaux, which was a most memorable experience. Merely a month later, having returned to Singapore, I received a call from Mabel Lee, translator of Gao's novels. As it turned out, she had read my dissertation at Gao's home in Paris and wanted to meet me in Singapore on her way back to Sydney. I am extremely grateful to her, as she has since been most encouraging and supportive of the publication of this book.

There are many more people to whom I am indebted. My degree examiners Michel Hockx and Sally Church, the first persons (besides Susan) to have read the earliest version of this book in its entirety, gave me invaluable comments and tremendous encouragement. Sally Church, Rajesh Krishnamuti, and Lim Song Hwee went through parts of the book to make it more readable. Editors Kirk Denton, Kwok-kan Tam, Leo Suryadinata, and Zhang Aidong provided critical feedback on earlier versions of chapters submitted for publication, which has helped my later revision. I am also grateful for comments by all the anonymous reviewers who read my manuscript, whether in part or in whole. I thank Lin Kehuan and Lu Min for sharing their views on contemporary Chinese theater when I interviewed them in Beijing in May 1999 and Xu Ping, who helped me procure video recordings of productions of Gao's earlier plays by Beijing People's Art Theatre. Thanks also to Ma Sen, Seto Hirosh, Chin Chung-lien, Ng How Wee, and Lee Huay Leng for assisting in gathering materials. Without the help of Henry Y. H. Zhao, I would not have made contact with Gao.

Earlier versions of some material in this book appeared as articles in *Asian Culture, Modern Chinese Literature and Culture,* and *Nantah Journal of Chinese Language and Culture,* and in Kwok-kan Tam's edited volume *Soul of Chaos: Critical Perspectives on Gao Xingjian* (2001).

My postgraduate study in Cambridge would not have been possible without full sponsorship from the National Institute of Education, Nanyang Technological University, Singapore. In this respect, I am thankful to Eddie Kuo Chen-Yu, Chew Cheng Hai, Leo Tan Wee Hin, and Koh Tai Ann for their support and recommendation. For students of modern Chinese literature, Cambridge has always been a dreamland inspired by the works of Xu Zhimo and Chen Zhifan. For me, the tranquility of Cambridge proved to be a perfect setting for reflection, writing, and living. Chen, incidentally, was a member of St. Edmund's College, with which I am affiliated. The reality of Cambridge life was in fact no great departure from the imagined, and I am grateful for the company of my fellow Cantabrigians, especially Lim Song Hwee and Raymond Oh, as well as Chiu Wei Li, an Oxonian occasionally seeking refuge in Cambridge.

Many friends have been supportive of my work. Lee Guan Kin has long encouraged me to pursue an academic career. Lim Song Hwee never fails to challenge me intellectually and always gives me worthy advice when I am at a crossroad. I especially enjoy the many exchanges with Ng How Wee, both in person and in writing, and he has enriched my imagination and worldview. Haresh Sharma and Alvin Tan have not only taught me what good theater is, they have also been there to share my moments of sorrow and happiness. The late Kuo Pao Kun, a most respected dramatist and intellectual in Singapore, had been a great inspiration to me as a mentor and a friend. It is unfortunate that, having seen this book in its dissertation form, he is unable to see it published.

Finally, I want to thank my sister Quah Sy Yi for her continual support both moral and financial, and my father Quah Chao Ping, who relieves me of worries by taking care of household matters. My biggest regret is that my mother Kao Seng Kow passed away while I was pursuing my studies in Cambridge. Her diligence as an educator and her passion for life will be inscribed in my memory forever.

Gao Xingjian, the Nobel Prize, and Transcultural Theater

Exiled Playwright and Nobel Laureate

In his now-classic book *The Theatre of the Absurd,* Martin Esslin pursues a detailed study of a generation of innovative and provocative dramatists in the 1950s and 1960s. From the experiences of those he calls the Absurdists, Esslin concludes: "New theatrical devices, new approaches to language, character, plot and construction of plays are necessary to the continued vitality of the theatre. Surprise, shock, the gasp of incomprehension are among the most powerful weapons in the armoury of the stage" (1991:430–431). Esslin's insightful analysis of these European dramatists is indeed a fitting description of the Chinese-French playwright Gao Xingjian (b. 1940) and his theater.

The first Nobel Laureate in literature (2000) to write primarily in the Chinese language, Gao Xingjian is one of the most controversial figures, both artistically and politically, in contemporary China. Between 1982 and 1985, three of his plays were staged by the Beijing People's Art Theatre—the most renowned theater company in the capital of the People's Republic, with a dominantly realist tradition—where he served as a professional playwright. However, none of Gao's plays had conformed to the realist tradition. Each one of these plays in fact shocked Chinese audiences and critics in its own way—aesthetically and ideologically. What Esslin called "the gasp of incomprehension," essentially an expression of fear and insecurity when one is faced with vigorous challenges, could be the latent force underlying the abundant condemnation targeted at Gao. Gao was not a martyr; neither did he aspire to be one. Twice he fled from apparent danger of suppression and persecution—to the remote hinterland of southwestern China in 1985 and then to the West, for good, in 1987.

At a time when realism was the officially sanctioned mode and ideology of theatrical representation—and in fact for all literary and artistic representation—as it had been in China since the early 1940s, Gao's nonconformist approach to theater appeared to be both novel in form and subversive in ideology. Gao and his collaborators cautiously attempted to avoid accusations that charged them as ideologically subversive by strictly containing any explanation of their works within the sphere of artistic experimentation (Gao 1998a). However, their experimentation not only provided an alternative to formal representation but also led audiences to adopt different perspectives in their reflection of the issues represented in the theater.

It is difficult to imagine how, after realism—and later socialist realism—had dominated artistic representation as well as the mindset of artists in China for forty years, Chinese writers and artists were able to break away from this tradition. In this respect, the Theater of the Absurd, especially that of the Irish playwright Samuel Beckett (1906–1989), was a great inspiration to Gao, who had access to it owing to his knowledge of French language and literature. These Western dramatists, their works and their aesthetics—little if not totally unknown to Chinese playwrights or audiences in the immediate post–Cultural Revolution years—offered a critical alternative approach to the current state of theatrical practice as well as to traditional Chinese theatrical aesthetics. The innovative and reflective spirit of dramatists such as Beckett formed the bedrock of Gao's continuous bold experimentation. In his later, postexile works completed while he lived in Paris, it is apparent that this spirit remains one of the key motivations of Gao's dramatic creation.

After Gao left China in 1987, the heated controversies that his plays had stirred up faded. When I interviewed scholars of contemporary drama in Beijing in 1999,[1] they concluded without hesitation that while Gao was one of the central figures in Chinese experimental theater in the mid-1980s, his influence had subsided to the extent that his name would not even be known to students of drama studies today. This obscurity is largely attributable to the fact that, after he vehemently denounced the Chinese government for its crackdown in Tiananmen Square (1989), both the publication and the performance of his works were banned in China. Meanwhile, however, there has been continued interest in Gao in Taiwan and Hong Kong,[1] more or less confined within academic circles.

It was little wonder that when the Swedish Academy announced Gao as the winner of the Nobel Prize in Literature in 2000, critics and journalists were bewildered.[3] It was especially baffling to people in mainland China, who had long hoped to be connected with the (Western) world, and one way would be to have a Chinese writer awarded the Nobel Prize in Literature. Those who had previously heard Gao's name were equally surprised, as the Gao they knew was a playwright who staged a few experimental works in the 1980s that by now were mostly forgotten.

Controversy surrounded Gao's identity. Upon hearing the news that Gao was awarded the Nobel prize, the Chinese Association of Writers maintained that Gao is a French writer, not a Chinese writer (Gao had acquired French citizenship), and that his winning of the prize had nothing to do with China. The Chinese Foreign Ministry criticized the Nobel committee for being politically motivated. In contrast, the news was enthusiastically embraced in Taiwan, where Gao was praised for having made Chinese people around the world proud (*Lianhe bao*, October 13 and 14, 2000). The opening line of the Swedish Academy's English-language press release says, "The Nobel Prize in Literature for 2000 goes to the *Chinese* writer Gao Xingjian" (italics mine), while the same organization gives Gao's nationality as French. The Chinese-language press release clarifies that Gao is a *"Zhongwen zuojia,"* literally a "Chinese-language writer," whereas the word "Chinese" in English could mean both "Chinese national" and "Chinese language." The ambiguity has added some dramatic effect to the controversy about Gao's identity, especially for those who have chosen to use the occasion to make a political statement.

Whether Gao has been overtly political in his works is debatable. He has always reserved his right to make political commentaries, although he never wanted to be involved in political activism (Gao 1996a:94). I would argue that Gao's works cannot be divorced from the political contexts in which they were produced. Even a play like *Bayue xue* (August snow; written in 1997, first published in 2000), the life story of a Chan Buddhist patriarch living in seventh-century China,[4] seemingly free of contemporary politics, can be read as a political allegory. It is indeed a traditional practice of Chinese intellectuals and writers to, as the old Chinese idiom says, use the past as a criticism of the present *(jie gu yu jin).*[5]

The Swedish Academy is not devoid of political inclination, either, as is clearly suggested in the Nobel diploma presented to Gao. With a piece of artwork on one side and the award citation on the other, the Nobel diploma is individually designed to capture the achievements of the laureate. In Gao's diploma, there are thirteen rows of eight neatly arranged red, five-pointed stars against a black background. The center of the artwork is superimposed with a white horizontal stroke, resembling the Chinese character *yi* (one) in running-style calligraphy. The horizontal stroke could be a symbol of the Daoist notion of *taiji*—from which the universe is born—representing Gao's artistic world and its genesis, which is profoundly influenced by the philosophies of Daoism and Chan Buddhism. The rows of orderly red stars, however, clearly suggest the communist regime in China. Does the design signify Gao's art and philosophy breaking away from the oppression of the government of the Chinese Communist Party and that, now liberated, Gao occupies a higher moral ground than the regime that ruled over his past?

It is indeed important to understand Gao Xingjian's past before studying his theater. To put Gao's art and thought in perspective, I will begin with a biographical account of Gao, with an emphasis on his encounter with theater and the development of his views on cultural, social, and political issues.[6]

The Early Years

Gao Xingjian was born in Ganzhou, Jiangxi province, on January 4, 1940. His ancestors were wealthy salt merchants living in Taizhou, Jiangsu province, until his great-grandfather used up almost his entire family fortune trying unsuccessfully to buy an official post. After the decline of the family, both his grandfather and his father worked for the Bank of China. Gao's mother graduated from a missionary school and later became an active member of the Chinese Young Christians Association Salvation Drama Troupe. Gao had, as he recalled, a comparatively stable childhood filled with happy memories, despite escalating warfare and the turbulence of the period—first the war against the Japanese invasion (1937–1945) and then the civil war between the Guomindang and the Chinese Communist Party (1945–1949). Because his father was a senior bank officer, the family's social circle included Chinese men and women who had some knowledge of Western culture, and English was occasionally used at social functions. Thus, as a child, Gao was exposed to Western influences.

Gao's encounters with drama began very early. After his parents married, his mother had to quit the traveling Salvation Drama Troupe, but her enthusiasm for drama remained. At home, she would sometimes write a short script and perform it to entertain herself. When Gao was older, under her direction, he would perform with his younger brother to their only audience, his mother. As a young teenager, Gao started to watch *jingju* (Peking opera) with his uncle,[7] who was a great *jingju* fan, and his father, although Gao's serious interest in traditional Chinese theater did not develop until much later.

Before 1951, because of poor health, Gao did not receive any formal education. After the family moved to Nanjing that year, he joined the last year of primary school and went on to Nanjing Number 10 Secondary School, which was formerly affiliated with the missionary-run University of Nanking. There Gao went through six years of education, which later proved critical to the development of his artistic inclination. The school had inherited the liberal atmosphere of missionary schools, and its teaching staff was competent. While Gao began to learn the violin at home, at school he also picked up oil painting and sculpture under the guidance of the renowned artist Yun Zongying. Gao's talent in painting prompted Yun to recommend him to the Central Academy of Fine Arts. The idea, however, was vehemently opposed by his mother, who had observed that, after the establishment of the People's Republic, the only job for artists was painting propaganda posters. What Gao gained from his early immersion in music and painting benefited him for the rest of his life. The most important of his theatrical concepts—multivocality *(duo shengbu)*—is borrowed from music. Moreover, after going into exile, he earned his living as a painter rather than a writer.

Before graduating from secondary school, Gao had to decide on his course of study at the university. His aspiration was to become a writer or to work in the theater. His first idea was to study Chinese literature, but he soon abandoned this option as he realized that it would not help him become a writer upon graduation. He also considered doing theater studies. However, he could not major in directing, as it required three years of work experience in a professional drama company; neither could he major in acting, as he was two centimeters short of the prescribed height of 1.7 meters. His final decision was an incidental one. Upon reading an article about the romantic and inspirational lifestyle of Parisian artists in the early twentieth century, Gao decided to read French literature and, in 1957, was offered a place at the Beijing Institute of Foreign Languages.

It was a year when numerous political movements followed one another in quick succession. As an undergraduate, Gao experienced for the first time a spiritually and intellectually repressive atmosphere. Students were swamped with materials relating to the antirightist campaign and were required to read works by Marx, Lenin, and Mao. Apathetic to political activities, Gao devoted most of his time to reading extracurricular books. Although there was already rigorous censorship of English materials, censorship of French materials was looser, and these were readily accessible to Gao. From the French editions of *Moscow News* and *Soviet Literature*, he read about the anti-Stalin and antitotalitarian movements in the Soviet Union that were intensely active in the 1950s. His readings made him more depressed about the situation in China.

As an undergraduate, Gao became actively involved in dramatic activities. In 1960, with some fellow students, Gao founded a drama society named "Seagull" in which he served as playwright, director, and literary advisor. He began to read books by the Russian director Konstantin Stanislavsky (1863–1938) and conducted workshops for members of the society. Later, he extended his reading to Evgeny Vakhtangov (1883–1923), Vsevolod Meyerhold (1874–1940), and Vladimir Mayakovsky (1893–1930). Eventually, he came into contact with the works of the German dramatist Bertolt Brecht (1898–1956), which would be important to the formation of Gao's own dramaturgy during the 1980s. The plays the society produced included *Uncle Vanya* by Anton Chekov (1860–1904), *The Good Person of Szechwan* by Brecht, and *The Center-Forward Died at Dawn* by the Argentine playwright Agustín Cuzzani (1924–1987). With the last, an avant-garde, absurdist-like play, Gao experimented for the first time with an empty-stage setting, which was a bold step that went beyond the realist conventions dominating the Chinese stage at the time.

Besides carrying out theatrical experimentation, Gao and his society members also watched many performances by the Beijing People's Art Theatre and the National Youth Theatre, the two most renowned theater companies in the Chinese capital. Gao was fortunate to have the opportunity to attend rehearsals at the National Youth Theatre and to receive personal guidance from its resident director, Deng Zhiyi, who happened to be a cousin of his schoolmate. In the rehearsal room, Gao learned the practical aspects of a play's production that were unattainable merely from reading books. One piece of advice from Deng that Gao never forgot was this: "A play is born in the rehearsal room rather than in the script. You have to be familiar with the theater before you write a play." By the time he graduated from university, Gao had written two stage plays and a screenplay. However, Deng advised him not to send them to literary journals for publication as they might invite trouble. Those plays were modern and revolutionary, but they might have appeared antirevolutionary at that time because they did not conform to realist conventions. Recognizing Gao's talents, Deng promised to help Gao attain a job in the National Youth Theatre.

Gao's initial hope of becoming a professional playwright, however, was not realized. Upon his graduation in 1962, he was assigned to work as a translator in the Foreign Language Bureau. Uninterested in translation work, Gao spent most of his spare time writing plays and stories, often working through the night. When the Cultural Revolution began in 1966, Gao had to burn all his manuscripts, including ten plays, an unfinished novel, and numerous poems and notes, which weighed almost forty kilograms in total. In 1969, Gao entered the cadre school. He soon realized that he was in tremendous danger of political attack in the cadre school, and he asked to be transferred to the countryside. In retrospect, he described this experience as fleeing: "A person is just like a little bug: it is impossible for him to confront the violence of a political regime. The only way out is to flee." In 1970, he began six years of rural life, first in the province of Jiangxi and later in Anhui.

During the years when he was lying low in rural villages, Gao began to write again, as he was engulfed by a deep sense of loneliness. Revealing his feelings and thoughts in conversation with others would leave evidence that could bring about subsequent attacks on him. Thus, the only person he could talk to safely was himself, and Gao started to acquire the habit of self-monologue, which he deemed essential to maintaining a person's consciousness: "The reason I am still alive is because I can carry on self-monologues. When ideological remolding goes on to the extent that self-monologue is extinct and you cannot hear your own voice, then you have already been thoroughly remolded." Unsurprisingly, self-monologue later became Gao's unique way of writing plays. He would use two tape recorders, one to play music to create a suitable mood and the other to record the dialogues that he recited verbally and spontaneously. He would later transcribe the recording, which usually formed part of his plays.

After China and the United States began to resume diplomatic relations following Richard Nixon's visit to China in 1972, the need for China to establish communications with the West increased. In late 1975, Gao was recalled to work in the Foreign Language Bureau, where he came into contact for the first time with the works of Samuel Beckett, which were to have a great influence on him. In order to improve the standards of the Chinese translators, a French Embassy official was invited to conduct lectures on modern French literature. The first text chosen was Beckett's *Wait-*

ing for Godot. Gao was fascinated by the Absurdist play and seized on the opportunity to borrow more works by Beckett from the French Embassy's library through the lecturer. Besides Beckett, Gao also read voraciously plays by Jean Genet (1910–1986) and Eugène Ionesco (1909–1994). Following his earlier encounter with Brecht's works, Gao was excited for the second time by a theater that subverted realist conventions. This time the subversion was both formal and ideological.

In 1979, Gao visited France with a delegation of Chinese writers, serving as the interpreter for the famous writer Ba Jin (b. 1904). Although this was his first trip to Europe, the Western experience did not surprise him, as he had read about the West in literary works and news reports, thanks to his translation job. In fact, it was the French writers who were surprised by his knowledge of Beckett and other modernist writers. Nevertheless, watching theater performances and talking to artists in France proved to be a refreshing experience for him.

After he returned later in the same year, Gao's first literary work, a novella titled *Hanye de xingchen* (Stars on a cold night), was published in *Huacheng,* a literary journal. From the end of the Cultural Revolution in 1976, Gao had begun writing prolifically, but his modernist works were perceived as "not storylike" and rejected by editors of many literary journals. When asked to write about the writing of modern fiction, he published a series of articles called *Xiandai xiaoshuo jiqiao chutan* (A preliminary discussion of the techniques of modern fiction). These articles were later printed twice as a collection and received enthusiastic responses. However, they also invited severe criticism, as Gao was accused of subverting realist tradition. Fortunately, veteran writers such as Ba Jin and Xia Yan (1900–1995) came to his rescue, and Gao managed to stay out of trouble. As it turned out, this was only the beginning of the political oppression Gao was to suffer later. In the same year, Gao was transferred to the Writers' Association in Beijing and traveled again to France and Italy, this time in the capacity of a writer.

The Mature Years

The turning point in Gao's life came in 1981, when he was transferred to the Beijing People's Art Theatre and became a resident playwright there. He was immediately asked by Yu Shizhi, vice president of the theater, to write a play. Within a week, he produced *Chezhan* (The bus stop). However, as the "Anti–Bourgeois Liberalization Campaign" was just beginning, the play, with its distinct Absurdist characteristics, had to be shelved. Gao was then requested to write another play in a more realistic style. With the help of Liu Huiyuan, a young man who used to work on a cargo train, Gao wrote a play about a train robbery, *Juedui xinhao* (Alarm signal).[8] Although this time he was cautious about using nonrealist modes of representation, the play was not approved for public performance by the Beijing People's Art Theatre Party committee because of its ambiguity in dealing with sensitive issues such as unemployment and China's future. Nevertheless, with Yu Shizhi's personal support, the play went on to rehearsal and was initially scheduled for an internal trial performance.

Upon reading *Alarm Signal*, Lin Zhaohua, a young director of the Beijing People's Art Theatre who had never directed a play on his own, was enthusiastic about the innovative ideas in Gao's play and volunteered to work with Gao. Lin was both well-trained in directing and open-minded toward new dramatic concepts. They formed a strong team as they exchanged their knowledge about theater and explored new representational modes. Lin became the sole director of all Gao's plays produced in China from 1982 to 1985. To a certain extent, the theatrical innovations of Gao's plays were a result of this collaboration, which also led Lin to become the most prominent director in Chinese experimental theater well into the 1990s.

Alarm Signal premiered in November 1982. In contrast to the suspicious attitude of some of the leaders of the Beijing People's Art Theatre, the play was warmly received by the invited guests, who were theater practitioners and students of drama studies. After each performance, the audience stayed back for the postperformance discussion, which sometimes lasted until after midnight. Reports and reviews in the newspapers were highly positive about the play. In view of the enthusiastic response, censorship was lifted and *Alarm Signal* went on to more than a hundred performances. Soon after, more than ten major drama companies across the country produced the play.

With the overwhelming success of *Alarm Signal*, Gao and Lin began to prepare for the production of *The Bus Stop*, though the Party committee of the Beijing People's Art Theatre still did not approve it for performance. This time, however, Gao attained verbal consent from Cao Yu (1910–1996), a veteran playwright and honorary president of the Beijing People's Art Theatre. In July 1983, Cao Yu came to the dress rehearsal and expressed his support for its public performance. Although *The Bus Stop* also excited the audience, its performance came to an abrupt halt after ten shows in the midst of the Anti–Spiritual Pollution Campaign. It then came under severe criticism and was labeled "anti-Party" and "antisocialist." Gao knew he had to flee from the situation, and, with the help of Yu Shizhi, he left Beijing and began his exile in southwestern China. From his experience in the Cultural Revolution, Gao realized that self-censorship would not necessarily keep him from political oppression and that fleeing was the best way of protecting himself.

During the following five months, from late 1983 to early 1984, Gao traveled through eight provinces and seven nature reserves, covering fifteen thousand kilometers in the Yangtze region. He had in mind collecting materials for his novel *Lingshan* (Soul mountain), which he had wanted to pursue since 1982. On his journey, Gao met anthropologists who were doing research on the primitive culture of ethnic minorities in China, and he was also attracted to the latter's folk arts and religious ceremonies. These encounters, coupled with the ideas of Daoism and Chan Buddhism, in which he was profoundly interested at the time, extended his understanding and perception of Chinese identity, which, in the context of modern China, had been molded predominantly by the urban Confucian literati tradition.

Gao returned to Beijing when the political campaign simmered down in mid-1984. Yu Shizhi again asked Gao to write a play so that Gao could be "rehabilitated." With his rural experiences fresh in his mind, Gao produced *Yeren* (Wild man), a play about the endangered natural environment and disappearing minority cultures, and planned to stage it at the Capital Theatre, the main performance venue of the Beijing People's Art Theatre. Gao's works had always been treated as experimental pieces and were produced in make-do studio spaces. To have a play staged at the Capital Theatre signified that Gao's work had been accepted as part of the Beijing People's Art Theatre tradition. Having acquired full support from the Beijing People's Art Theatre, Gao carried out a large-scale experiment that aimed to offer a totally different theatrical experience from that of existing spoken drama *(huaju)*. He called it "total theater" *(wanquan de xiju)*, which included elements of traditional Chinese theater and songs and dances of ethnic minorities. When *Wild Man* premiered in May 1985, it immediately ignited another round of heated debate, this time directed not at the content but at its mode of representation, which was unprecedented in the strong realist tradition of the Beijing People's Art Theatre.

Soon after the success of *Wild Man*, Gao wrote *Bi'an* (The other shore) in 1986. It was intended primarily to train actors in all-around performing abilities, as Gao and his director Lin Zhaohua had planned to set up an experimental theater workshop. However, neither the realization of *The Other Shore* on the Chinese stage nor the establishment of the workshop materialized.[9] As it turned out, *Wild Man* was Gao's last play to be produced in China before he left his country in 1987.

While Gao was encountering political censorship in China, his works had gained recognition outside the country. As early as 1983, the French newspaper *Le monde* hailed the production of *The Bus Stop* as signifying "the birth of Chinese avant-garde theater," and Geremie Barmé (1983b) published an article in *Renditions* introducing Gao with translated excerpts from *The Bus Stop*. In 1984, *The Bus Stop* was staged by a theater group in Yugoslavia and broadcast on the Hungarian state radio station. Between 1985 and 1986, with invitations from various European governmental and arts organizations, Gao attended seminars and play-reading sessions in Germany, France, Britain, Austria, and Denmark. At the same time, his literary and critical works were translated and his plays produced in many European countries.

In May 1987, Gao was invited by the Morat Institut für Kunst und Kunstwissenschaft of the Federal Republic of Germany to be a visiting artist. The Chinese authorities initially refused him permission to go. Only after intervention by a senior official in the Ministry of Culture was Gao given clearance to leave the country. By this time, Gao realized that he would always be subjected to political attack. When he packed to leave for Germany, Gao had decided not to return to China. Later that year, Gao moved to Paris and made it his new home.

When he accepted the invitation from the Morat Institut, Gao wanted to make sure that he would be able to earn a living as an artist. His Chinese ink paintings were already well known in West Germany, where his first solo exhibition had been held in 1985 at Berliner Kunsterhaus Bethanien. Since then, his paintings had been exhibited throughout Europe and collected by European art galleries and museums. While residing in Paris as a successful painter, free from worry about either material or ideological constraints, Gao continued to write plays and novels.

Most of Gao's later plays were commissioned by arts organizations in Europe. In these plays, he embarked on the exploration of humanistic themes, especially the predicament of alienation in modern times. In 1989, he wrote *Taowang* (Fleeing), based on the Tiananmen Incident of June 4, for an American theater. However, as the parties had different perceptions of the incident, the theater wanted Gao to revise the play, which he refused to do on the principle that freedom of expression was the fundamental right of a writer. *Fleeing* was later premiered by Kungliga Dramatiska Teatern of Sweden in 1992. Another play, *Shengsi jie* (Between life and death) was commissioned by the French Cultural Ministry in 1991 and premiered by the Renaud-Barrault Théâtre in Paris in 1993. The play *Duihua yu fanjie* (Dialogue and rebuttal) was commissioned by France's Maison des Auteurs de Théâtre Étrangers and premiered by Austria's Theater des Augenblicks in Vienna in 1992 with Gao directing the play himself. France's Beaumarchais Foundation commissioned the play *Yeyou shen* (Nocturnal wanderer) in 1993, and it was premiered by Théâtre des Halles in Avignon in 1999. *Zhoumo sichongzou* (Weekend quartet) was commissioned by France's Bibliothèque Municipale de Joué-les-Tours in 1995, and its first public reading was held in 1999 in l'Isle-sur-la-Sorgue. (The premiere was scheduled for September 2003.) Gao's latest play, *Kouwen siwang* (Inquiring death), will be staged in December 2003.

In contrast to the above-mentioned plays, three other projects first conceptualized in China were later completed in Paris. Thematically related to China, these works were part of Gao's attempt to propose an alternative idea of Chineseness. Originally written for the dancer Jiang Qing, *Mingcheng* (The nether city) premiered as a modern dance piece by the Hong Kong Dance Company in 1988. (It was reworked into a full-length play in 1991.) *Shanhaijing zhuan* (The Story of Shanhaijing [*The Classic of Mountains and Seas*]) was originally proposed to the Beijing People's Art Theatre in order to attain approval to leave China in 1987. The play, a large-scale re-presentation of ancient Chinese mythology, was eventually completed in 1993 but remained Gao's only major play to go unstaged. Gao's first novel, *Soul Mountain*, for which he had begun research in 1982, was completed in 1989 and published in Taiwan the following year. With the completion of these three projects, Gao claimed that he wanted to sever his relations with China and begin a new life.

In June 1989, after the crackdown on the student demonstrations in Beijing's Tiananmen Square, Gao voiced a strong protest and formally sought political asylum from the French government. In 1991, at a conference in Stockholm, he announced that he would "never return to a totalitarian China." In 1998, after living in Paris for more than a decade, he became a citizen of France. On the surface, it might seem that Gao is determined to sever all connections with China and is enjoying his newfound freedom to express himself and his humanistic concerns. However, this is not entirely true. Although he claimed, after completing the play *The Story of Shanhaijing*, that "China doesn't even appear in my dreams," the cultural and artistic aspects of China as well as his experiences in China were not completely erased. Gao's recent dramatic work *August Snow* (which premiered in Taipei in December 2002 with Gao as the director) is the life story of the Chinese Chan Buddhist patriarch Huineng (638–713). Another novel, *Yige ren de shengjing* (One man's bible, 1999), is based on his experiences during the Cultural Revolution. As he continues to wander freely in exile, China and Chinese culture remain important sources for his creative efforts.[10]

Transcultural Theater and Its Significance

As evident from the above biographical account, Gao Xingjian not only is at ease in and moves freely between different cultures, he has also reflected profoundly and extensively on cultural issues and the notion of culture. I therefore propose to read Gao's theater as a transcultural entity. I am not so much interested in understanding how different cultures become integrated in the process of Gao's theatrical creation (that is, with issues relating to the creator's intention) as in examining the different cultural elements in his theatrical products; that is to say, I see Gao's theater as a cultural and intellectual sphere in which an interaction of different cultures takes place. An analysis of the representation of cultures and the occurrence of cultural exchanges in Gao's theater requires close attention to how different cultures—Chinese and French, traditional and modern, literati and folk, mainstream and peripheral—carry on a dialogue with each other.

Before I begin such an analysis, the notion of transculturalism should be interrogated. In the fields of theater and performance, is transculturalism a concept of artistic representation or of cultural politics? Does transculturalism merely allude to or actively appropriate a theatrical form originating from a different culture? At what levels do cultural exchanges take place, and what are their effects on the individual culture? When an instance of cultural exchange occurs, is it always possible to detect its occurrence or trace its cultural origins? What is the significance of transculturalism in the present cultural, social, and political contexts of globalization?

Scholars have used different terms to discuss the concept of transculturalism and related notions, such as intercultural and intracultural. For the French scholar Patrice Pavis, intercultural theater "creates hybrid forms drawing upon a more or less conscious and voluntary mixing of performance traditions traceable to distinct cultural areas." In this process of hybridization, the original forms are usually undistinguishable, giving way to the formation of a new aesthetic. The "transcultural," Pavis contends, "transcends particular cultures on behalf of a universality of the human condition," as practitioners of transcultural theater "are concerned with particularities and traditions only in order to grasp more effectively what they have in common and what is not reducible to a specific culture" (1996:6–8, 18–19). Indian theater practitioner and critic Rustom Bharucha, in contrast, disapproves of Pavis' seeming distancing from the realities of history, political struggle, and nationalism, which he condemns as "apolitical," "asocial," and "subtly orientalist." Using examples drawn from the Indian subcontinent, Bharucha instead proposes the notion of "intraculturalism," whose objective is "not to reconstruct 'dying' traditions, but to create new possibilities of interaction and exchange within and across a wealth of 'living' traditions from vastly different time frames and cultural contexts" (2000:27, 62–63).

When using the term "transcultural," I am aware of the inherent cultural politics demonstrated by Bharucha's critique of Pavis. While I agree that certain characteristics may connect two or more different cultures, a recourse to "universality," however, must not subsume the specificities of individual cultures. As I shall elaborate below, Gao's transcultural theater embodies aspects of cultural exchange and integration that are at times collaboratory and at times contradictory, and encompasses the myriad cultural practices and politics highlighted by both Pavis and Bharucha. Moreover, as part of a cultural and intellectual movement at the turn of the twentieth century, modern Chinese theater has always been an alien form of art appropriated from the West, bearing little or no connection to traditional forms of theater in China. To posit Gao's theater as transcultural is to recognize both the historical genesis of modern Chinese theater as well as Gao's indebtedness to that tradition. More important, Gao's theater is not confined to a single area of cultural exchange but, in the context of China and beyond, ambitiously embraces the intercultural, the intracultural, and the transcultural as described above. As such, I have chosen the more generic term "transculturalism" for its inclusiveness.

Intercultural Dialogue as a Discourse of China's Reality

Gao Xingjian first became the center of controversy as a playwright with the production of *Alarm Signal* in 1982 and *The Bus Stop* in the following year. Scholars often regard these early plays together with *Wild Man*, Gao's third and last play staged in China, as his critique of contemporary China.

In the first book-length study in English of Gao's theater, Henry Zhao lists these plays under the category "explorative/socially committed plays" together with *Fleeing*, which was written in 1989 when Gao had already attained freedom of expression in exile. Zhao believes that Gao's works have the explicit intention "to lecture the audience on social issues" and that they became political targets because of their provocative social messages, whereas "whether they were experimental in technique was of secondary importance" (2000:9).[11] Zhao's view is valid in terms of the perception of Gao's plays by the Chinese authorities. I would, however, argue that the relationship of theatrical form to their content and message should not be dismissed. The form of Gao's preexile plays, in particular *The Bus Stop*, is not secondary to its message; on the contrary, the appropriation of a Western theatrical form in these plays has predetermined the nature of their message.

The history of modern Chinese drama is, from its inception, a history of wholesale appropriation of a Western dramatic form. In his seminal account of modern Chinese drama of the twentieth century, the Taiwanese scholar Ma Sen (1991) underlines two periods in which influence from the West was at its height, the May Fourth era and the post-1980s, which he describes as "dual Western tides" *(liangdu xichao)*. Kwok-kan Tam, a Hong Kong scholar, also argues that Western ideologies have dominated modern Chinese drama through the export of dramatic form, proposing the concept of discursive formation for analyzing modern Chinese drama. Tam summarizes its hundred-year history into three discourses: the realist, the socialist-realist, and the postmodernist, all Western-influenced traditions (2000:142).

A common view of both Ma and Tam is that Chinese dramatists have played a significant role in effecting the impact of Western ideologies on modern Chinese drama in the twentieth century through their highly conscious effort in introducing and appropriating Western dramatic forms. These novel and provocative Western forms have clearly directed Chinese audiences to adopt perspectives on social issues that would have been inaccessible had they been represented in a familiar form. In his discussion of *The Bus Stop*, often labeled as the "first Chinese absurdist play," Tam argues that Gao's play begins with a realist setting and gradually unveils a world of absurdity, disorder, and confusion, challenging social unfairness with the use of dramatic techniques such as collage, repetition, juxtaposition, alienated narrator, and objective commentaries. In so doing, Tam contends, Gao has transformed the play into a process in which members of the audience are required to assume an active role in the reflection of their world (2000:142). Evidently, Gao's adoption of an absurdist form is not merely arbitrary but a deliberate effort to provoke the Chinese audience into interrogating their social realities.

Many critics have compared Gao's *The Bus Stop* with Samuel Beckett's *Waiting for Godot*, pointing to similarities such as the theme of waiting and its relationship to the bleak condition of human existence (Tam 1990). Others, however, perceive *The Bus Stop* as a critical-realist play despite its shared formal characteristics with Western avant-garde theater (Tay 1990). Though Gao denies that *The Bus Stop* is a Chinese version of *Waiting for Godot*, many techniques appropriated from the latter are noticeable in the former. These include the use of music as a motif and multivocality (two or more characters speaking at the same time, forming an orchestration of utterance, which I will discuss further in chapter 2).

The social issues represented in *The Bus Stop* were not atypical of China in the 1980s. However, because of the strangeness of the form, the audience experienced a Brechtian alienation effect. In a reversal of how Brecht's concept of the alienation effect *(Verfremdungseffekt)* was inspired when he first saw a performance by the great *jingju* actor Mei Lanfang (1894–1961), Chinese audiences in the 1980s were led to take up a new approach in their perception of familiar issues through a novel Western form. Were it not for the novel absurdist form, the overfamiliar social issues in *The Bus Stop* would have come across as yet another exercise in realist expression. In this case of transcultural interaction, the appropriation of a Western form has distinctively determined the delivery of the content in Gao Xingjian's theater.

Intracultural Dialogue as a Challenge to Cultural Hegemony

Transculturalism in Gao's theater not only expresses itself as an interaction between Chinese and Western cultures (what Pavis calls "interculturalism") but also as an interaction between different cultural systems within the geographical boundaries of China (what Bharucha calls "intraculturalism"). I will focus in this section on the latter and its interrogation of the notions of "Chinese culture" and "Chineseness" by citing three of Gao's plays, namely, *Wild Man*, *The Nether City*, and *The Story of Shanhaijing*. In these plays, Gao gives expression to cultural elements from regions, ethnicities, periods, and ideological systems that do not belong to the mainstream, orthodox, central plains *(zhongyuan)* Confucian culture, thereby using intracultural dialogue to pose a challenge to these cultural hegemonies.

Wild Man is a product of Gao's 1984 escape to the Yangtze region in southwestern China, in which the folk and tribal materials that he collected (the origins of which are noted in the postscript of the dramatic text) are dramatized as a representation of the frontier ethnic peoples and communities. For example, drawing inspiration from folk cultures in Hubei province, "Team of Sisters" comprises songs originally sung at wedding ceremonies in Shennongjia district; the exorcist mask dance is based on Daoist ritual performance and the *nuo* dance of the northeastern region of Gan; and the roof workers' song and the grass-weeding song originate from folk music in the Shennongjia and Jingzhou districts (Gao 1985a:273–274). Admittedly, marginal cultural elements are made central to the theatrical representation of these minority peoples and their cultures. The excavation of these cultural elements from their origins in various rural locales and their transportation to a modern urban environment may be seen as a challenge to cultural hegemony, an example of "the periphery invading the center" *(difang baowei zhongyang)*, even at the risk of exoticizing these minority cultures. *Wild Man* can be seen as an important first step in Gao's experimentation with the representation of peripheral cultures in modern Chinese theater.

The Nether City and *The Story of Shanhaijing* demonstrate Gao's ambition to construct a new, personal version of national mythologies. The dramatic structure and characterization of these plays as well as the playwright's explanatory notes illustrate that Gao's reflection on Chinese cultures is a challenge to mainstream Confucian literati culture. To counter the hegemonic culture of the Yellow River region, Gao upholds the marginalized cultures of the Yangtze region, which have an equally long history; to counter the canonized, dogmatized Confucian culture, Gao valorizes the cultures of secular Daoism and Chan Buddhism, which have strong folk and ritualistic characteristics; to counter the rigidified literati culture, Gao promotes an array of folk arts that are inextricably linked to people's everyday lives. Gao's ambitious version of national mythologies is significant, because not only has he launched a comprehensive challenge to mainstream culture, he has also provided an interactive space for various peripheral cultures in his theater. In this imaginary yet physical space, marginal cultures are given an opportunity to conduct a dialogue among themselves as well as to interact with the mainstream culture represented by the audience and the modern urban environment where Gao's plays are staged.

Gao, therefore, actively appropriates these cultural elements for his theater. In the postscript to *The Nether City,* he explains,

> When this play is being staged, there should be no attempt to represent a verisimilitude of reality. In order to achieve this, the following devices are used: the masks of *nuo* dance, the face painting of *jingju*, the *bianlian* [rapid changing of face masks] technique of *chuanju* [Siquan opera], the tilt-walking of folk performance, drums and gongs, the style of accentuation of traditional Chinese percussion, colorful makeup, acrobatics, and magic tricks. The use of these elaborative elements is to recapture the function of entertainment and play, which is lost in modern theater. (Gao 1995c:68)

This point is reiterated in the postscript to *The Story of Shanhaijing:* "This play is an attempt to return to ancient Chinese dramatic traditions in the search for modern dramatic forms. . . . The writer suggests using something similar to a carnival performance" (Gao 1995d:108).

It is clear that Gao's objective is to create a vibrant form of modern theater by appropriating elements from various cultural systems for which he attempts to provide a discursive space in his theater. Notably, in his selection of cultural elements to be represented, Gao repeatedly stresses the importance of their entertaining, playful, and carnivalesque nature. Gao's emphasis on playfulness is not meant to make his theater appear frivolous; to the contrary, playfulness is valued by Gao precisely because it can serve a serious purpose. For Gao, playfulness is an effective weapon for challenging the oppression of the overly solemn and inviolable mainstream literati culture. As I will illustrate (see chapter 3), Gao's targets include, first, Confucian literati culture, which inculcates traditional ethics and doctrines, and second, the realist and socialist-realist modes of representation, which emphasize the function of social criticism. Gao's deliberate appropriation of these playful cultural elements in his theater marks a clear departure from the self-burdened mainstream tradition that has preoccupied generations of modern Chinese intellectuals.

Transcultural Dialogue in the Form of Theatrical Representation

One key issue in the study of transcultural theater is the comparison between the essences of two or more cultures—or whether such a comparison is possible at all. On the one hand, there may not be a common ground for comparison between cultures with origins in disparate social and historical circumstances. On the other hand, it may be meaningless to make a comparison when the essences of different cultures are stripped down to some elusive basic human nature. Pavis has cautioned about "turning intercultural theatre into a vague terrain for comparing themes or cultural identities" (1996:2). While I do not intend to engage in a philosophical discourse, I do propose to examine how Gao transforms philosophies into forms and uses them in terms of theatrical representation for the contemplation of the modern human condition.

When *Dialogue and Rebuttal* was staged in Vienna, a local newspaper carried the headline "Zen in the Theater of the Absurd" (*Der Standard,* September 24, 1992, cited in Gao 1996a:211). Gao's play, as suggested by the headline, is seen as an integration of two seemingly unrelated entities, both culturally and historically. How, then, does the integration of Chan and the Theater of the Absurd happen, and at what level? Is the integration a result of a similarity in the way the world is represented in their philosophies, or is it based on the comparison between the cosmic view of ancient Chinese Chan and that of modern French Absurdism?

Gao's kinship to the Theater of the Absurd and his deliberate appropriation of its form have been mentioned earlier in this chapter. With respect to Chinese traditions, most scholars concur that Chan Buddhism is an essential component in Gao's thought and theater. Henry Zhao categorizes *Dialogue and Rebuttal* under the label of "Zen/*xieyi* plays,"[12] which he claims to be hitherto unseen in the history of world drama (2000:22). In Zhao's view, the corpus of Gao's later works in this category (which also include *The Other Shore, Between Life and Death, Nocturnal Wanderer,* and *August Snow*) has its aesthetic origin in Chan, while its style of stage representation is *xieyi* (ibid.:156). It is apparent from the title of Zhao's book, *Towards a Modern Zen Theatre,* that he considers Zen (Chan) to be the fundamental spirit of Gao's theater. In his introduction to *The Story of Shanhaijing,* the Chinese scholar-in-exile Liu Zaifu points out that the play is a return to Chan *gongan,*[13] which reflects the predicament of human incommunicability (Gao 1993:9). Liu also claims that, in Gao's plays, the essence of Chan culture has been preserved and developed to its fullest extent (2000:9). Such critics attempt to unveil the spiritual aspects of Gao's theater, tracing the source of his influence to a philosophical if not a religious origin.

The significance of philosophy as a form in Gao's theater, in my view, deserves a deeper understanding. In this respect, the Theater of the Absurd is a good point of departure. In the works of European dramatists such as Samuel Beckett and Jean Genet, Martin Esslin observes, "the Theatre of the Absurd has renounced arguing *about* the absurdity of the human condition; it merely *presents* it in being—that is, in terms of concrete stage images. This is the difference between the approach of the philosopher and that of the poet . . . the difference between theory and experience" (1991:25, italics in original). Esslin's insightful statement reminds the audience of the Theater of the Absurd to pay more attention to the "how" rather than the "what" of theatrical representation. The subject matter is expressed through a unique form that, according to Esslin, "separates the Theatre of the Absurd from the Existentialist theatre" (ibid.). Gao's theater could be studied in a similar way. The form of Chan Buddhism (in this case, Gao's choice is *gongan*) is used as a means for contemplating modern conditions. Represented in the form of *gongan*, the problems of modern existence go through a process analogous to light going through a prism. A study that focuses on form would set out to understand how white light becomes an array of splendid colors. Gao's theater may be seen, on the one hand, as a successor to Chan Buddhism, and on the other, as subverting the philosophy of Chan Buddhism by appropriating its form for the representation of problems that exist in a different temporal and spatial context.

While scholars have analyzed how the philosophy of Chan has influenced the subject matter of Gao's theater, the playwright himself has called attention to his use of Chan as a theatrical form and a mode of representation in *Dialogue and Rebuttal*: "The play's dialogic *form* is inspired by the *gongan* style of question and answer in Chinese Zen Buddhism. The play has no intention of promoting Buddhism, and there is no need for the director to devote his time and effort in expounding the meaning of Zen Buddhism. The author only wants to propose that this kind of dialogue and cross-questioning is capable of being dramatized as a *form* of stage performance" (Gao 1999a:136, italics mine).[14] I have earlier argued, with reference to *The Bus Stop*, that the appropriated absurdist form has transformed the way its content and message are perceived. Similarly, in the case of *Dialogue and Rebuttal*, the form of Chan *gongan* has invariably mediated how modern conditions are represented.

One subject of *Dialogue and Rebuttal* is the problem of verbal communication between two characters, a Man and a Girl. They attempt to speak to each other after they have had a brief sexual encounter only to realize that physical intimacy does not necessarily bring about spiritual closeness. Their failure to communicate also results in their retreating to their respective isolated worlds. Their problem is illustrated in the following scene toward the end of the play:

Man:	*(Talking to himself.)* Behind that door, perhaps there is nothing.
Girl:	*(Asking herself.)* No memories?
Man:	*(Ruminating.)* That door, behind that door, perhaps there is really nothing, do you believe that?
Girl:	No fantasies?
Man:	That's right, there's nothing behind that door, you thought there was something, but there's nothing.
Girl:	And no dreams either?
Man:	*(To audience.)* That door, behind that door, there's nothing.
Girl:	She can't remember anything.
Man:	*(To himself.)* There's absolutely nothing behind that door. *(Giggles.)*
Girl:	*(To audience.)* What happened?
Man:	*(Softly, his back facing Girl.)* That door, behind that door, there is nothing.
Girl:	*(Softly.)* And no memories.
Man:	Absolutely, absolutely.
Girl:	And no fantasies.
Man:	Absolutely, absolutely. *(Nods his head.)*
Girl:	And no dreams either.
Man:	Absolutely, absolutely! *(Becoming contemptuous, his head to one side.)*
Girl:	*(More softly.)* Can't say.
Man:	*(Very softly.)* Why?
Girl:	*(With certainty.)* Can't say.
Man:	Why can't you say it?
Girl:	*(Almost whispering.)* Can't say!

(Gao 1999a:129–130)

From the words of the two characters, it is obvious that they are neither speaking to nor responding to each other, although a dialogue is seemingly going on. The dialogue, according to the playwright, is presented in question-and-answer form, with inspiration from Chan *gongan*. Along with the *gongan* style, the dialogue is imbued with a nonsensical, paradoxical nature, which resonates with the senselessness and futility of the characters' being. In what follows, the dialogic characteristic of *gongan* is incorporated in the monologue:

Girl: She can't believe that she actually said it, she said something that can't be said, but she said it, clearly this can't be said but why did she have to say it? It ought not to be said it can't be said but she said it regardless, it's her misfortune, it's her disaster, it's her sin.
. . .

Her sin, well, if she feels guilty then she's guilty. She's afraid of this, afraid of that, afraid, afraid, afraid, but she's not afraid of her, not afraid of herself. But what happens if she's also afraid of herself? Then wouldn't she be not afraid?

(Gao 1999a:130–131)

In this way the paradox is further internalized by the character, suggesting that senselessness does not arise from incommunicability with the other but with oneself. In Gao's play, the form of Chan *gongan* serves, on the one hand, as a means of constructing the dialogue while demonstrating, on the other, the impossibility of this construction.

As represented in Gao's theater, Chan *gongan* is not an abstract idea, nor is it alienated from the mundane world, but it is a form for dealing with problems of the modern conditions of human existence. Subjects such as the meaninglessness of words and alienation in human relationships are perennial issues in modern times and have been frequently dealt with by many Western modernist writers. Under the same modern conditions and faced with dilemmas of similar nature, Gao engages these problems from a different viewpoint. By employing Chan *gongan* as a form in his theatrical representation, Gao's response is imbued with a transcultural perspective.

---— PART I ———

Exploration within Context

Chapter 1
Searching for Alternative Aesthetics

The Early Introduction of Brecht

It should come as no surprise that mainland Chinese (and some overseas) responded disapprovingly to Gao Xingjian being awarded the Nobel Prize in Literature in 2000. Political reasons aside, Gao's theatrical works have always been at the periphery of modern Chinese theater and have generally been perceived as an alternative, if not a direct challenge, to mainstream realist theater. Being alternative, fundamentally, is to adopt a reflective and sometimes interrogative attitude toward conventions, norms, and the status quo. Not only are dominant modes of theatrical representation scrutinized, but also the frame of mind with which a theatrical piece is to be perceived, understood, and interpreted. In this sense, alternative aesthetics are an ongoing process, always searching and never resolutely established. For such a process to take shape, a reasonably open and conducive intellectual space is necessary. The most ardent search and dynamic mediation by dramatists of the People's Republic era first happened during the late 1950s and early 1960s, and then reemerged in the late 1970s, with the repressive Cultural Revolution set in between. Many critics have discussed the political and cultural vibrancies of the 1980s with little reference to earlier periods, hence presenting the 1980s as an era detached from earlier contexts. I shall thus begin my discussion with a detailed account of what Gao and his predecessors, especially the veteran director Huang Zuolin, have done in their search for alternative dramatic aesthetics since the late 1950s. The following discussion will show that many controversial topics of the 1980s—such as the use of Brechtian techniques to break away from realist conventions and the revisiting of traditional Chinese aesthetics—were in fact raised and contemplated by some foresighted dramatists in the late 1950s, with Huang being the strongest advocate.

Indeed, after the Cultural Revolution ended in 1976, the repression of intellectual and artistic life in mainland China was, to some extent, mitigated, and artistic composition began to regain some vitality. The decade or so up to 1989—when the Tiananmen Incident marked the end of a relatively liberal period of artistic and intellectual expression—came to be known as the "New Era" (Xin shiqi), during which an extensive search for alternatives to the dominant orthodox ideologies and representational modes of artistic expression was in progress. In the field of theater, playwrights and directors first discovered the dramaturgy of the German playwright/director Bertolt Brecht as an effective alternative. Later, they realized that a return to traditional dramatic aesthetics was essential to the establishment of new theatrical aesthetics. Modern Chinese theater became a creative space for transcultural practice in which Western forms and Chinese aesthetics underwent a process of integration. What are the elements they deemed useful in the theaters of Brecht and other Western dramatists? How were they inspired by their own traditions? How does their search for alternative aesthetics relate to the sociocultural context of the 1980s? And how have aesthetics intervened and constructed alternative ideologies?

The search for alternative dramatic aesthetics does not begin with the so-called New Era. As early as in the late 1950s and early 1960s, some Chinese dramatists considered the dominance of realist drama to be suffocating and advocated enriching the modes of theatrical representation. Although Gao was only a young student during this time, his early experiences proved to be essential to the later development of his dramaturgy.

One issue that arises with the discussion of alternative aesthetics is the definition of realism. Realism as a dramatic representational mode, with its ideological connotations, is a target to be challenged, deliberately or otherwise, when Chinese dramatists propose or practice alternative artistic means. In China, the evolution of the notion of realism has been closely related to political developments. After 1949, "socialist realism" became the orthodox mode of representation, although in the late 1950s new terms like "revolutionary realism" *(geming de xianshi zhuyi)* and "revolutionary romanticism" *(geming de langman zhuyi)* came into the official discourse. A typical Chinese definition of realism, by the Chinese scholar Hu Xingliang in his study of literary trends in modern China, is that which truthfully reflects social reality, constructs typical characters in typical circumstances according to the true features of life, and depicts the truth of everyday life (Hu 1995:347). Yang Lan adds to that definition an emphasis on the functional and ideological aspects of realism, stating that socialist realism is "to idealise realistic life according to communist ideological standards" and "to educate people in socialist ideology and spirit" (1996:94–95). These characteristics are usually defined within the official political discourse. The use of the term "orthodox realism" in the following discussion refers to such characteristics. The search for alternative aesthetics can thus be seen, in general, as a challenge to the official orthodoxy of a sanctioned representational mode that propagates official ideologies.

The proclamation that realism can be the only means of literary and artistic creation climaxed when Gao Xingjian began his initial exploration into alternative modes of representation. Gao was a fourth-year undergraduate at the Beijing Institute of Foreign Languages in 1960 when he, with some fellow students who were also drama enthusiasts, founded a drama society named "Seagull" (Hai'ou jushe). From the fact that they named their group after the famous Russian play *The Seagull,* by the realist master Anton Chekov, it could be suggested that their involvement in drama started with an interest in realism. In an era when realism had been legitimized as orthodoxy and the performance system of the Russian director Konstantin Stanislavsky was predominant,[1] Gao and his peers' starting point was understandable. However, they were not content with staging Chekov's plays or adopting the training method of Stanislavsky for long. Gao recollects their departure from orthodox realism, stating that he felt the need "to look for a more vigorous drama" because he was "suffocated by the confinement of the fourth wall constructed by Stanislavsky" (Gao 1988b:153). The fourth wall, a concept first applied to naturalist drama and later associated with performance in the Stanislavskian method, is an imaginary wall constructed between the stage and the audience enabling actors to concentrate wholly in what the Russian director called the "closed creative circle" (Stanislavsky 1967:148). It has become a Chinese synonym for Stanislavskian realism, which, in practice, impedes actor-audience interaction. Faced with the overwhelming dominance of a single dramatic school, Gao felt the need to explore other alternatives.

Initially, Gao turned to other Russian dramatists such as Evgeny Vakhtangov and Vsevolod Meyerhold. Then, he discovered the German dramatist Bertolt Brecht. The discovery of Brecht had such a forceful impact on Gao, as he recounts it, that it "immediately overturned my respect for Stanislavsky," whom he had admired when he first became interested in drama (Gao 1988b:52–53). Brecht interested him, Gao suggests, because his dramatic concepts and styles differed greatly from dramas that "attempted to re-present the true features of life and strove to fabricate an illusion of truth on the stage. He reminded me there is another kind of modern drama" (ibid.:156). In Brecht's plays and theoretical writings, Gao found an alternative to orthodox realist drama. He made this discovery early compared to most drama students of the time.

During the pre–Cultural Revolution period, besides adopting Stanislavsky's system to enhance realist drama, some dramatists were contemplating the assimilation of elements of traditional Chinese theater in the indigenization *(minzu hua)* of spoken drama. Both of these dominant directions were essentially nationalistic in nature, making an extensive effort to establish a drama with Chinese characteristics. Voices that did not hail Stanislavsky's system and traditional Chinese theater were weak and generally unheeded. For example, Ouyang Yuqian (1889–1962) and Huang Zuolin were two of the rare few who expressed reservations about the dominance of Stanislavsky's system. Ouyang pointed out in 1960 that "while we are studying Stanislavsky's system, we should also pay attention to the study of other countries' advanced traditions and experiences of performance" (1990: 370). Huang, in his 1962 talk, suggested the integration of Stanislavsky, Brecht, and Mei Lanfang to form a new dramaturgy. However, the foresighted call from both Ouyang and Huang did not attract much if any attention. Huang's 1962 talk became famous only in the early 1980s, when Chinese dramatists began a more extensive search for alternative dramatic aesthetics and recognized Huang's insight.

Unsatisfied with the monotony of Chinese spoken drama, the members of Seagull Drama Society, in 1960, two years before Huang gave his talk, began their exploration in a school of drama until then generally unheard of among Chinese dramatists, let alone the public. Though their goals were vague at this early stage, this was the beginning of a process of establishing new modes of representation as a challenge to Stanislavskian realism. Eventually, their search for alternatives was to lead to their discovery of Brecht.

Huang Zuolin's introduction of Brecht and his theater into China was a significant event in the history of Chinese theater, especially with respect to the search for alternative dramatic aesthetics. In 1959, Huang, an eminent Shanghai director who had been active since the 1930s, produced the first Brecht play performed in China, *Mother Courage and Her Children*. In 1962, he made a public speech in which he discussed the

German dramatist in detail. Huang had first encountered an English translation of Brecht's writing on traditional Chinese theater in 1936,[2] when he was a student in directing in London. In 1951, he delivered a detailed speech on the differences between traditional and Brechtian theaters, which, according to Adrian Hsia, was the first systematic introduction of Brechtian theater in China. During the six-hour speech, Huang talked about the content of Brecht's plays, how they were produced, and the history and characteristics of Brecht's notion of epic theater (Hsia 1982:46–47). The speech was addressed internally to the members of Shanghai People's Art Theatre, where Huang was the deputy head. Brecht was first mentioned publicly in Huang's famous speech to the All-China Forum on Spoken Drama, Song Drama, and Children's Drama in Guangzhou in March 1962.[3]

Young students in Beijing had already discovered Brecht in the course of their own explorations. In an interview with the author, Gao recalled that he first came across Brecht's plays and his famous article "A Short Organum for the Theater" in a Chinese translation with restricted circulation. As he had already read French modernist works and other Western works before, he was open to and enthusiastic about anything new. Though excited by his discovery of Brecht, he did not know how a Brechtian play should be staged. His opportunity to find out came in late 1963—three years after he had actually directed one himself—when he watched Huang Zuolin's *Jiliu yongjin* (Surging ahead against the current).

In the meantime, he went to the Beijing National Library and found a book profusely illustrated with pictures of the mise-en-scène of *Life of Galileo* directed by Brecht himself. Although they might not have had a thorough and precise understanding of Brecht's dramaturgy, through a process of experimentation Gao and the society's members staged Brecht's *The Good Person of Szechwan* in French, using the painted face masks of *jingju* and adopting a *xieyi* (see below) style of performance. Even this brief description makes it clear that their production differed from the realist style of performance and therefore was highly significant as an experiment in staging.

It is only in retrospect that the performance can be described as *xieyi*. The term "*xieyi*" was used by Huang Zuolin in his 1962 speech to highlight the nonrealistic style of Chinese theater in contrast to the *xieshi* (realistic) style of Western realist drama. But Huang did not invent the term "*xieyi*." In an article published in 1926, Yu Shangyuan (1897–1970) explicitly described traditional Chinese theater as *xieyi* in contrast with

Western drama's *xieshi*. An actor of the *xieshi* school, Yu summarized, denies the virtual nature of stage representation and disowns his or her self-identity when on stage. A *xieyi* actor, in contrast, acknowledges the fact that he or she is a performer with the objective of moving the audience with his or her art. Yu too was aware that the fourth wall had separated the audience from the performers, and he contended that some Western dramatists had been trying to demolish it (Yu 1986:150–151). Interestingly, what Yu argued in this early era resonates with some of the most important beliefs of Huang and Gao when they launched their challenge against realist drama. While there is no evidence that either Huang or Gao was influenced by Yu's arguments, the fundamental disparity in the nature of Western and Chinese theaters becomes obvious when they are compared. Nevertheless, although "*xieyi*" had been used earlier to describe the traditional style of performance, Huang first advocated it in his call for the renovation of spoken drama.

As *xieyi* is a concept derived from traditional Chinese ink painting and conventionally used for traditional Chinese theater, it is difficult to find an appropriate English translation. Huang used several English terms for his concept of *xieyi* drama at different times, namely, "intrinsicalistic," "essentialist," and "ideographic" (Fei 1991:192–193). In addition, Adrian Hsia uses the term "imagistic" (1982:62), while Xiaomei Chen uses "suggestive" (Chen 1995:130). These terms delineate the nature of *xieyi* to different degrees without, however, capturing its entire essence. Huang's concept of *xieyi* later sparked a nationwide debate, one of the most extensive on dramatic topics during the post–Cultural Revolution era, which culminated in the mid-1980s.[4] In 1962, however, Huang stood alone as he presented a comparison of three masters of different dramatic traditions.

In his discussion of the dramatic concepts of Mei Lanfang, Stanislavsky, and Brecht, Huang divided the world's drama into three categories, namely, realistic drama that attempts to construct an illusion of life on stage, *xieyi* drama that aims at breaking that illusion, and an integration of both. He argued that Stanislavsky believed in the fourth wall, Brecht wanted to pull it down, and for Mei, the fourth wall did not exist at all (Huang 1962). It is apparent that Huang reserved his highest praise for traditional Chinese theater, in this instance represented by the superb art of Mei.[5] In an article published twenty years later, the main argument of which was the same as that of this talk, Huang discussed the nature and superiority of traditional Chinese theater in greater detail (Huang 1982). But in 1962, when the Stanislavsky school was firmly entrenched, he chose to emphasize Brecht as a means of breaking away from Stanislavsky's fourth wall.

Huang, in his talk, made a great effort to delineate the history of the construction of the fourth wall. He related the fourth wall to the emergence of naturalism in the late nineteenth century and confirmed its contribution, in the progression toward realism, as a means in uncovering vices and problems of the bourgeoisie. However, when the influence of the fourth wall became so great that some dramatists maintained that it was the only means of drama, it had become a restriction to their creativity. Hence, in order to break away from its restrictions, Huang argued, Brecht had advocated demolishing the fourth wall and shattering the illusion of life on stage with the notion of the alienation effect.

Although in 1962 Huang did not and could not explicitly state that his advocacy of Brecht was directed against the Stanislavsky school, his intention was nevertheless obvious. In an interview in 1979, he admitted that he had formally raised this issue of Brecht's dramaturgy in 1962 hoping to demolish the fourth wall. "It [Huang's proposition] was being opposed. No one had formally engaged in a debate with me, but they opposed it in their heart. . . . Brecht wants to demolish the fourth wall: that is why I am interested in Brecht" (Huang 1983:1–2). In Huang's view, Brecht demanded that there exist a distance between the performers, the characters, and the audience in order to prevent the theater from being surrounded by mystification and generating a hypnotizing effect. Both the performers and the audience should be in possession of a clear and critical mind to discern the playwright's message and to comprehend the ideological and philosophical contents of the play. If they overindulged in the story and emotions of the play, Huang concluded, "they would not be able to make rational use of their sober and scientific minds to recognize life and reality and hence to transform life and reality" (Huang 1962).

Although Huang identified Mei Lanfang, Stanislavsky, and Brecht as the three masters of realism, the talk elaborated on the arts and ideas of Mei and Brecht with little mention of Stanislavsky. There was only one paragraph discussing similarities between Stanislavsky and Brecht, which had little relevance to the issue he was addressing. According to Huang, both were realists and were militantly against naturalism. Huang argued that although Stanislavsky had often been mistaken for a naturalist, he asserted that real life should be presented on stage only after artistic processing. The only specific similarity Huang mentioned was that both dramatists stressed that the emotions of a character should be expressed with physical actions on stage. In contrast, their differences were repeatedly delineated. In Huang's discussion, it appeared that there were many more similarities between Brecht and Mei, made evident through the extensive, unreserved praise Brecht had for Mei. Brecht admired the objectivity displayed by Mei in his rejection of "complete conversion" from an actor to the character. Huang quoted Brecht as acclaiming, "What Western actor of the old sort (apart from one or two comedians) could demonstrate the elements of his art like the Chinese actor Mei Lan-Fang, without special lighting and wearing a dinner jacket in an ordinary room full of specialists [of dramatic arts]?" (Huang 1982:166, English quotation from Brecht 1974:94). Clearly, Huang's objective was to suggest an alternative to the Stanislavsky school that he thought would be more vibrant and suitable for Chinese drama.

The Spirit of Revolt and Its Initial Setbacks

Twenty years before the more open and dynamic 1980s, both Huang and Gao had displayed a spirit of revolt against the existing dramatic and ideological orthodoxy. Their revolt was engendered by their dissatisfaction with realist forms, which were pervaded by political motivations and hence circumscribed free exploration in both form and content. A cursory parallel can be drawn with a similar revolt of some modern Western dramatists since the late nineteenth century. As suggested by Robert Brustein, the work of dramatists such as Ibsen, Brecht, and Artaud could be characterized as the "theater of revolt," in contrast with the traditional theater of communion. The traditional theater, Brustein argues, was a place "where traditional myths were enacted before an audience of believers against the background of a shifting but still coherent universe," while the modernist dramatists' theater of revolt displayed rebellious spirit and took place "in a flux of vacancy, bafflement, and accident" (1991:4).

While the target of Chinese dramatists differed fundamentally from that of their Western counterparts, there were similarities in the course of their revolt. They were estranged from orthodoxy, and hence the establishment, as they rejected artistic or ideological conventions. In turn, they were alienated and forced to pursue their creative life in exile, either as physical fugitives from their homeland or isolated in a state of spiritual exile. Especially in the case of the Chinese dramatists, their aesthetic pursuits remained a personal ordeal.

For most playwrights and directors in 1950s China, drama, like other forms of literature and the arts, was required to be created in accordance with socialist ideology and as a means to portray positive and absolutely perfect revolutionary images for the education of the masses. The Chinese Communist Party used drama as a revolutionary weapon and imposed strict control over dramatic themes and modes of representation. In this milieu, very rarely would an artist not submit his or her creativity to the hopeful future promised by the socialist state, just as the majority of intellectuals had "welcomed or at least complied with the Party's policy" (Goldman and Cheek 1987:11). Even Huang Zuolin had directed such plays as *Bubu jin'gen Mao Zhuxi* (Following Chairman Mao every step of the way) and *Ba yisheng jiaogei Dang* (Dedicating my life to the Party), displaying his enthusiasm for the establishment of the People's Republic (Fei 1991:79).

However, such nationalistic appeals, combined with such extreme ideological repression, could not sustain the true artist in his or her aesthetic pursuits. As Brustein argues, the practical and utilitarian concerns of the dramatist will always give way to aesthetic imagination. Although concerned about political and social reality, the dramatist is more absorbed in the "imaginative reconstruction of a chaotic, disordered world," and its artistic expression (Brustein 1991:8–9). Inevitably, a desire and need for personal expression and divergence from authorized modes of expression will emerge, although the divergence need not be political in motive. Such an artist may not have set out to subvert orthodox ideologies but, in fact, was more inclined to aspire to a state of "heteroglossia," to borrow Bakhtin's term, in expressive forms and styles of artistic creation.[6]

Huang Zuolin's concept of *xieyi* drama manifested this spirit of revolt when he incorporated Brechtian theater. He cautiously identified Brecht, together with Mei Lanfang and Stanislavsky, who were generally accepted at that time, as the three main foundations for his new dramatic concept that would "liberate us from the restrictive situation of having only one dramatic concept" (Huang 1962). In his 1962 talk, Huang did not discuss thoroughly the *xieyi* nature of traditional Chinese theater but highlighted it through his appropriation of Brecht. He related Brecht's narrative technique to that of traditional *pingtan* (storytelling and ballad singing) artists. Brecht's intention in using the narrator was to achieve the effect of alienation, which forced the audience to observe and think critically. Huang, however, perceived the technique of using narration as an effective means for the development of plot, the depiction of characters' inner selves, and the illustration of authorial subjectivity. He concluded that Brecht's scripting began with the establishment of actions rather than the construction of characters, the reverse being normally practiced in the scripting of conventional realist plays. By considering these issues, Huang had probed into the very root of the limitations of realist drama. By placing emphasis on action in place of character, he was suggesting a new dramaturgy that was directly in conflict with the socialist belief in the positive portrayal of heroic proletarian figures, although this ideological challenge might not have been his deliberate intention.

Huang's efforts to practice Brechtian techniques and to realize his ideal of *xieyi* drama did not go smoothly. As an established dramatist in the 1950s, he started to incorporate Brechtian concepts into his directing. When in 1959 he directed Brecht's *Mother Courage and Her Children*, response from the audience and from critics was unenthusiastic. Huang had earlier adopted, with much effort to accord with the expectations of the cast and the audience, some elements of epic theater in two productions of Chinese plays. In 1951, he led a team in Shanghai to produce *Kang Mei yuan Chao dahuobao* (A great live report of resisting America and assisting Korea). In 1958, he directed *Bamian hongqi yingfeng piao* (Eight red flags are fluttering). Both plays reportedly incorporated the Brechtian concept of epic theater to overcome the limitations of the realist setting and were similar in having several independent scenes that delineated vast temporal and spatial spans. However, not much attention was paid to his pioneering experimentation. After the outbreak of the Cultural Revolution, the introduction and performance of Brecht's plays was automatically discontinued and, worse, became a target of denunciation.

Adrian Hsia analyzes the reasons for the lackluster response to *Mother Courage*, providing a glimpse of the reception of Brechtian theater in China during the 1950s and early 1960s, from three angles. First, the subject of the play, which was the Thirty Years War in Europe in the seventeenth century, was too distant from the concerns of the Chinese audience. Second, the color scheme was dull and unattractive to an audience accustomed to the bright and colorful costumes of traditional operas. Third, in his play, Brecht intended for the audience to exercise reasoning and judgment, and this was unfamiliar to audiences used to the unequivocal message of Chinese drama, which was until then didactic in nature (Hsia 1982:51–52).

The relevance of the subject matter, Hsia's first point, is utterly essential to the audience's reception. *Mother Courage* was written in 1938, when the outbreak of war was imminent. While that provided a basis to which the European audience could relate (Brecht 1974:229), the Chinese production did not have a similar referential context. While Hsia's second point does not differentiate the audience of spoken drama from that of traditional Chinese drama, a nonrealist set would undoubtedly have seemed strange to audiences who were, until then, only familiar with spoken drama in realistic style. Third, Brechtian theater aimed at transforming the passivity of the audience. This goal presupposed the existence of an unfavorable oppressive sociohistorical environment seen in terms of class conflict. This environment could not be invoked in China, as the communist state had just been established. In addition, the audience had to be prepared in logical and critical thinking in order to respond to the reflective style of a Brechtian play, and the Chinese apparently were not used to such an exercise at that time.

What Hsia has not mentioned that is equally important is the attitude of the production team, their preparedness to adopt and effectively execute a new and progressive mode of theater. As Brechtian theater had just been introduced to the Chinese stage, the director and his production members were only beginning to understand and experiment with this theatrical concept with excitement and unfamiliarity. The leading role of the cast is important as is their intellectual consciousness. Brecht put high demands on his actors, whom he said should be "demonstrating their knowledge . . . of human relations, of human behaviour, of human capacities . . . consciously, suggestively, descriptively" (1974:26). Only when the performers are certain of their mission and upholding an objective view are they able to execute their task in a Brechtian theater effectively. Apparently, neither the Chinese performers nor the audience were ready to understand and appreciate a theater that was drastically different from the realist drama they were used to.

If conventional realist drama serves as a one-way instructional didacticism, Brechtian theater displays a similar didactic purpose but demands active participation from the audience. While in the realist drama the contact between audience and stage is based on empathy, Brecht intends to make the audience adopt an attitude of inquiry and criticism in its reception. Hence, in a Brechtian theater, the audience constitutes a vital component as important as the performance. The transition from conventional drama to Brechtian theater therefore signifies a shift of emphasis from the stage toward the audience. As Walter Benjamin suggests: "Epic theatre is always intended for the actors quite as much as for the spectators. The essential reason why the didactic play [of Brecht] falls into a category of its own is that, through the exceptional austerity of its apparatus, it facilitates and encourages the interchangeability of actors and audience, audience and actors" (1983:20). Members of the audience do not stay on the passive receiving end but have to involve themselves actively in the interpretation of the incidents presented by the actors. In fact, in this process of participation, Benjamin argues, "every spectator can become one of the actors." However, as the reception of *Mother Courage* in China revealed, this interactive relationship was far from established during the 1950s.

From a different perspective, taking into consideration the ideological aspect of Brechtian theater, this relationship between play and audience appears to be even more critical. Being a Marxist, Brecht took as the task of his theater to suggest a possible way of constructing a Marxist social structure. His intention was therefore to evoke a "radical transformation of the mentality of our time" with a "radical transformation of the theatre" (Brecht 1974:23). Brechtian theater, as Colin Counsell argues, "sought to depict what he believed to be the real relations of power that lay beneath the patina of appearance, to show his audience the true nature of society, thereby empowering them to change it" (1996:81). In this context, the audience is the oppressed subject under bourgeois rule and hence the vital force that will transform that oppression. In Huang's experimentation in this early period, it is apparent that the spirit of revolt he displayed was neither concerned with revealing oppressive conditions nor appealing for ideological subversion. His main concern was to adopt Brecht's theatrical techniques for the establishment of a dramatic ideal. The relationship between the audience and the performance in the Chinese context was essentially different from that intended by Brecht. Nevertheless, the social and political environ that persisted provided a foundation for this relationship. It was not until the end of Cultural Revolution, however, that a favorable environment appeared for Huang and other dramatists to pursue their aesthetic exploration.

Brechtian Theater in the Post–Cultural Revolution Era

Since the late 1970s, the reception of Brecht in China has improved greatly. In 1979, *Life of Galileo*, the second of Brecht's plays to be produced in China, was staged. In contrast to the first production, it was received enthusiastically across the board. One of the reasons, as underlined by

Adrian Hsia, is that "the Chinese would equate ecclesiastical suppression in the play with socialist fascism" (1982:58), since the Cultural Revolution had just ended two years before. The reasons for selecting the play to be staged in this particular juncture were spelled out by codirector Chen Yong: "Our choice of *Galileo* was not just a matter of an artistic experiment for the sake of introducing another dramatic school to the Chinese public, nor did we merely intend to criticize the mental imprisonment and the cultural dictatorship under the Gang of Four, we introduced this artistic product to Chinese society mainly because of the meaning of the play" (1982:89). Although Chen does not explain what she means by "the meaning of the play," the other reasons she mentions should not be ignored. In fact, the significance of *Galileo* to the Chinese audience is twofold. First was its thematic relevance to the concerns of the contemporary Chinese people. Chinese audiences who had a fresh memory of the Cultural Revolution readily related to Galileo's struggle against the religious authorities. Furthermore, Galileo was portrayed in the play as at once a great scientist and a cowardly individual. To an audience used to seeing either heroes who were all good or villains who were all bad, this human, flawed protagonist, with such contradictory features, opened up a totally new theatrical experience. One important aspect of this experience is that it is essentially a realistic one, in contrast with socialist realist drama that pretends to be realistic but actually creates completely unreal worlds and unreal characters. Second, as the political and cultural atmosphere had loosened up, exploration of alternative aesthetics beyond that of orthodox realism became possible. Huang Zuolin, the director of *Galileo*, with his special interest in Brecht, thus commenced this new endeavor and began to realize his dramatic ideal.[7]

Other factors that had contributed to the failure of *Mother Courage* were dealt with by Huang. Huang, apparently, had understood and learned from his first experience staging a Brecht play. While the previous team had rushed their production of *Mother Courage*,[8] in *Galileo*, Huang made great efforts to get the cast and crew well prepared. The production was not entirely Brechtian. Huang presented his cast with "a mixture of Stanislavsky and Brecht" (Sun 1987:142). The Stanislavskian method, especially in the style of acting, would be more familiar to and easily acceptable by the Chinese audience. Furthermore, the team attended talks by specialists, carried out study and research, and visited places like the planetarium and a Catholic church (Hsia 1982:60). All preparatory work was aimed at ensuring that the team had a good understanding of

Brechtian concepts as well as the background and content of the play. Huang's other task was to consider the needs and habits of reception of the audience.[9] The production had more elaborate scenes than originally intended. Dancing and singing were included as concessions to popular taste. The singing bards were expanded into narrators-spectators-actors, who appeared in every scene instead of just the carnival scene as in the original script (Hsia 1982:61). These adaptations, along with other conscious efforts by the team, resulted in the successful reception of Brecht. Still, without the mental and psychological shift that took place after the Cultural Revolution, affecting both theater practitioners and the audience, success would have been almost unimaginable.

The post–Cultural Revolution era witnessed dramatic and unprecedented changes, socially, economically, politically, and culturally, in the history of the People's Republic. Although the dominance of realist drama on the Chinese stage had molded the receptive habits of the audience, transformation of the external environment had unquestionably prepared them to receive other artistic forms and styles. In fact, other dramatic schools were never totally unrepresented on the Chinese stage. As early as in the 1920s, romanticism and neoromanticism,[10] together with realism, received equal attention from Chinese dramatists.[11] However, with the intensification of the leftist political movement and the Japanese invasion of the early 1930s, proletarian drama *(puluo xiju)* and national defense drama *(guofang xiju)*, both essentially realist forms, took over center stage. In the following decades, politics had permeated the consciousness of the arts and the audience's perception of the arts.

The general atmosphere emphasizing the collective and repressing individuality came to a turning point forty years later. The formulation of the reform and open-door policies in the late 1970s not only heralded vibrant development in the economy but also induced the possibility of relaxation of creative and intellectual control. Effects of the deliberate shift toward a market economy permeated other spheres of life. This process of marketization eventually allowed for a certain degree of autonomy in both the production and the reception of art. As Terry Eagleton suggests, "Once artefacts become commodities in the market place, they exist for nothing and nobody in particular, and can consequently be rationalized, ideologically speaking, as existing entirely and gloriously for themselves" (1990:9).

Once assured of their audience's openness, dramatists of this era were keen to experiment with different dramatic forms and styles. To challenge the orthodox dogma in the arts became an irresistible temptation for artists who were dissatisfied with the current situation. They were looking for an effective means to express divergent points of view. In this context, long-lasting conventions were progressively contested through the introduction of alternative aesthetics or, in Raymond Williams' words, "structures of feeling." Williams argues that an alternative aesthetic begins as an individual experience that has no external counterpart in existing conventions. As a new structure of feeling emerges, it will receive criticism or rejection from the established formations but will gradually be accepted as the experience is shared by others (Williams 1993:17–19). The introduction of Brecht by Huang Zuolin and Gao Xingjian in the early 1960s, which was confined to a very small group of dramatists surrounding them, had failed as they were unable to establish a new structure of feeling within the boundaries of orthodox realism. However, thanks to the social structural transformation that took place in the post–Cultural Revolution era, the impact of Brechtian dramaturgy was more comprehensive and intensive during that time. After the success of *Galileo*, more and more dramatists began to show interest in understanding Brecht and adopting Brechtian techniques in their works.

Just as intellectuals had launched realism to develop the intellect of the populace during the May Fourth era, the artists of the post–Cultural Revolution era made a similar attempt to break away from forms they perceived to be oppressive. Yet their chosen course was different from their predecessors' in the sense that they did not emphasize so much the subversion of existing ideological formations. They confined themselves —consciously or unconsciously, nevertheless, cleverly—to the exploration of forms and styles. While censorship over ideological issues was still carried out, there was greater space in which to advocate new modes of representation.

With their attempt to introduce new dramatic forms and styles, dramatists were establishing a new discursive formation through alternative aesthetics. What is the significance of this achievement? Eagleton describes modern aesthetics as having a spectrum of preoccupation with such issues as freedom and legality, spontaneity and necessity, self-determination, autonomy, particularity and universality, and so on. He then argues: "The category of the aesthetic assumes the importance it does in modern Europe because in speaking of art it speaks of these matters too, which are at the heart of the middle class's struggle for political hegemony. The construction of the modern notion of the aesthetic artefact is thus inseparable from the construction of the dominant ideological forms of modern class-society, and indeed from a whole new form of human subjectivity appropriate to that social order" (1990:3). Although Chinese dramatists were not taking fire directly at the official ideology— not even the most daring dramatists had done this explicitly and emphatically at this stage—dealing with the notion of aesthetics already "provides an unusually powerful challenge and alternative to these dominant ideological forms" (ibid.). Brecht himself understood well the power of theater to challenge dominant ideologies when he said, "It is precisely theatre, art and literature which have to form the 'ideological superstructure' for a solid, practical rearrangement of our age's way of life" (1974: 23). While not necessarily intending to employ an alternative aesthetics in order to launch a dissenting discourse, the intellectual and ideological concerns of Chinese dramatists would, consciously or otherwise, be reflected in their aesthetic choices.

Huang Zuolin, in his 1962 speech, claimed that one of the reasons Chinese dramatists of this era were especially interested in Brecht was that Brecht opposed the bourgeois class as well as the idealist and aesthetic arts of the bourgeoisie (Huang 1962). The Chinese scholar Ding Yangzhong described Brecht's dramatic philosophy as "dialectic materialistic epistemology" (1985:25). Undoubtedly, as a declared militant Marxist and realist, Brecht was a safe choice for Chinese dramatists to explore and exploit in this era. Interest in Brecht was thus much stronger than interest in Western dramatists such as Samuel Beckett or Jerzy Grotowski (1933–1999).

Brecht is a realist who is paradoxically against realism. In his response, posthumously published ten years after his death, to Lukács' attacks on expressionism during the great literary debate in the 1930s, Brecht asserts that form is not the exclusive essence of realism; other forms, including expressionism, are equally adaptable to the dramatist's needs if they suit the needs of the literary work in question. It is what Brecht called "a realistic point of view" that constituted the essential nature of the realist (1980:70–76). His belief that "literature cannot be forbidden to employ skills newly acquired by contemporary man" (Brecht 1980:75) makes him a realist who is proficient in subverting obsolete forms and engaging new forms of expression to consolidate the spirit of realism. His method was to use realism as the basis for incorporating different artistic forms. Hence, realism in its essence is more ideological than aesthetic, more substance than form, as seen in his definition: "Our concept of realism needs to be broad and political, free from aesthetic restrictions and independent of convention. Realist means: laying bare society's causal network/writing from the standpoint of the class which has prepared the broadest solutions for the most pressing problems afflicting human society/emphasizing the dynamics of development/concrete and so as to encourage abstraction" (Brecht 1974:109). It is apparent that Brecht is not against realism as a political and ideological notion but realism with limitations in its form of expression. It is this spirit of Brecht that gave Chinese dramatists leeway to explore different modes of representation; it was a starting point that did not instantly threaten the status quo of the orthodox ideologies.

Emerging Alternative Aesthetics

The significance of the performance and influence of Brecht in the post– Cultural Revolution era is not only that Brecht provided Chinese dramatists with a new aesthetic, but that he opened up a path to numerous possibilities. Many playwrights and directors of this era claim that their works embody, to some degree, elements appropriated from Brecht. These elements may appear to be authentically Brechtian or, as in most cases, they may not. However, there can be no doubt that these dramatists were inspired by Brecht to commence their own aesthetic exploration.

Raymond Williams contrasts Brecht's drama with that of the naturalist in four domains.[12] First, Brechtian theater evokes the spectator's ability to observe and awakens his or her capacity to act. Second, it presents a view of the world that the spectator confronts and is made to study. Third, it makes each scene exist for itself and develops by sudden leaps so as to stimulate independent perception and reflection on each incident. Fourth, whereas conventional drama takes the human being, in the run of its action, as known, given, and inevitable, Brechtian theater shows individuals producing themselves in the course of the action and therefore subject to criticism and to change (Williams 1993:278). Naturalist drama, by contrast, is a closed and confined entity, which not only restrains the involvement and reflection of the audience, but also rigorously defines the action and interpretation of the performance. Brechtian theater attempts to stimulate the audience's rational and intellectual participation. The nature of this drama is thus open—to both the audience and the performers—and on what Walter Benjamin calls a "public platform" (Benjamin 1983:22), Brechtian theater establishes itself through the deposition of Stanislavskian realism.

This "public platform" provided the space for contemporary Chinese playwrights to demonstrate their modest exploration of Brechtian techniques immediately after the 1978 production of *Galileo*. Generally perceived to be the first experimental post–Cultural Revolution play, *Wuwai you reliu* (Hot spring outside, 1980) by three young Shanghai playwrights, Ma Zhongjun, Jia Hongyuan, and Qu Xinhua, displays a significant appropriation of Western dramatic techniques. The writers claimed to be inspired by Huang's concept of *xieyi* drama. The play presents the conflict between Zhao Changkang, a courageous and selfless worker in Heilongjiang province, and his younger brother and sister, two materialistic urban youngsters. Although he dies in a snowstorm, Zhao is still a heroic figure. His appearance as a spirit is unconventional in spoken drama. The playwrights intentionally adopt an unrealistic style by portraying a spirit character in a generally realistic setting. (In fact, the appearance of spirit characters is not unfamiliar in traditional Chinese theater.) More interesting, as Zhao pleads for the salvation of the youngsters' lost souls, he turns and points to the audience, questioning their unresponsiveness and appealing to them for reflection. Later, as the younger brother and sister realize Zhao is dead, they too turn to the audience, asking for their help in bringing him back to life. In this play, direct address to the audience is within the capacity of the characters rather than narrators detached from the incident. While in Brechtian theater this technique is employed to activate the audience's objective judgment, here it is used to stimulate their emotional response. Although empathy is the playwrights' foremost concern, this play took a significant step in breaking away from the fourth wall.

Another play, also staged in 1980, with a more obvious appropriation of Brechtian techniques is Sha Yexin's *Chen Yi shizhang* (Mayor Chen Yi). Chen Yi (1901–1972), a former mayor of Shanghai and foreign minister who was ousted early in the Cultural Revolution, became one of the most frequently portrayed characters in post–Cultural Revolution drama, symbolizing unjustly persecuted veteran cadres. Before Sha, Chen Yi appeared as the protagonist of plays such as *Dongjin! Dongjin!* (Eastward! Eastward! 1978) by Suo Yunping and Shi Chao and *Chen Yi chushan* (The resurgence of Chen Yi, 1979) by Ding Yisan. Chinese critics singled out *Mayor Chen Yi* for its novel portrayal of the protagonist. In Sha's play, there are ten scenes, loosely related and spanning a period of slightly more than a year chronologically, depicting different incidents surrounding Chen Yi. This structure markedly resembles the episodic structure that is characteristic of Brecht. In fact, Sha admitted that this play was inspired by Brecht's *Fear and Misery of the Third Reich* and gave this appropriated structure a Chinese name meaning "a string of candied fruits" *(bingtang hulu shi)* (Sha 1981:120–121).

Because it delineates various aspects of life in Hitler's Reich, *Fear and Misery* has been described as "un-Brechtian" and "naturalistic" (Esslin 1984:270), and the usual Brechtian alienation devices, such as subtitles, heightened speech, or songs, are absent (Willett and Manheim 1983:vii). It is apparently out of convenience that Sha adopts this particular structure that suits his need in portraying the complicated and diversified incidents in *Mayor Chen Yi*, rather than a conscious advocacy of Brechtian techniques.

This manner of appropriation was in fact a common practice among the dramatists of this era. They demonstrate little concern for the relation between form and ideological significance that is manifested by Western playwrights. Brecht's narrative mode and episodic structure have an essential relevance to the content he depicts and the message he wants to relay. Chinese dramatists took these techniques out of their ideological contexts, arbitrarily and yet creatively, and appropriated them to express their own interests. None of them, including Huang Zuolin, the strongest advocate and practitioner of Brecht in China, thought of becoming a militant and "authentic" Brechtian. Brechtian theater was only one of the many schools of Western drama from which Chinese dramatists could learn and appropriate techniques in the process of forming their own aesthetics.

If his intention in advocating Brecht in the 1960s was to break away from the monolithic dominance of the Stanislavsky school, Huang Zuolin, in the post–Cultural Revolution era, displayed his idea of *xieyi* drama in a more mature form with the appropriation of Brecht. As a director in the late 1970s, Huang did not hold slavishly to Brechtian dramaturgy but adapted some of Brecht's notions to establish his own ideal. He once again advocated the notion of epic theater, however, with the prefix "Chinese-style." Brecht defined epic theater as "narrative" that "turns the spectator into an observer, but arouses his capacity for action" (1974:37). "Epic," originally an Aristotelian term, is a form of narrative briefly defined by John Willett as "a sequence of incidents or events, narrated without artificial restrictions as to time, place or relevance to a formal 'plot'" (1977:169). The term "epic theater" is commonly translated into Chinese as *"shishiju"* (literally, historical poetic drama). This translation is not accurate but is widely accepted. There exists a less used but more accurate translation, *"xushiju"* (literally, narrative drama).

When he uses the term *"shishiju,"* Huang Zuolin interprets the first *shi* as "history, reflecting realistic life" and the second *shi* as "an artistically created conception that has its foundation in real life and that produces artistic works that are more elevated, more powerful, more concentrated, more typical, more idealistic, and more universal than life" (Huang 1988:1). It is apparent that Huang has misinterpreted the Brechtian term based on the earlier mistranslation. This is an example of what Lydia Liu calls "translingual practice," in which "new words, meanings, discourses, and modes of representation arise, circulate, and acquire legitimacy," and meanings are not so much transformed from one language to another as invented within the context of the latter language (Liu 1995:26). Whether Huang fully comprehends the original meaning of the Brechtian term "epic" is, in this instance, of little significance. What is more important is that Huang has intentionally misinterpreted and appropriated it for the presentation of his ideal of drama, which is essentially Chinese in nature.

In the 1982 article that is a revised edition of his 1962 talk, Huang attempts to outline the different natures of Western and Chinese theater using painting as an analogy. Western paintings, he suggests, are basically realistic and portray what the eye sees, while Chinese paintings are mainly *xieyi* and portray what the mind observes. Huang has offered an English translation, "essentialism," for *xieyi*, generated from the word "essence" *(benzhi)*, which he deems appropriately captures the nature of Chinese art. In his conclusion, Huang asks, "Can we say the fundamental nature of Western arts is *xieshi* (realism) and that of Chinese arts is *xieyi* (essentialism)?" (1982:169).[13] It should be noted that when he uses the English term "realism" for *xieshi*, Huang means the realistic form and style but not the ideological denotation of realism, which Chinese usually translate as *"xianshi zhuyi."*[14] He is basically addressing techniques to be engaged for the presentation of ideas. This pursuit of Huang is exemplified in his definition of *"shishiju,"* quoted above, which is to make use of an effective artistic means to portray the reality of life. In this sense, interestingly, the dramatic concepts of Huang and Brecht appear to have much in common.

From Brecht to Traditional Chinese Theater

With his profound knowledge of both Chinese and Western theaters, Huang Zuolin established his own aesthetics, appropriating Brechtian theater as a foundation. Gao Xingjian, with his distinctive interpretation of Brecht, appropriated certain Brechtian techniques to create some of the most provocative and innovative works of the 1980s. Brecht's works pointed Chinese dramatists to new possibilities in their search for alternative aesthetics. At the same time, his theatrical concepts have somehow inspired Chinese dramatists to look back to their traditional theater.

The rediscovery of traditional Chinese theater that took place in the 1980s was not a simple transplantation of traditional forms onto the contemporary stage. Instead, Chinese dramatists made a close investigation of traditional theater until they achieved a deep understanding and then selectively assimilated the essence of its spirit. In the course of this process, Chinese dramatists came to the important realization that traditional theater could be a means to set free a theater restricted by the fourth wall.

Besides the alienation effect, the notion of narrativity in Brecht's epic theater is also a distinct characteristic of traditional Chinese theater. While Huang does not pay much, if any, attention to this characteristic, Gao values this particular aspect of Brechtian dramaturgy and uses it to expand his creative space. Gao writes in one of a series of articles published in 1982 and 1983:

> Brecht has reconfirmed the status of the dramatic actor as a narrator and has rejuvenated the narrator with *the consciousness of a modern human being.* Once the narrator with a modern consciousness emerges, the Ibsenian dramatic structure is completely smashed. Hence, drama requires a different way of writing; it does not create conflicts that are resolved nor does it fabricate intertwining plots. It is like writing novels in that it narrates and comments *freely* on incidents. (Gao 1988b:54, italics mine)

Gao perceives Brechtian theater as possessing the qualities required to overcome the predicament of Chinese drama. He regards orthodox realism as passé and challenges it from a broad perspective. First, he discards the notion that drama is an "art of words" *(yuyan de yishu).* This term itself was a product of the leftist drama movement. In 1928, Hong Shen (1894–1955) suggested adopting the term *"huaju"* (spoken drama) in place of *"xinju"* (new drama) (Ge 1990:119). Since then, the term has been canonized, and drama, confined by the term *"huaju,"* is generally defined exclusively as an art of words. As a result, other aspects of drama have been overlooked. Second, Gao argues that drama should not be didactic but should provide the audience with both entertainment and artistic gratification. This view is probably directed at the practice of using drama to serve politics, which culminated in the highly politicized model plays during the Cultural Revolution. Third, he suggests that drama should exploit whatever techniques are available, be they Western or Chinese, to present an experience of reality that the audience may not have had in life. And finally, he specifically criticizes Ibsen and Stanislavsky, whose dramatic ideas were appropriated by the Chinese and resulted in restriction of artistic expression.[15] Gao is emphasizing that Chinese drama should break away from the existing dramatic dogma and face the needs of the contemporary era while at the same time expanding its expressivity. With "the consciousness of a modern human being," an artist will be able to perceive current social and political circumstances. With means that enable the artist to present his or her ideas "freely," he or she will then be able to search for individual and unique forms of expression.

Through advocating Brecht, Gao also stresses the importance and value of traditional Chinese theater. One of his foci is the similar employment of narrative mode in both kinds of theater. Mode of narrative is one of the most important innovations in Gao's works, apparently inspired, at least partly, by Brecht. While Brecht adopts a Western narrative language previously employed by novels and reportage in his theater, Gao contends that narrative elements including those borrowed by Brecht are also present in traditional Chinese theater, such as the prologue *(kaichangbai)*, the self-revelation of one's history *(zibao jiamen)*, and the aside utterance *(pangbai)* (Gao 1988b:15). In Brechtian epic theater, the narrative mode is a means more than an end. This mode, among other techniques such as screen projection and singing, functions in the process of "literarization of the theater," intending to spur the audience to "intellectual activities" and "[provide] access to 'higher things'" (Brecht 1974: 43–44). Gao, by contrast, is interested in the narrative mode as a means per se. He has an interesting analogy:

> In Chinese calligraphy, there are [styles such as] *kaishu, xingshu, caoshu*, and even *kuangcao*. Within *kaishu*, there are different schools such as those of Yan [Zhenqing], Liu [Gongquan], and Zhao [Menghu]. Each calligrapher has a strength. In the hands of contemporary calligraphers, all schools

have been integrated into one. Those with the highest degree of proficiency can even reach a level where they can invent their styles freely. The relationship between dramatic means and content is quite similar to that between calligraphy and the [Chinese written] characters. It is apparent that they can be differentiated for separate study, and [the emphasis on dramatic means] will not be mistaken as formalism.[16] (Gao 1983c:122)

This passage does not imply that Gao disregards content; rather, it reveals what he saw as his immediate task. On the employment of the narrator in Brechtian and traditional theaters, Gao proposes that the future lies in reevaluating the traditions of Chinese theater. Indeed, he found the use of the narrator to be the most powerful weapon for launching an attack on the Stanislavsky school. The objective of a Stanislavskian actor is to enter the heart of the character and experience his or her feelings, blend with the character fully, and always avoid direct communication with the audience. The narrative mode of acting, however, prevents the Brechtian actor from being completely transformed into the character he or she is portraying. It provides a certain distance from the character. Although Gao has never said so explicitly, the use of a narrator provides a vital breakthrough. Once the actor is released from the enclosed Stanislavskian "creative circle," he or she is no longer circumscribed by the life and feelings of the character. Resuming the identity of an actor on stage, the actor is free to employ all possible means of performance, including manipulating the dual functions of actor and character.

With numerous possibilities awaiting his exploitation, Gao never confined himself to any single school of drama. For Gao, Brecht's significance lies in his effectiveness in expanding the range of artistic experimentation. However, he does not wish to be encumbered by Brechtian dramaturgy. When he was asked to name the dramatist he found most influential, Gao answered, "It is very difficult," adding that "it is definitely unhealthy to consume only one type of vitamin" (Gao 1988b:60). Brecht was only his point of departure. In fact, his nourishment came from a long list of Western dramatists, from Beckett to Genet, from Artaud to Grotowski.

Gao perhaps most admired Antonin Artaud (1896–1948), whose idea of total theater appealed to his search for an unfettered and comprehensive mode of representation. Gao does not discuss the ideological aspects of the French director—the notion of the Theater of Cruelty, Artaud's manifesto "to restore an impassioned convulsive concept of life to theatre" by incorporating "themes and subjects corresponding to the agitation and unrest of our times" (Artaud 1993:81)—these are only mentioned briefly in Gao's account of the development of modern dramatic concepts (Gao 1983b:28). Instead, he chooses to emphasize total theater, Artaud's effort to establish a theater that presents powerful physical actions, which was inspired by Balinese folk arts, Japanese Kabuki, and Tibetan religious rituals.

The significance of total theater, in Gao's view, is that it inspires the major trend in the West of rediscovering ancient theatrical means and concepts (Gao 1988b:19). Artaud calls the elements from these Asian traditional arts "ancient magic powers" (1993:66) and appropriates them into a theater that is essentially contemporary. The traditional arts do not exist purely as an object of great antiquity to be admired, neither are they renovated and reinstalled in modern theater to preserve their original appearance. On the contrary, it is the contemporary consciousness of the artist that calls for the integration of traditional elements into contemporary life and claims that they are related to contemporary human spiritual needs. Gao has followed a similar path. With a consciousness that arises from contemporary circumstances rather than a desire to conserve antiquity, Gao has advocated the importance of looking back to traditional Chinese theater since his very first discussions of drama.

A question that could be raised at this juncture is: Did Gao discover and acknowledge the worth of indigenous art forms only when inspired to do so by Western dramatists? The answer does not lie in whether he first encountered traditional or Western theater. Xiaomei Chen, who has discussed this issue in detail, argues that in a situation of "retro-influence" such as Gao's, "there is no hierarchy in any scheme of reading, but only an exchange of shared properties or of differences" (Chen 1995:110). Examining the text of Gao's *Wild Man*, a play at once perceived as Chinese and Western by readers from different cultural backgrounds, she suggests that it is difficult to determine the source and subject, in her words, the emitter and receiver, of influence. Whether traditional Chinese theater or Artaudian/Brechtian theater constitutes the foundation of Gao's plays is thus not a simple task of studying the "presence of two distinct and therefore comparable entities" (Chen 1995:110–111). Consequently, attempts to differentiate these intertwining elements may be futile and even trivial.

Gao's endeavor to integrate theatrical elements from both Western and Chinese traditions should in fact be perceived from a broader perspective within the historical context of the international and intercultural exchange of traditions that his predecessors experienced in the early twentieth century. In 1930, Mei Lanfang toured the United States, where he received unanimous praise and met film stars such as Charlie Chaplin, with whom he became close friends (Cosdon 1995:182–185). In 1935, Mei was invited to perform in Moscow. Many of the most eminent European dramatists congregated to witness his performance, including Stanislavsky, Meyerhold, Eisenstein, Gorky, Tolstoy (who were members of the welcoming committee), Tairov, Tretiakov, Brecht, Craig, and Piscator. After seeing his performances, some of them were inspired to integrate Mei's acting into their aesthetic schemas (Banu 1986:153–158).

The greatest significance of this occasion, during which *jingju* was presented to the West by Mei, was probably the experience of a theater patently different from the realist drama that had had a stranglehold on the stage in both Europe and America. With Mei's appearance in America, Cosdon suggests, realism was challenged (1995:182). It is not surprising that, five years later, across the Atlantic Ocean, European dramatists such as Meyerhold, Eisenstein, and Brecht were more enthusiastic about Mei's performance than others, as they had long been searching for alternatives to realist drama.

Mei's theater helped to corroborate Brecht's lifelong pursuit of a theater that is independent from illusion and empathy. Soon after seeing Mei perform, he wrote his famous article "Alienation Effects in Chinese Acting," in which for the first time he used the term *"Verfremdungseffekt"* (alienation effect or A-effect). The traditional Chinese actor is, in Brecht's perception, highly aware of the audience's presence, and he rejects complete convergence with the character he is playing. During his performance, the actor observes the audience as well as his own acting. He is able to maintain objectivity as he "portrays incidents of utmost passion, but without his delivery becoming heated." From his observation of Chinese acting, Brecht finds support for his own ideas: "The alienation effect intervenes, not in the form of absence of emotion, but in the form of emotions which need not correspond to those of the character portrayed. . . . The alienation effect does not in any way demand an unnatural way of acting. It has nothing whatever to do with ordinary stylization. On the contrary, the achievement of an A-effect absolutely depends on lightness and naturalness of performance" (Brecht 1974:94–95). Brecht's perception of alienation effects in Chinese theater, as Leonard Pronko observes, arises from his unfamiliarity with Chinese stage conventions. It is, in fact, the norm for a Chinese audience to react emotionally to the performance of traditional theater. Brecht's feeling of coldness in Chinese acting is the result of subjective misunderstanding. The reason for this peculiar reception, Pronko suggests, is that "the unfamiliar always causes us to focus our attention on the exterior until we are capable of going beyond it to the emotions within" (1967:57). In such a process of what she calls "creative misunderstanding," Xiaomei Chen see positive results of "cross-cultural communication" (1995:112).

I would argue that the supposed influence of Chinese theater on Brecht is not merely a case of Chinese acting giving rise to or inspiring Brecht's dramaturgy. Rather, it is the formation of a new aesthetic in the process of creative interaction between two cultural traditions. In this instance, the characteristic elements of Chinese acting were integrated into Brechtian dramaturgy and did not remain a differentiable entity with its original peculiarities. The relationship between Brecht's alienation effect and Chinese theater has been debated feverishly. Martin Esslin has argued that the Asian theatrical influence on Brecht "should not lead one to overlook the large extent to which the Brechtian theatre represents a return to the main stream of the European classical tradition." He further quotes Jean-Paul Sartre's observation that "the 'Verfremdungseffekt'. . . was one of the basic principles of classical French tragedy" (Esslin 1984: 129). John Willett has also shown that Brecht previously used the term "*befremden*" (seem odd to) in 1927 and "*Entfremdung*" (alienation) (Willett's translations), possibly in January 1935, before he watched Mei Lanfang's performance. Willet goes on to delineate the direct influence of the Russian critic Viktor Shklovskij's "*Priem Ostrannenija*" (device for making strange) (Brecht 1974:19–20, 76, 99). From these arguments and Brecht's own writings, it becomes clear that Brecht did not attain his idea of the alienation effect just from this brief encounter with the performance of Chinese theater.[17]

Besides the two interacting traditions—West and East—a third factor may have been the essential catalyst in the process. Brecht explicitly identifies his target to be conventional Western theater, because it discourages the audience's intellectual involvement. It is precisely within this context that he hails the art of Chinese acting for being at once objective and passionate, alienating and intriguing. He is therefore proposing a new aesthetic, from a "realistic point of view," that is inseparable from his consciousness of contemporary social and political circumstances. Although it could be argued that the meeting of Brecht and Mei was a coincidental one, the birth of that particular aesthetic nevertheless emerged from the specific historical context of that meeting.

Gao's embrace of the two traditions was similar in a certain respect. His discovery of Brecht was preceded by his encounter with Stanislavsky and Meyerhold. In his dissatisfaction with Chinese orthodox realist drama based on Stanislavsky's system, he first turned to Meyerhold, who proposed a theater that diverged from Stanislavsky's mode of representation. Then, Brecht's epic theater pointed him toward indigenous Chinese theater. In the process of establishing his dramaturgy, one of Gao's foremost concerns was to search for a mode of expression that would prove to be more effective in representing contemporary life and consciousness. Brecht, Artaud, and several other Western dramatists have guided Gao in his understanding of the connections between theater and contemporaneity. Some of these influences may have further stimulated his awareness of the contemporary significance of indigenous Chinese theatrical art.

In 1982, in the context of a comparison of traditional *xieyi* theater with Western realist theater, Huang Zuolin summarized the characteristics of traditional Chinese theater as fluidity *(liuchangxing)*, flexibility *(shensuoxing)*, sculpturality *(diaoshuxing)*, and formality *(guifanxing)* (Huang 1982:164). Gao's perception of Chinese theater was engendered within a similar context. Furthermore, Huang and Gao were both inspired by Brecht's creative misinterpretation of Chinese theater. It could be argued that, if it had not been for Brecht's perception of Chinese theater as "alienated," the Chinese dramatists Huang and Gao would not have realized the significance of indigenous theater in a contemporary sense. Although it is impossible to trace back to a traditional theater that is "uncontaminated" by foreign interpretations, the creative process of misinterpretation has continued, in this instance, a further misinterpretation by the Chinese based on the former misinterpretation by their Western predecessors.

In formulating his distinctive aesthetics, Gao appears to be more akin to Artaud than to Brecht, although, again, he has not adopted Artaud's ideas without creative distortions. Artaud aspires to a theater that "will recapture from cinema, music-hall, the circus and life itself, those things that always belonged to it." By employing all possible actions and issues, this theater attempts to invoke the senses and intellect of its audience, numbed by popular psychological theater and cinema (Artaud 1993:64–67). Artaud's total theater is therefore inseparable from his notion of the Theater of Cruelty, which attempts to present physicality resisting pacification and subduing social reality with its powerful universal and primordial forces. Gao's concept of theater displays discernible traces of Artaudian theatrical intensity, but with the appropriation of Artaud's notion, Gao identifies traditional Chinese theater as possessing the essence of total theater. Clearly, Gao has again integrated two genealogically unrelated entities, in this instance Artaudian theater and Chinese theater, in the development of his own aesthetic.

Gao delineates the three dominant characteristics of traditional Chinese theater as syntheticality *(zonghexing)*, suppositionality *(jiadingxing)*, and narrativity *(xushuxing)*.[18] First, he explains, traditional theater is a synthetic combination of the arts of singing *(chang)*, reciting *(nian)*, acting *(zuo)*, and acrobatic performance *(da)* that relies on the high level of performing techniques achieved by the actors. Second, it always clearly presents itself as acting and does not attempt to re-present reality or create an illusion of reality. Both the actors and audience are aware that what happens on the stage is suppositionally displayed. It is through this suppositional performance that the audience's imagination is being manipulated as it becomes convinced by the actors' performing skill. Third, the structure of traditional theater is narrative in nature, both in the script and the actors' performance. It therefore provides ample space and freedom, which require neither temporal-spatial objectivity nor Aristotelian dramatic unity (Gao 1988b:80–82).

Making use of a wide range of theatrical means and particularly emphasizing its kinship to the syntheticality of traditional theater, Gao designates his experimentation with the label "total theater" *(wanquan de xiju)* (Gao 1988b:133). While Artaud's notion has provided him with openness and freedom in theatrical exploration, elements of traditional Chinese theater are the substantive means by which Gao attempts to integrate his contemporary experimentation. Gao's assimilation of traditional Chinese theater and the indigenization *(minzu hua)* of spoken drama of the early 1950s are essentially different in their approaches. While the latter focused mainly on the adoption of the traditional theater's formalized representation, Gao's idea is to understand and incorporate the spirit of traditional theater and to apply it to contemporary theater creatively without the restraints of rigidity of form. I would argue that the emphasis on stylized formal appropriation in the effort at indigenization carried out in the 1950s did not work very well, as it was unable to probe into the intrinsic essence of traditional theater. Some of the more successful examples, such as Lao She's *Chaguan* (Teahouse, 1957), portray indigenousness in theme and content, but the mode of representation is patently none other than Stanislavskian realism.

Compared with Huang Zuolin's *xieyi* drama, Gao provides a different perspective for contemporary theater to work from. Huang was a man of great ideas, and his concept of *xieyi* freed Chinese realist drama from its ideological restrictions. However, *xieyi* is such a comprehensive concept that, on the one hand, it allows great freedom for interpretation and experimentation (Huang himself never confined his directing to any particular style or school). On the other hand, *xieyi*'s abstractness defies being pinned down to a specific direction in the search for alternative aesthetics. Huang's concept of *xieyi* works only through practice, and it always works with the results of disparate creativities. In contrast to Huang, Gao's total theater displays concrete methods of performance that are able to guide the director toward the realization of a dramatic text. In other words, Gao offers a workable dramaturgy. Gao's dramaturgy suggests how the characteristics of traditional theater can be assimilated to enhance the expressivity of contemporary theater. At the same time, with the notion of suppositionality, which derives from traditional theater, Gao's total theater provides freedom in the creative employment of different representational modes. What Huang and Gao suggest, successfully, in my view, is an open mode of artistic creativity. If one pictures a Venn diagram in which orthodox realism is one set of aesthetics among the various overlapping "sets" within the "universe," the alternative aesthetic proposed by Huang and Gao is not just another set but essentially opens up to the entire universe beyond that enclosed set.

The odyssey of Huang Zuolin, Gao Xingjian, and other post–Cultural Revolution dramatists in their search for alternative aesthetics can be seen in a different light by placing it within the greater historical context of the development of Chinese modern drama. During the early introduction of modern drama, dramatists of the May Fourth era generally set their agenda in political and social terms. As in other literary and intellectual spheres characterized by C. T. Hsia's (1971) notion of the "obsession with China," the foremost target of the dramatists was to educate a people they deemed to be backward and ignorant. Furthermore, those dramatists were prepared to launch attacks on traditional Chinese theater, which they perceived as being divorced from reality and generating a paralyzing effect. They therefore appropriated Ibsenian realist drama to construct a fourth wall, until then nonexistent on the Chinese stage, so as to present an illusory reality for didactic purposes.

Once erected, the fourth wall stayed intact for almost half a century. In the post–Cultural Revolution era, contemporary dramatists have reversed what the May Fourth dramatists painstakingly established. They demolished the fourth wall that their predecessors had constructed. They rediscovered and embraced the traditional theater that their predecessors had discarded and attacked. This is not a historical cycle in which erection and demolition of the fourth wall will recur alternately. Evidently, for the dramatists of the two eras, the nature of their ordeal is essentially different. While the May Fourth dramatists adopted a utilitarian approach, Huang, Gao, and their contemporaries took off on an endeavor in the exploration of dramatic aesthetics.

Chapter 2
Exploration in Action

The Context of 1980s China

The search for alternative aesthetics, enthusiastically and consistently pursued by Chinese dramatists, was carried out against a background of fluctuating official control over artistic and intellectual activities. In the post–Cultural Revolution era, as in the previous three decades under communist rule, policies toward artists and intellectuals were "characterized by cycles of relative restriction and relative tolerance" (Hamrin 1987: 275). While changes in official control still had political significance, the relatively long periods of relaxation in the 1980s provided some room for artistic exploration. In the field of drama, the challenge to Stanislavskian representation continued to be an important part of dramatists' endeavors. On the one hand, exploration into new areas, especially modernism and humanism, forced realism to face "a self-subverting crisis" (Chen Xiaoming 1996:160) and intensified the reexamination of realist representational modes. On the other hand, the establishment of a new aesthetic suggested different ways of representing reality and thus provided alternative perspectives on how reality could be perceived.

The formation of alternative aesthetics through experimentation with forms and styles had taken place without directly endangering, at least on the surface, orthodox ideologies. That pursuit had begun as early as the late 1950s with Huang Zuolin's introduction of Brechtian theater. With the relative relaxation of official control in the 1980s, this process was able to develop into a major dramatic trend. After the staging of *Hot Spring Outside* in 1980, many plays that diverged stylistically from realism had been produced. Each one invited fervent discussions, confined within the perimeter of aesthetics. These productions were labeled *"tansuo xiju"* (exploratory drama) for their experimental formal and stylistic characteristics. It is thus not surprising that *Hot Spring Outside*, generally perceived by Chinese critics as one of the first exploratory plays, even acquired official endorsement with the conferment of an award by the Chinese Ministry of Culture. The reason *Hot Spring Outside* received such an enthusiastic response was due more to its novel form than to novelty in content. While it had surmounted the realistic setting by adopting techniques such as direct address of the audience and dialogization of characters' internal feelings, its thematic concerns nonetheless continued to be the current social issues found in other more conventional works.

In this respect, *Hot Spring Outside* can be seen as a transitional piece of work, combining formal exploration with contemporary social concerns. From 1977 to 1979, the expression of grief and resentment that came to the surface with the end of the Cultural Revolution had resulted in plays condemning the Gang of Four and praising revolutionary veterans. Examples of these plays were Bai Hua's *Shuguang* (The light of dawn, 1977) and Zong Fuxian's *Yu wusheng chu* (Where there is silence, 1978). These works were akin to the so-called literature of the wounded *(shanghen wenxue)* and literature of reform *(gaige wenxue)* of the same period. The writers anxiously attempted to reveal the psychological and physical predicaments of the Chinese people brought about by political suppression during the previous decade. They also hailed the modernization process initiated by the current leadership by depicting positive and heroic figures at different societal levels. The hidden significance of this celebration of the current social and political regime should not be overlooked, Xiaomei Chen suggests, as it was "on many occasions used as a cover-up for criticizing the communist system in general, a system that produced a Maoist regime as well as a Dengist one" (Chen 1995:51). Chen may be overestimating the climate of revolt, especially in the early period. However, first with the reintroduction of Western nonrealist plays, then with the appropriation of Western nonrealist techniques, Chinese playwrights had embarked on their own form of exploration.

The term *"tansuo xiju"* is generally recognized and adopted in critical discourse, although terms such as *"xianfeng xiju"* (avant-garde drama), *"shiyan xiju"* (experimental drama), and *"xinchao xiju"* (new wave drama) have been used interchangeably to describe a similar corpus of works. As one critic points out, the term *"tansuo"* is confusing and imprecise. Since exploration is one of the fundamental characteristics of all arts, he asks, "is there a drama that is 'nonexploratory'?" (Ding 1991:4). The essential issue is therefore what kind of exploration was being carried out. Was it merely an exploration in form per se, or was there the further complexity of a combination of formal and thematic exploration?

As revealed by the different terms used to refer to it and by the example of *Hot Spring Outside*, exploratory drama began with experimentation in form. In general, Chinese critics perceived the effort at formal renovation of drama to be a direct response to dwindling audiences. Since 1980, the attendance rate at theater performances had started to fall, hitting its lowest point in 1984. Critics attributed this trend to the popularity of commercial television and movies, and the monotony of the many "social problem plays" that had stifled audiences' interest (Tian Benxiang et al. 1996:9–10; Gao Wensheng et al. 1990:43–44). While these factors may have spurred such formal exploration, the basic impetus to formal renovation of drama had arisen earlier. The production of Western plays such as Brecht's in the late 1970s had widened the Chinese conception of dramatic representation, and the endeavor to establish alternatives to orthodox realism had been an ongoing process. The critics' emphasis on domestic social factors not only discounted the significance of the earlier influence of Western aesthetics as well as traditional Chinese theater, it also ignored the conscious challenge dramatists were presenting to a stultified form and the repressive ideological institutions that supported it.

It would be too simplistic to assume that the ideological institutions inherited from previous eras had been conveniently subverted and that realism had arrived at an impasse. In fact, although strongly challenged by alternative aesthetics, the notion of realism, in the post–Cultural Revolution era, survived and even underwent self-adjustment and transformation to remain the most all-embracing and multifaceted mode.

In the literary and ideological sphere at large, the literary critic Liu Zaifu argued that realism should be released from the restrictions of political ideologies. Liu observed that the self-reflective process that took place in Soviet literary circles in the late 1970s had resulted in the conclusion that realism was unbounded in its objective perception of ever evolving realities and the view that realist writers should be free in their selection of subject matter and methods of representation. Proposing the notion of a "historically open system," he professed that mechanical reflectionism that attempts to "depict nature in its reality" had become obsolete and that a strong consciousness of authorial subjectivity had enabled writers to incorporate different styles in carrying out their literary experimentation (Liu 1986:15–18). As Liu separated mechanical reflectionism from realism and highlighted the flexibility of subjectivity, he made it appear that almost all other modes of representation could readily be incorporated into realism.

Realism in dramatic arts experienced a similar intrinsic expansion in scope. In fact, as early as in the 1930s, Brecht had envisioned a realist drama that possessed the flexibility to employ new forms. In the 1980s, Chinese critics were quick to react to the possible crisis realism would face if it were to further rigidify as a closed aesthetic entity. Some common views included a call for the integration of realism and modernism "on the foundation of realism" (Tian Benxiang 1988:39) and the manifestation of a more open sort of realism that "can also adopt artistic means such as absurdity, symbolism and imagination" (Chen Long 1995:14). Admittedly, these attempts to redefine realism displayed an effort to sustain the legitimacy of realism as an existing ideological institution. "Neorealism" *(xin xianshi zhuyi)* is the term by which some critics designated the revived and expanded representational mode. Within the specific sociocultural context of 1980s China, the transformation and reformation of realism could also be seen as an effort to legitimize the experimentation with new forms.

In this renewed capacity, realism was not only rejuvenated, but also changed and expanded to accommodate most exploratory drama. A single author might discuss the same dramatic pieces on different occasions or in different chapters as both exploratory drama and realist drama. For instance, all three plays by Gao Xingjian that were staged in China were generally perceived as successful examples of exploratory drama. They were also acclaimed for their contribution to "enriching and expanding the dramatic concepts of realism" and "intensifying its substance" (Hu Xingliang 1995:356; Tian et al. 1996:87). Such an ambiguous demarcation between the two literary subgenres suggests a deep ideological reconstruction in progress. On the one hand, the emergence of exploratory drama was founded on a craving for liberalization in form. However, its newly acquired forms inevitably forced it to adopt different points of view toward the same contemporary sociocultural issues. In this process, not only did an alternative aesthetic emerge, but an attempt was made to establish an alternative discursive formation.

As the challenge from exploratory drama appeared to be vigorous and even subversive, writers and critics who stressed the importance of holding onto realism were forced to reflect on its validity and flexibility. In practice, realist playwrights began to incorporate techniques from other schools when they produced plays such as Liu Jinyun's *Gou'er ye niepan* (Father Doggie nirvana, 1986), which was claimed to be one of the classic examples of so-called neorealist drama. Ideologically, the expansion of realism enabled it to accommodate exploratory drama and therefore transformed the existing challenge into an impetus within its own perimeters. In so doing, a possible external power relationship was internalized. The modernist spirit of exploratory drama therefore was not only an external challenge to realism, but also constituted an integral part of that discursive structure.

In fact, the attempt of realism to accommodate exploratory drama may have backfired. Not only did the modernist spirit of the latter not disintegrate, but realism, in the process of incorporating a modernist spirit, became involved in the construction of a Chinese modernity. In the literary arena at large, Xudong Zhang discards the dichotomy of realism and the avant-garde as a "self-deceptive, complacent mythology" and argues that both are involved in a symbolic sphere in which modernism, as a massive social-symbolic shifter, "moves the social experience engendered by the sphere of social praxis into a better equipped symbolic space" (1997:111, 120–121). Modernism, at once hailed by the intellectual elite as an alternative aesthetic and denounced by the Chinese authorities as reactionary, nevertheless permeated the post–Cultural Revolutionary era. Both as an end and a means in the construction of modernity, the modernist spirit in Chinese drama did not display, from this perspective, a challenge to any external target, but an ongoing challenge to itself.

The experience of modernity is not new to the Chinese. The genesis of this idea can be traced to the late Qing period, and, as Leo Lee (1983) suggests, its appearance in Chinese literature has been particularly visible since the last decade of the nineteenth century. After the fervent pursuit of modernity during the May Fourth era, it faded from the center stage in the politically suggestive literature under the Communist regime. David Wang (1997) argues that there were various notions of modernity in the late Qing that were "repressed" by the May Fourth discourse. After the Cultural Revolution, however, the pursuit of modernity was gradually resumed against a more open and economically oriented backdrop. The determination to achieve modernization in material life eventually brought the Chinese people an experience similar to that of the development of capitalism in the West.

The experience of modernity, as Marshall Berman observes, permeates all spheres in an era of capitalism and industrialism. Berman argues that modern people are situated in environments that bring about fulfillment as well as disillusionment in both material and spiritual realms. Modernity is thus "a paradoxical unity, a unity of disunity: it pours us all into a maelstrom of perpetual disintegration and renewal, of struggle and contradiction, of ambiguity and anguish" (Berman 1983:15). That experience is essentially a process of self-reflection, self-realization, and self-recuperation. In the post–Cultural Revolution era, orthodox ideological institutions as well as historical and cultural traditions were confronted with conscious and vigorous reevaluation. External influences, especially Western ideologies, combined with the comparatively more open and vibrant socioeconomic climate left the Chinese cultural and intellectual elite with the task of defining a new public sphere.

In this endeavor contemporary Chinese dramatists demonstrated a spirit similar to that of their predecessors during the May Fourth era. Quoting C. T. Hsia's classic notion of the "obsession with China" as the dominant theme of modern Chinese literature during the first half of the twentieth century, Leo Lee asserts that, to the May Fourth writers, modernity appeared as an iconoclastic revolt against tradition; their revolt arose from China's sociopolitical conditions. Writers were generally preoccupied with content rather than form and deliberately chose realism as the mode to make sense of their immediate environment (Lee 1983:451–452). A similar obsession was present in the post–Cultural Revolution era. The critic Hu Xingliang in proposing the notion of neorealism suggests that dramatists' "modern consciousness" (xiandai yishi) was a vital constituent of the dramatic scene of the 1980s. He argues that this consciousness is manifested in the contradictory actions and sophisticated emotions of modern characters, while at the same time, he perceives that dramatists have a consciousness of standing at a "higher historical level" (Hu 1995:359–361). While this may not be true for all dramatists, many have displayed a sense of "moral burden" similar to that of the May Fourth elite.

Although the task of these dramatists to understand and represent reality is somewhat unitary in conception, they chose vastly disparate means to accomplish it. In the process of exploration, form became a motif in the representation of modernity. Geremie Barmé's pessimistic comment that it was unlikely that Chinese modernism would "flourish and result in a revolution in content and not just a faddish experimentation with artistic forms" (1983b:377) underestimates the ideological significance of form. In the modern era of late capitalism, Terry Eagleton suggests, "aesthetic becomes the guerrilla tactics of secret subversion, of silent resistance, of stubborn refusal." He further argues that in the modern aesthetic form becomes its content, "a form which repulses all social semantics and might just allow us a glimpse of what it might conceivably be like to be free" (Eagleton 1990:369). In this light, the dialectics of form and motif deserve a closer and more thorough scrutiny. Through an examination of the forms adopted by Chinese dramatists and their appropriation of these forms, a clearer picture of their ideological intentions and intellectual consciousness can emerge.

It is within the context of form as constituting content that Gao Xingjian must be considered. Well versed in modern Western literature, especially French, and displaying a strong modernist spirit, Gao began his career as a playwright with cautious and humble experimentation. Gradually he presented his aesthetic and intellectual views with bolder creativity. Discussion in this chapter will focus on Gao's three major plays— *Alarm Signal* (1982), *The Bus Stop* (1983), and *Wild Man* (1985)—which were produced before he left China in 1987. All were staged by the Beijing People's Art Theatre. Gao's last play written in China, *The Other Shore* (1986), will not be considered here, as in this play he shows larger concerns that are not circumscribed by the Chinese sociocultural context.[1]

Appropriation as a Creative Process

In his formal innovations, Gao Xingjian is usually perceived as the playwright most influenced by Western avant-garde theater and especially the Theater of the Absurd. For critics who approve of his experimentation, he is a "self-conscious and courageous explorer" who has led the renewal of modern Chinese drama (Ye 1989:1–2). For those who disapprove, however, Gao has merely displayed "a product of the blind worship and mechanical copying of the social viewpoints and creative theories of modernist drama in the West" (He 1983:390). Traces of appropriation are discernible in his dramatic works, especially elements from the dramatic works of Samuel Beckett. I shall attempt to show below that many novel formal techniques employed by Gao, such as the use of sound effects as a dramatic character and the complex structuration of multivocality, indeed have their origins in Beckett's plays. However, just as his so-called absurdist plays deserve a different definition from the Theater of the Absurd, Gao has creatively appropriated forms from Beckettian theater for the construction of his own dramaturgy. While Gao has not duplicated the pessimistic outlook of such theater (he even opposes Beckett's subversion of the conventional idea of dramatics), an alternative viewpoint has inevitably emerged in his new mode of representation. Gao has attempted in his early plays appropriating Western theatrical techniques —and this is especially visible in *The Bus Stop*—to reveal human subjectivity, a quality previously repressed in conventional realist theater.

The first play Gao wrote after he was transferred to the Beijing People's Art Theatre in 1981 as a professional playwright was *The Bus Stop*. Critics have no difficulty labeling it the first Chinese absurdist play (Barmé 1983:373), and they rightfully observe its close resemblance to Samuel Beckett's *Waiting for Godot* (Tam 1990:23). However, as Gao had become a target of the campaign against capitalist liberalization then under way, the play was rejected.[2] Subsequently, Gao was asked to write a play that was more realistic in style. He did so and produced *Alarm Signal*, which he called, in retrospect, a "product of conscious compromise" (Gao 1998a). Although *Alarm Signal* was Gao's first play to be staged, it was not initially approved for performance. The reason was not strictly political, though the issue of unemployment presented in the play was undoubtedly taboo at the time. Instead it was disallowed because its proposed form of representation was a breach of the tradition of socialist realism in the Beijing People's Art Theatre.[3] In the name of a "trial performance" *(shiyan yanchu)*, the play was scheduled for just two performances and opened to a restricted audience from drama circles. However, because it had a personal endorsement from Yu Shizhi, vice president of the Beijing People's Art Theatre, and overwhelming support from the invited guests, it went public and set a record of more than one hundred performances in a studio theater accommodating about one hundred spectators that had been converted from a rehearsal studio.

Alarm Signal is a play with a conventional structure: it has an introduction, development, climax, and denouement. Its plot and characters are both constructed in a realist manner. The play presents the love affairs and the phenomena of social entrapment, such as unemployment and crime, experienced by three youths, all typical of early 1980s China. Heizi is unemployed, filled with uncertainty about the future, and is tempted to help rob a cargo train. Mifeng, Heizi's girlfriend, although also unemployed, is optimistic and idealistic in nature. Xiaohao, the third youth, is more fortunate as he will succeed his father in his job and is an apprentice train guard. However, instead of being happy about this state of affairs, he is disappointed because his original aspiration was to play the trumpet and because his love for Mifeng has not been fulfilled. The suspense heightens as the Senior Train Guard begins to suspect that Heizi is about to commit a crime in collaboration with a robber who is on board the train in disguise.

Although the play was said to mark "the birth of avant-garde theater in China" by the French newspaper *Le monde,* the only technique it uses that can be regarded as nonrealist is the externalization of characters' thoughts and feelings. This externalization takes place in three areas: psychological activities, recollections of the past, and imagination. While engaged in these activities, the characters are isolated from the realistic setting and enter a different theatrical space. This space is defined by the use of special lighting and sound effects that diverge from the usual realistic setting. In this separately defined space, the characters' behavior is distorted from their normal behavior in real life to accord with their psychological states.

Compared to his later plays, *Alarm Signal* is a humble and cautious preliminary experiment. The issues portrayed that are highly relevant to people's daily lives stimulated fervent reactions in the audience, and Chinese critics responded overwhelmingly and positively to its formal novelty. In a conventional performance, recollection of the past is usually presented as a realistic experience of the characters. With the help of technical effects, Gao makes a powerful portrayal of a type of subjectivity that is virtually absent in conventional realist plays. In a scene where Mifeng's aspiration is expressed through her imagination, a soft light is cast on her to show her naïveté and optimism. At the same time, an eerie green spotlight is on Heizi, the suspect, and this light disrupts the harmony of the setting. The internal conflicts experienced by Mifeng are not presented in her physical actions but through technical effects, and these suggest her subjectivity.

This effect is more apparent in the scene where Mifeng and Heizi exchange their inner thoughts in a dreamlike ambience. The characters step away from the realistic setting while the lighting changes. By separating the characters' interior thoughts from the realistic mise-en-scène, the repressive reality is temporarily sidestepped. The characters' subjectivity, represented by their hidden feelings for each other, is released and expressed in a symbolic manner. As this technique is used throughout the play, the audience is consistently reminded of and confronted with the subjectivity that is unexpressed in conventional situations and thus usually perceived as nonexistent. The externalization of the characters' thoughts and feelings is therefore not merely a technical innovation but an intentional effort to embark on experimentation with a new aesthetic.

A further and more thorough appropriation of Western theater is exemplified in *The Bus Stop*. In this first play that Gao wrote as a professional playwright, it is probable that he deliberately appropriated elements from *Waiting for Godot*, for which he had expressed admiration in his earlier essays. Gao knew the political danger in admitting to any relation of himself or his play with absurdist drama and cautiously rejected any suggestion that there was such an association. To be labeled as an "absurdist" was tantamount to being called a "reactionary." More important, as I shall show below, he attempted to establish an aesthetic essentially different from the works of Western absurdist theater. With seven characters covering the spectrum of typical suburban people, the play begins as they wait at a bus stop heading toward the city. At the beginning, they squabble and shove each other. As time goes by, buses speed past and never stop. Eventually, they realize that ten years have passed and they are unable to accomplish their tasks in the city. As the plot suggests, the play revolves around the notion of "waiting." In this process of waiting, each of them experiences hope, despair, frustration, and anxiety.

With *The Bus Stop*, Gao was perceived as a pioneer in introducing elements of the Theater of the Absurd to the Chinese audience. However, Geremie Barmé has rightly pointed out a fundamental disparity: while Beckett exhibits total disillusionment in humankind, Gao's play, at least insofar as the text is concerned, expresses a "positive view" toward Chinese society (Barmé 1983b:375). However, because this play was produced in China, it need not be taken as fully expressing Gao's attitude toward reality. In fact, Gao asserts that all his plays produced in China are "products of conscious compromise" (Gao 1998a). He exercised a certain degree of self-censorship to enable production of his plays. Nevertheless, a comparison between *The Bus Stop* and *Waiting for Godot* based on analysis of the printed text may prove helpful in perceiving what Gao intends to represent by selectively appropriating elements from Beckett's play.

"In *Waiting for Godot*," Martin Esslin summarizes, "the feeling of uncertainty it produces, the ebb and flow of this uncertainty—from the hope of discovering the identity of Godot to its repeated disappointment —are themselves the essence of the play" (1991:45). While Beckett's protagonists do not know who Godot is, when he will come, and what will happen when he comes, the seven characters in *The Bus Stop*, by contrast, are completely certain about what they want to do. Their initial optimism is conveyed by a silent character in addition to the seven anxious passengers. The Silent Man, who has waited for the bus together with the other passengers, halfway through the play starts his journey unnoticed. As intended by the playwright, the staging of *The Bus Stop* was preceded by Lu Xun's *Guoke* (The passer-by), and the same actor played both the Passer-By in Lu Xun's play and the Silent Man in *The Bus Stop*. In planning this conjunction of plays, Gao attempted to borrow Lu Xun's image of the wayfarer, easily recognized by the Chinese audience, who proceeds with his journey regardless of uncertainty, in stark contrast to the other characters who hesitate.

At the end of *Waiting for Godot*, because the long awaited Godot has not come, Vladimir asks, "Well? Shall we go?" Estragon replies, "Yes, let's go." And the stage direction reads, "They do not move." Their failure to move despite having agreed to leave only shows that the stagnant situation has not changed after all. They have displayed their sense of futility through their nonaction. *The Bus Stop* ends in a similar situation. The seven characters are finally ready to set off on their journey to the city. Although the characters are indecisive and hesitant, they are reminded that the situation of "waiting" is expected to change if they are determined to start their journey and demonstrate the power of human will. Action or the willingness to take action is the message in Gao's play. In this light, *The Bus Stop*, despite Gao's professed indebtedness to *Waiting for Godot*, is not a descendant of the Theater of the Absurd but a so-called absurdist play of a different nature.

In Martin Esslin's account, "the Theatre of the Absurd strives to express its sense of the senselessness of the human condition and the inadequacy of the rational approach by the open abandonment of rational devices and discursive thought" (1991:24). It is apparent that this sense of absurdity does not form the essence of *The Bus Stop*. What Gao presents in his play is more appropriately defined in the common-sensical usage of the word "absurd," which Esslin quotes as "out of harmony with reason or propriety; incongruous, unreasonable, illogical" (ibid.:23). The absurdity in Gao's play, in this sense, serves as a means to reveal the characters' subjectivity rather than to portray pessimism toward reality.

The first half of *The Bus Stop*, showing the seven characters beginning to shove each other and argue about current social issues, is adequately realistic in style. It is only when they find out with shock they have waited for the bus for one year that the situation turns absurd:

Carpenter: Hey, sir, what time does your watch say?

Bespectacled: *(Looks at his watch and is shocked.)* What? What . . .

Carpenter: Isn't it working?

Bespectacled: It would be better if it wasn't. . . . Goodness, one year has passed!

Girl: You're lying!

Bespectacled: *(Looks at his watch again.)* It's true, we have already waited at the bus stop for a whole year!

. . .

(The Girl runs away, burying her face in her hands. Everyone is grave and silent.)

Mother: *(Talks to herself.)* They have no more clothes to change into. He can do nothing, he can't even mend his torn trousers. Peipei will be crying her heart out for mom, my poor Peipei. . . .

(The Girl squats down. Everybody slowly gathers around her.)

Bespectacled: *(Softly.)* What's wrong with you?

Carpenter: Are you hungry? I've still got a piece of pancake in my bag.

Old Man: Stomachache?

Director Ma: *(Shouts at the audience.)* Where is the doctor? Someone who knows medical treatment come and take a look!

Mother: *(Controlling herself, walks over and bends toward the Girl.)* Where aren't you feeling well? Tell me. *(Strokes her head.)*

(Gao 1985a:99–101)

Through the unfamiliarity of their current situation and the estrangement of the characters from the reality that they are used to, Gao strips off their social façade and unveils their inner subjectivity, which is normally concealed. Some of them start to reveal their genuine emotions and show concern for others. The absurdity in the play is therefore a means to reveal subjectivity. By releasing repressed emotional subjectivity and overcoming psychological rationality, paradoxically, the first half of the play, which is supposed to represent objective reality, appears irrational and thus absurd. In the transformation from real-life absurdity to the situational absurdity of fantastic imagination—the turning point comes at the time when the characters realize that they have waited for ten years at the bus stop—the playwright has constructed a surreal locality for the expression of individual subjectivity. In this light, *The Bus Stop* is not an example of Theater of the Absurd but essentially anti-absurdist, that is, against the abstraction of action.

Critics have argued that the conventional perception of *Waiting for Godot* as an antiplay of nonaction, because of its lack of plot and logical movement, and its digressions, is debatable. Waiting as an action, Andrew Kennedy suggests, albeit indirect and ambivalent, forms a never-ending cycle "of expectations and let-downs, of uncertainty and of run-down." He further asserts that the repeating acts of waiting "underline the endless action-in-non-action cycles, suggesting an infinite series" and that this is achieved by parodying, changing, and counterpointing the conventional expectations of drama (Kennedy 1989:25, 42–43). This formal characteristic of Beckett's play is inseparable from its philosophical outlook, which constitutes the essence of its absurdity.

Viewed from this perspective, Gao has clearly adopted a different attitude in his appropriation of Beckett. Although he admits that absurdity is the motif of *The Bus Stop*, Gao asserts that, while Beckett has transformed drama into a forum for contemplating metaphysical issues, he retains drama's human and artistic sensibility. What Gao wants to achieve is not purely a philosophical discussion through dramatic representation but an exciting dramatic experience in the audience. Action, in particular, is the fundamental constituent of Gao's dramaturgy. In his theater, different forms of action—physical, verbal, psychological, and even actions expressed by lighting and sound effects—are employed to achieve a kaleidoscopic dramatic effect.

Although he rejects the abstraction of action in Beckettian theater, Gao was undoubtedly inspired by some of the formal representational techniques in Beckett's plays. For instance, both Beckett and Gao try to maximize the use of sound effects. To Gao, sound effects are not only an integral part of his theatrical performance, but they are further portrayed as an autonomous character. In *Alarm Signal*, the sound of a traveling train recurs in variations at different junctures. At the beginning, it is sluggish and monotonous. Later, the blaring noise of the passing trains characterizes the unrealistic scenes of recollection and imagination. Using terms derived from music to describe the speed of the train, Gao indicates an increase in the speed of the traveling train from "adagio" to "andante," then "allegro," and finally "presto" (Gao 1985a:82). In this sense, the sound serves as both a mood setter and a leitmotif in the play, and represents dramatic action as well.

Gao introduces music as a separate, autonomous character more explicitly in *The Bus Stop*. Interestingly, Beckett employed such a technique in plays like *Words and Music* and *Cascando*. As Beckett displays a highly developed musical sensibility in these plays, the identification of music as an autonomous character is sometimes perceived as the "collapse of faith in verbal language" (Kalb 1994:131). In contrast, Gao's musical character in *The Bus Stop* represents a personified dramatic counterpoint to the situational development. After the Silent Man has left quietly, a musical motif, which the playwright designates as the "music of the Silent Man," is heard nine times in variations. At first, the music is faint and indistinct, but gradually it becomes clearer and faster, and develops into an all-encompassing march. If the seven characters who have been waiting impatiently for the bus represent the ordinary Chinese people in general, the Silent Man perhaps symbolizes someone who has the foresight to reflect on reality and set himself free from the absurd situation by voluntarily taking his own action. Although the Silent Man leaves the scene of waiting early, the consciousness of this prescient loner does not retreat entirely. It continues to reappear as a musical motif, significantly always along with the sound of a bus speeding away, thus serving to remind and urge the characters to realize the absurdity of their situation.

The "music of the Silent Man" is therefore a form—a sound effect in the form of music—that is transformed into the alter ego of the Silent Man. As a musical motif, it continues to intervene in the actions of the other characters in a transcendent manner. Like the exhortative voice of a prophet, it is a reflection of the playwright's subjective consciousness. In this sense, *The Bus Stop* is not an absurdist play in which all beings are trapped in the futility of repeating and endless cycles of meaningless existence. Dramatic actions seem to be in a process of development, because the musical motif continually reminds the characters and makes them more determined to take up their own course instead of waiting incessantly. However, whether their aspiration will ever be realized in the conclusive action of leaving the bus stop is doubtful. The play ends as they are all ready to move on, and Director Ma, one of the seven characters, halts the group to tie his shoelace. With this suggestive action by Director Ma, the play comes to an end. However, unlike the end of *Alarm Signal*, it is an end without a clear solution, to which Chinese audiences have become accustomed, to the problems raised throughout the play.

When asked about his attitude toward Chinese society, Gao explicitly expressed the pessimism and despair he felt as early as his writing of *The Bus Stop* (Gao 1998a). By making the Silent Man and the recurrent musical motif into dramatis personae, Gao indicates the presence of both alienation and sobriety in his intellectual consciousness. He neither entirely negates the existence of humankind and its future like Beckett, nor does he indulge in the "obsession with China" of many of his predecessors and contemporaries. In fact, Gao appears to be a silent loner, himself a passer-by in the contemporary Chinese context. The image of solitariness that first appeared in *The Bus Stop* reemerges as the Old Singer in *Wild Man* and becomes a recurring motif in his later works, especially those written in exile.

Inspiration from Tradition

Although Gao Xingjian is usually considered a modernist playwright who has been greatly influenced by Western ideas and has appropriated Western dramatic techniques on a large scale, the art of traditional Chinese theater continues to be an essential component of his creativity. Yet when he takes a close look at the traditional theater, he has to reexamine it in the context of both modern theater and modern times. While trying to assimilate its spirit, he displays a pessimistic attitude toward the vitality of traditional theater. This attitude has led him to contemplate traditional and folk cultures, especially those being marginalized, in which a similar pessimism is exhibited.

Having been exposed to traditional *xiqu* since he was a child, Gao has a deep understanding of it and even writes about its reformation. Gao's idea of the reformation of *xiqu* displays his respect for its traditional artistry. Whereas he opposes reforming *xiqu* with Stanislavskian realism (as was commonly practiced during the 1950s and 1960s), he suggests discarding any rigidified elements and combining an understanding of its essential spirit with the addition of new modes of expression. For example, he suggests the incorporation of *xiangsheng* (cross-talk) and *wushu* (martial arts), both forms of Chinese folk art, to enrich *xiqu* performance (Gao 1988b:71–76). These suggestions are in fact consistent with his treatment of *xiqu* in his modern plays.

In almost all his plays, traces of the creative assimilation of traditional *xiqu* are discernible. It is not a case of grafting traditional forms onto modern theater but of assimilating the spirit and ideas of traditional theater to establish a new dramatic aesthetic. When Gao talks about traditional forms, he often addresses the role they can play in the creation of a modern theatrical experience. From the reference to traditional acting skills in *Alarm Signal* to the creation of a theater in the spirit of traditional arts in *Wild Man*, Gao has engaged himself comprehensively in the contemplation of his tradition. As he revisits and assimilates traditional theater, he re-creates the traditions with a modern consciousness.

In *Alarm Signal*, he advises in a postscript that the actors use the technique of *pangbai* (aside) from *jingju* for the representation of the characters' inner feelings (Gao 1985a:83). In using this technique, the performers dissociate themselves from their dramatis personae and assume a different role, normally acting as a narrator, to introduce the characters or to explain the dramatic situation. Although the function of this change of role is similar to that of Brecht's narrator, Gao stresses that it originates from traditional *xiqu*. His intention is to achieve swift changes of role to enhance the effect of the different psychological states of his characters. The reference to traditional theater is even more explicitly elaborated in *The Bus Stop*, where Gao emphasizes that the performance should not achieve verisimilitude in detail, but should seek an artistic abstract or "likeness in spirit" *(shensi)*. He requires his actors to learn from *jingju* artists like Mei Lanfang and Zhou Xinfang (1895–1975), especially from their execution of the highly respected quality of "transmitting the spirit and delivering the idea" *(chuanshen dayi)* (ibid.:135).

The notion of *shen* (spirit) has been a central issue in traditional aesthetics. In his interpretation of the relation of *shen* and the external world, as discussed in the seminal work *Wenxing diaolong* by Liu Xie (c. 465–522), Stephen Owen suggests that it maintains both "a freedom and an absence of motive." *Shen* neither loses itself in the external world nor sees the latter as mere object, but participates "with them" (Owen 1992: 203–204). Like traditional *xieyi* ink painting, in which the aim of the representation is not verisimilitude but to convey the *shen* of the object, Gao's actors must attain the spirit of the theme and characters, and represent a level of truth about reality, not merely reproduce reality.

With his emphasis on *shen*, Gao does not merely transplant traditional forms into modern theater; his treatment of traditional elements is highly self-conscious. In the process of assimilation, he strongly advises against formalization and exaggeration in acting (Gao 1985a:83, 135). He attempts to choose creatively from *xiqu* the ideas that can enrich his modern theater. For example, in *Alarm Signal* and *The Bus Stop*, the set is minimal. He claims that it is thus similar to that of *xiqu* and also that the concepts of space and time are delivered through acting rather than realistic sets (Gao 1988b:45–46). As such, even formalized performing techniques from *xiqu* can be rejuvenated and given new life in his theater. His request that the actors learn from *xiqu* performers should therefore be seen in light of this intention.

Gao's attempt to integrate the ideas of Western and Chinese theater is more comprehensively exemplified in *Wild Man*, which epitomizes the extent of his experimentation in China. Although he adopts Antonin Artaud's notion of "total theater" to describe his concept of theatrical performance, his elaboration of the idea is intimately related to artistic representation in traditional Chinese theater:

> It is necessary for theater to gather up the many artistic means it has lost in the past century. This play is an attempt of modern drama to return to the traditional concept of *xiqu*. In other words, it not only emphasizes the art of spoken language, but also fully employs the techniques used in *xiqu*, such as singing, recitation, acting, and acrobatic performance. The director should try to bring the performers' potential in all these areas into full play. They might choose to emphasize their physical appearance, posture, speech, acting, singing, or dancing. There are also sections written [in the dialogues] especially for reciting. It is therefore a kind of total theater *(wanquan de xiju)*. (Gao 1985a:272)

For Artaud, the powerful physical action of primitive rituals and folk arts forms effectively counter the mechanical and stultified mentality of contemporary people. His idea of total theater, which incorporates such physicality, evokes people's sensibility and spirituality. By contrast, although he employs the artistic means of traditional Chinese theater, Gao's total theater is concerned with the revitalization of the sensibility and spirituality in the theater. There is a distinct line of demarcation between his works and what he called the "dead art" of *jingju*. His theater is not a revival of traditional *xiqu* but a newly established dramatic aesthetic.

In *Wild Man*, Gao incorporates such elements of Chinese traditional and folk arts as the epic *Hei'an zhuan* (Song of the dark), the grass-weeding dance, the exorcist mask dance to drive away drought, the roof workers' song, and the wedding song *Pei shi jiemei* (Team of sisters).[4] In Bruno Roubicek's opinion, these elements, connected with primitive rituals and shamanism, "may be seen as an attempt to return to the very roots of performance in China." Roubicek further suggests that Gao's concern in the employment of such elements is "in taking a Western approach to the exploration of elements from the earliest types of Chinese performance" (1990:188). Whether Gao has taken a Western approach in the representation of these traditional folk arts is debatable. Gao might have been inspired by Western dramatists such as Artaud and Brecht in adopting an approach toward his indigenous culture that is different from that of his Chinese counterparts.

By assuming that because of his professed interest in Western theater Gao is taking a Western approach, Roubicek has displayed a Westerner's point of view on the issue of interaction between Western and Chinese cultures. Interestingly, Gao has spoken about this issue, and his view is starkly different from that of his critic. He says: "A modern Chinese will not refuse to learn from modern Western culture. Being an Easterner, however, you digest Western culture in an Eastern way. Similarly, when Western artists turn to Eastern arts, their works inevitably encompass the spirit of the West" (1988b:179–180). Nevertheless, Gao's attitude toward Chinese cultural tradition deserves closer scrutiny.

Gao designates *Wild Man* as "multivocal modern epic theater" (*duo shengbu xiandai shishi ju*). In a somewhat similar approach to Roubicek's, the term "epic" instantly directs the attention of the researcher Jiping Zou to the West and to Brecht's notion of epic theater (Zou 1994:123). In fact, Gao is aware that Brecht's epic theater is more appropriately translated as *"xushi ju"* rather than *"shishi ju."* Although he has also extensively employed the narrative mode of Brecht's epic theater, his use of "epic" in this context refers to a primitive poetic narration of national myth and legend, in his own words, "the original meaning of epic, which describes the genesis of a nation *(minzu)*, such as the *Iliad* and the *Odyssey*" (Gao 1998a). Along with his use of other components of traditional and folk arts, Gao is making an ambitious attempt in *Wild Man* to redefine Chinese cultural traditions. These components are therefore not ornate forms to enrich his theatrical representation but the subjects of the play.

Gao's perception of the traditions he includes in *Wild Man* emerged in an era in which Chinese artists and intellectuals alike were recontemplating and reinterpreting their traditions as these traditions confronted a crisis of disengagement and dissipation. The discussions of these artists and intellectuals were part of the cultural discourse of the early 1980s and peaked in the "Great Cultural Discussion" (Wenhua da taolun) or the so-called Cultural Fever (Wenhua re), in 1985. Among other cultural and political discourses, the debates on traditions revolved around the question of how and what parts of traditions were inherited and whether the inherited traditions have any relevance in the contemporary era. Most of the participants in the Cultural Discussion belonged to a generation that had come to feel alienated from its cultural traditions as a result of repressive political demands on literature and the arts since Mao Zedong's "Talks at the Yan'an Forum" in 1942. Some of them felt that entire traditions had been negated by the May Fourth Movement. Consequently, reassessment of the various traditions became their priority, and viewpoints differed on how to conceptualize the notion of tradition.

Among these intellectuals, some, like Liu Zaifu, called for the revitalization of traditions. Others opposed the idea of reviving a tradition that they deemed stagnant and rigidly confined to the past, possessing neither creativity nor vitality in its present existence. Gan Yang, a radical intellectual and one of the leaders in the Cultural Discussion, asserts this notion emphatically. He claims: "Traditions are a process that flows through the entire temporality of the past, present, and future but do not solidify into substance. . . . Traditions have not been circumscribed; they are forever in the process of producing and creating, forever open toward the unlimited possibilities and possible worlds of the future" (Gan 1989: 21). Hence, the revitalization of traditions is seen, at least by some, not simply as a process of continuing and maintaining what has been created in the past, but as searching for elements that are fundamentally relevant to the current pursuit and can be adapted to establish a new way of living. In this process of revitalization, intensive reflection upon traditions becomes necessary. The spirit of reflection about the past, as Xudong Zhang summarizes, "places a distinct emphasis on history, a history that must be structured culturally." He further asserts that "Chinese culturalists view this structuration as an urgent anxiety, [and] this sense of urgency is an urgency to understand history in a language that sets forth the particular time and space in which historical events not merely take place, but take place as someone's own history" (Zhang 1997: 53–54).

In the midst of such discourses on cultural traditions, Gao went off in a different direction. Gao's interest in such issues had predated the nationwide fever for such discussion. He had begun his investigation into southern Chinese cultures for the writing of his first novel, *Soul Mountain*, as early as in 1982. The production of *Wild Man* came at the time when the public discussion peaked in 1985.[5] While some members of the intellectual elite were more interested in the modernization of mainstream Confucian traditionalism, Gao regards the primitive and peripheral non-literati cultures *(fei wenren wenhua)* of the Yangtze River as more attractive, lively, and universal than the northern literati culture of the Han people. He discusses four dominant formations in Chinese culture:

First, the orthodox culture that is closely related to the imperial rulers of Chinese feudal dynasties. . . . In correspondence to it are the moral doctrines and self-cultivating philosophy of Confucianism. . . .

Second, Daoism, evolving from primitive shamanism, and Buddhism, introduced from India and Sinified, although occasionally promoted and exploited by the feudal rulers, and preserved as independent religious cultures. . . .

Third, the folk cultures, including multinational mythology and legends, customs and practices, folk songs, folk rhymes, storytelling, folk dancing, and even *xiqu*, which evolved from sacrificial rituals, and *huaben xiaoshuo* (fictional scripts for storytelling).

Fourth, a quintessentially Eastern spirit, represented mainly by the naturalist philosophy of Laozi and Zhuangzi, Xuanxue philosophy of the Wei and Jin dynasties, and the philosophy of Chan Buddhism, which is divorced from its religious formation. (Gao 1996a:179)

Gao is most interested in the latter three of these cultural formations—those he deems to possess the most potent creativity. As an orthodox ideology, used over centuries by ruling regimes, Confucian traditionalism has been dogmatized and hence stultified. In his search for vitality in indigenous traditions, he turns primarily to the sphere of folk arts, which have been forgotten by the erudite elite and are barely preserved in the Yangtze region.

From this perspective, *Wild Man* is not about the "wild man" but about the destiny of marginalized cultural traditions in the modern era. Critics have readily noted the play's engagement with issues such as environmental controls, deforestation, and the dilemmas of modernization. The ultimate motive of the playwright, Roubicek perceives, is to use "the problems associated with nature conservation as a catalyst for exploring the fundamental social and political questions associated with change and modernisation experienced in a society still dominated by ancient beliefs and customs" (1990:187). These issues, undoubtedly, are components of the multilayered and complex plot of *Wild Man*. However, at a different level, they are constructed as a background against which cultural traditions face their destiny of disappearance. Such traditions were first marginalized by a dominant Confucian culture and then further marginalized in a modern era pervaded by utilitarianism and greed.

Wild Man is structurally divided into three "movements" *(zhang)*. (Again, Gao appropriates a musical concept, namely, the symphony, in the structuration of this play.) Throughout the three movements, the Old Singer appears in different capacities closely related to the respective motifs. First, the Old Singer's idyllic folk singing becomes the quiet backdrop for the massive destruction of the natural environment that takes place in the name of progress. Second, the frantic hunt for the wild man and the frenzied process of deforestation are juxtaposed with the Old Singer's *Song of the Dark*, which narrates the legendary creation of the world. Finally, the death of the Old Singer is ironically contrasted to a joyous wedding ceremony and the ending of a boy dancing with the wild man in his dream that symbolizes aspirations for a better future. In the second movement, the three primary motifs are juxtaposed, with the epic *Song of the Dark* forming a central image.

Song of the Dark depicts the story of Pan Gu, an archetypal representation of the creator of Heaven and Earth in Chinese folk legend. While the ensemble actors forcefully denounce the excessive exploitation and evil destruction of nature, the Old Singer drums and recites the story of how Pan Gu created the world. *Wild Man* shows, on the one hand, the genesis of the universe and humankind represented in an epic and, on the other, the evil of the arbitrary actions of humankind that lead to the destruction of all forms of life. The scene thus encompasses both creation and destruction. The figure of a primitive man appears while the Old Singer is narrating the legend of Pan Gu. While the actors perform the act of felling trees, the primitive man is surrounded. When a gigantic tree finally falls, he collapses and disappears (Gao 1985a:252–253). The legendary Pan Gu provides an image of the wild man (the other one appears only at the end of the play) who has been exterminated by such aggressive acts of destruction. Ironically, at the same time, a crowd of scientists, journalists, and officials agitatedly search for the wild man to study and report on as an anomaly. As the play suggests, their search is futile. Metaphorically, the destiny of the epic (a symbol of peripheral cultural traditions) will be the same as that of the wild man. The Old Singer's death in the third movement further symbolizes the predestined tragic loss of cultural traditions.

Gao's attitude toward all Chinese traditions, be they orthodox Confucian or otherwise, seems to be pessimistic. Is there a parallel derivable from his comment that *jingju* is a "dead art"? While he perceives the traditional art of *jingju* as unrenewable in the modern era, he also accepts without regret the fate of Chinese cultural traditions that are in the process of either irreversible rigidification or irretrievable disintegration. Questioned about the links between *Wild Man* and the root-searching literature of the same period, Gao asserts that, while the latter displays a mixed sense of nostalgia and repression, "I don't need to search for the roots, they are already within me" (Gao 1998a). In his attempt to establish a dramatic aesthetic of his own, he paradoxically discards and absorbs traditions that, according to him, he has already fully internalized.

The character of the Silent Man in *The Bus Stop* is assumed to be a figure that the playwright identifies with. Is there a character in *Wild Man* with whom he identifies? Some critics have suggested that the Ecologist is vaguely a self-portrait of the playwright (Gao 1988b:173). However, with his view of Chinese peripheral cultural traditions, I think that Gao identifies more deeply with the Old Singer, the only person in the world who knows the epic *Song of the Dark*, his alienation in modern society, and the fear that he too will suffer the destiny of extinction.

Multivocality: Form as a Motif

From the theaters of Brecht and Beckett to traditional *xiqu*, Gao Xingjian has visited the dramatic aesthetics of both the West and China. He advocates formal experimentation but seldom talks about ideology or the content of his plays. He has a specific goal, that is, to establish a "modern Eastern theater" *(xiandai de dongfang xiju)* in what he calls the first stage of experimentation (Gao 1998a). Although he has never explicitly defined his notion of "modern Eastern theater," it is clear that it involves a modern consciousness and techniques from both Western and Chinese theaters. The philosophies of Daoism and Chan Buddhism also constitute a vital part in this creation. *Wild Man*, according to Gao, was the final product of this first stage. The second stage, which began with *The Other Shore*, was terminated owing to the climax of the Anti–Bourgeois Liberalization Campaign in 1986. It was never resumed, as Gao left China a year later.

As a focal point for Gao's experimentation, *Wild Man* is a multifaceted play, both formally and thematically, and its inspiration can be traced to various sources. The playwright himself sees it first as an example of his ideal of "modern Eastern theater." In concluding my discussion of Gao's works written before he left China, I intend to highlight the concept of multivocality, essentially a crystallization of his ongoing program to establish a new aesthetic in his first stage of experimentation. The multivocality demonstrated in *Wild Man* is also a significant breakthrough in theatrical representation that came out of his 1980s search for alternative aesthetics. With the use of multivocality, the linear structure of realist drama is fundamentally deconstructed, while several motifs are presented at once, strongly suggesting an interreferential interpretation. Not only is multivocality a bold innovation in theatrical representation, but it is also a deliberate attempt to transform the audience's habitual perception of the representation on stage.

Multivocality *(duo shengbu)* is a theatrical representational mode that Gao consciously applies, and it was inspired by techniques in musical composition. As if writing a musical piece harmoniously formed of different melodic parts, Gao appropriates the technique of counterpoint to establish a vocal ensemble in his theater. The basic expression of multivocality comprises two or more performers speaking at the same time, harmoniously or otherwise, forming a contrapuntal effect. In addition, Gao asserts, "not only is [performers'] speech sometimes multivocal in itself, but speech combined with music and sound effects also forms a multivocal structure, even in contrast to visual effects" (1985a:273). Other playwrights, most significantly Samuel Beckett, have employed similar techniques. In his one-act play, titled *Play*, three characters (actually talking heads—the actors' bodies are hidden in large urns throughout the performance) are speaking all at once.

W1: Yes, strange, darkness best, and the darker the worse, till all dark, then all well, for the time, but it will come, the time will come, but it will come, the time will come, the thing is there, you'll see it, get off me, keep off me, all dark, all still, all over, wiped out—

W2: *(Together.)* Yes, perhaps, a shade gone, I suppose, some might say, poor thing, a shade gone, just a shade, in the head—*(Faint wild laugh.)*—just a shade, but I doubt it, I doubt it, not really, I'm all right, still all right, do my best, all I can—

M: Yes, peace, one assumed, all out, all the pain, all as if... never been, it will come—*(Hiccup.)*—pardon, no sense in this, oh I know... none the less, one assumed, peace... I mean... not merely all over, but as if... never been—

(Beckett 1990:307–308)

Perceived as a "deliberate reduction of stage figures to talking automata," *Play* demonstrates Beckett's continuous abstraction of action from the physical world (Kennedy 1989:92). Although Beckett provides precise notation for the above "chorus" in his postscript, the unintelligibility of the overlapping speeches during performance is unavoidable and offers "a pointer to its own shadowy setting, a place of diminution, an unspecific underworld" (Beckett 1990:93). Gao's idea of multivocality strongly resembles such a technique in its formal features but, as is usually the case in Gao's appropriation of Beckett and other dramatists, does not intend to negate all dramatic actions so totally. On the contrary, Gao has attempted, in an accurately orchestrated manner, to present his characters' subjectivity through forceful and individualized actions.

Gao first employed multivocality briefly in *Alarm Signal*. As the Train Guard becomes certain of the robbery plan, he orders Xiaohao to set off the alarm signal for the train to stop at the next station. Everyone on board notices something serious has happened, and the situation turns chaotic.

Train Guard:		Are you going to own up?
Train Robber:	(Almost together,	Damn it! (Jumps to his feet.)
Mifeng:	loudly.)	Ah, it's really happened!
Heizi:		It's all over.

Train Guard: Now do you get it? (Points his flashlight at the Train Robber.)

Xiaohao: Absolutely! (Also points the signal lamp at the Train Robber and Heizi.)

Train Robber:		You've screwed up everything!
Heizi:		Leave me alone!
Mifeng:	(Boisterously.)	Heizi . . . Xiaohao, what's all this?
Train Guard:		Watch out!
Xiaohao:		Mifeng, stay away!

Everybody: (A sudden moment of agitation and chaos. None of their utterances can be heard clearly.) Ah—yi—wu—ha—ai—ah!

(Gao 1985a:73)

Gao asserts that such multivocality is fundamentally a reflection of reality in which two or more persons speak simultaneously, creating commotion (Gao 1988b:124). What he attempts in this initial stage of experimentation, which is essentially different from what Beckett does in the first example, is to present the multivalence of real life using simultaneous actions and speech on stage.

With the same objective of representing real-life situations, Gao uses multivocality more extensively and achieves a deeper structural intricacy in The Bus Stop. In this play, there are more instances of two or three characters speaking at the same time. Furthermore, there is one scene in which the seven characters are bunched into three groups, and dialogue takes place within all groups simultaneously. Toward the end of the play, the seven characters drop their theatrical personae and appear to the audience as actors and deliver lengthy utterances all at once. In the dramatic text first published in *Shiyue*, each of the actors' utterances is scripted, one after another, in a conventional manner. However, in the later collected edition, these utterances are notated to display an orchestrated effect.[6]

Actor A playing the Girl: Why aren't they leaving?

Actor B playing Director Ma: Sometimes people

Actor C playing the Carpenter:

Actor D playing the Mother:

Actor E playing the Old Man: Comedy is harder than

Actor F playing the Dolt: Don't understand.

Actor G playing the Bespectacled:

A: Hasn't that all been said?

B: are fated to wait. Tried lining up to buy fish? Oh, you

C: It's okay to wait. People wait because there is

D: Mother says to son, Let's go,

E: tragedy.   Say tragedy, if the audience doesn't weep

F: It's like

G: Really don't understand.

                                                        (Gao 1985a:130)

Comparable to the effect of a symphony, the interplay of the seven vocal parts forms an integrated composition. This symphonic effect is further enhanced by the accompanying music and sound. In this instance, similar to the choral effect in Beckett's *Play*, the unintelligibility of the utterance becomes a deliberate effort to break away from conventional drama, which is dominated by spoken words and relies on the meaning of utterances. What Gao has achieved with multivocality is a new aural experience rather than another mode of relaying meaningful messages. What's more, as the play was staged in theater-in-the-round, with the audience sitting right in front of the performers, members of the audience would have been able to discern the utterances of performers nearer to them more clearly than those of others. In contrast to conventional realist plays, which usually guide the audience through a linear progression of consecutive focal points, Gao has created a multifocal situation that requires the audience to exercise subjective selection in its attention. Such a technique provides greater spatial scope in that it allows for the representation of several subjects at the same time as well as for intertwining relationships between those subjects to exist. More than just a novel mode of representation, multivocality is essentially a seminal breakthrough in dramatic structuration.

Multivocal structure is further employed for thematic representation in *Wild Man*. The motif of primitiveness versus civilization is presented through a contrast in the folk singing of the Old Singer and his Assistant, on the one hand, and the choral recitation of the history of urbanization and deforestation, on the other.

Male and female actors A:

  The magnificent and tranquil

B: Never disturbed

C: Chopped

D: Trampled

E: Burned

F: Plundered

G: Never stripped

H: Like a virgin

A: A forest that has preserved its primitive lives!

The actor who plays the Ecologist: *(In a mixture of sounds and voices, sonorously.)* You go up the river against the current, the turbid and filthy river is polluted with mud and industrial waste, and rubbish from the city on the shores. Where can you find a stretch of green forest that is able to restore the ecological balance already disturbed by human beings?

(The sound of a horn fades away gradually.)

Assistant: *(Sings.)* Sister rides on a mule,

Old Singer: *(Sings.)* Passes by the paddy field,

Assistant: *(Sings.)* Calls her lover,

Old Singer: *(Sings.)* Asks for a ladle of cool water,

Assistant: *(Sings.)* Three sharp blasts from the horn,

Old Singer: *(Sings.)* A clear stream flows,

Assistant: *(Sings.)* He dismounts from his white horse,

Old Singer: *(Sings.)* Passes by the paddy field,

Assistant: *(Sings.)* Sister dismounts from her mule,

Old Singer: *(Sings.)* Drinks a ladle of cool water. . . .

(Gao 1985a:206–207)

While the chorus of performers poses a direct and forceful charge against the overwhelming scale and speed of deforestation in a style resembling the recitation of verse *(langsong)*, the Old Singer and his Assistant present the beauties of pastoral life in a lyrical mode. If the multivocal technique in *Alarm Signal* and *The Bus Stop* effected the complexity of real-life situations, in *Wild Man* it is meticulously designed to display powerful contrasts between rhythmic recitation and lyrical folk singing, a boisterous crowd and a leisurely duet, intense agitation and relaxed enjoyment, and, finally, anxiety about an unpromising future and nostalgia for the past. Multivocality intervenes and restructures the representation of motifs. When presented contrapuntally, different motifs are displayed and contrasted with each other, indirectly exerting a strong presence of authorial subjectivity.

In another scene, several locales are presented simultaneously on stage and through sound effects. Against the sound of torrential rain, the strident tones of a radio appeal calling for residents to retreat from the afflicted area can be heard. In one corner, the Ecologist is seen silently witnessing the disaster. On the main stage, the residents are panicking and lamenting, while the flood control workers are busy monitoring the situation. At the same time, a group of performers narrates, "The town is beneath water level / The floodwater is above the people's heads" (Gao 1985a:212–213). Within the limited theatrical space, different levels of concern pertaining to the disaster are presented at once. There are the residents and flood control workers, who are emotionally involved at the center of the tragedy. There are also the performers, who view the scene objectively and report what is going on. And there is the Ecologist in the background, who offers an even more detached comment on the disaster. With multivocality, not only is a more comprehensive representation of an incident possible, but several points of reference can be provided for perception and reflection.

The significance of multivocality as a form is threefold. First, it breaks away from the conventional linear narrative mode. With two or more focal points presented on stage, the audience's subjectivity is aroused by their selection of certain parts of the performance for their attention. In this sense, multivocality is somewhat similar to the effect of introducing a narrator to comment on the events—it alienates the audience and prevents it from becoming emotionally involved in the plot, while leaving it intellectually engaged with the motif. Second, by producing an integrated theatrical experience, multivocality subverts any attempt to produce a simple, idealized representation like that in Aristotelian drama and instead provides a multilayered and multitextual structuration. From the beginning, Gao has deliberately avoided dividing his plays into acts or scenes. In so doing, he discards the conventional linear structure and adopts one with greater flexibility. Third, this fundamental restructuration, by the use of multivocality as a form, inevitably leads to new ways of reading the motifs presented. Different motifs that complement or contradict each other are represented at a single time and therefore provide a platform for textual interreferentiality.

Gao adopts the term *"fudiao"* (polyphony) for this mode of representing motifs. Gao's polyphony has nothing to do with Mikhail Bakhtin's idea of polyphony as "a dialogic sense of truth and a special position of the author necessary for visualizing and conveying that sense of truth" (Morson and Emerson 1990:234). Gao's polyphony, directly borrowed from musical composition, is similar to his idea of multivocality. He sometimes uses the two terms interchangeably.[7] However, Gao also mentions that in *Wild Man* "several motifs are intertwined, constituting a kind of polyphony, sometimes overlapping harmoniously or inharmoniously, and forming certain counterpoints" (Gao 1985a:273). It is in *Wild Man* that Gao for the first time demonstrates comprehensive polyphonic techniques that create ambivalence in the reading of the juxtaposed motifs.

There are four primary motifs in *Wild Man:* the destruction of nature in the process of modernization, the personal predicament of the modern age, the frantic search for the wild man, and the disappearance of a peripheral epic. Each of them is an issue weighty enough around which to build an entire play. However, Gao's ambition is to portray the interrelatedness of these issues, to create an epic of modern times (hence the subtitle "modern epic theater"). These motifs are represented fragmentarily and developed with reference to each other. With the use of juxtaposition and montage, they form a network of interwoven issues resembling the complex situation of modern life. Among these four motifs, the first two are social issues that will directly evoke the audience's empathy and emotional involvement. To be sure, Gao has dealt with pressing and sensitive social issues in all three of his staged plays. However, in *Wild Man*, these motifs do not confront those issues directly. Instead, the search for the wild man operates at a metaphorical level. Toward the end of the third movement, when a debate on the existence of the wild man is going on, the agitated utterance of an American professor hints at this metaphorical level:

Professor: We are having a discussion on science, and science is a serious profession. Regarding the existence of the Saskatchewan, the Snowman, or the wild man, before a living specimen is captured, everyone can either believe in it or not believe in it. But I think what should not be disturbed are the human emotions engendered by it. Such beings remind us of people's childhoods. They are also a substance of our personal imagination, hallucination, and nightmare. Even the demons in the mythologies and legends created by people's collective consciousness are related to them.

(Gao 1985a:268)

Among a number of assertions and denials that are based on absolute scientific rationality and that express a measure of indifference toward human feelings, the link between the existence of the wild man and human consciousness suggests a more passionate approach to the issue. Although the message in the American professor's speech appeals to be direct and didactic, its reference to other motifs in the play suggests that a more intrinsic reading is needed. Dramatically, the frantic search presents a situational absurdity that is reminiscent of the meaningless waiting in *The Bus Stop*. Metaphorically, as the search is juxtaposed with other motifs, its absurdity serves as either a parallel or a contrast. To the predestined disappearance of *Song of the Dark*, the search provides an ironic contrast. The rationality and indifference of modern people to the past has unwittingly caused the disappearance of a cultural tradition while at the same time serving as an allegorical reminder of the extensive destruction of nature brought about by modernization. The futile search for the wild man prophesies a tragic end to materialistic pursuit in modern times.

The modern epic is a tragedy. Yet Gao represents it as a combination of tragedy, comedy, farce, lyricism, and narrative. The employment of various traditional and folk arts that are intended to establish a modern Eastern theater in *Wild Man* continues to remind people of the innovative formal creations in his theater. When asked if the image of the wild man was a symbol for nature, Gao responded: "Are you talking about the wild man who appears in Ximao's dream? Or the wild man who is being hunted and discussed? Or the wild man as signified in the title?" (Gao 1988b:191–192). To give a definite answer is not Gao's style or philosophy. Perhaps if it were, he would have been content with conventional realist theater. With multivocality in form and structure, Gao has created a new aesthetic mode; and with polyphony in his representation of motifs, he has created a theater of ambiguity. In the context of contemporary China, it is this ambiguity that provides him with ample space simultaneously to deal with current social issues that interest the Chinese audience and to present his personal reflections on the sociocultural sphere in which he lives.

"Compromise Endings" and an End to Compromise

The production of Gao Xingjian's plays was never a smooth and easy process. Gao and his director Lin Zhaohua knew only too well that their unconventional formal experimentation would unavoidably invite political attacks. They cautiously described their first production of *Alarm Signal*, therefore, as a "modern play" *(xiandai ju)* instead of "avant-garde theater" *(xianfeng xiju)*. They proclaimed the nature of the play as "realist" and not "modernist"; what they were doing was a "theatrical experiment" *(xiju shiyan)* and not "experimental theater" *(shiyan xiju)*. Although the main theme of *The Bus Stop* is the absurdity of reality, Gao named it a "lyrical comedy of daily life" *(shenghuo shuqing xiju)* and avoided talking about its relation to the Theater of the Absurd (Gao 1998a). In fact, all the plays he staged in China were carefully presented with a certain degree of self-censorship, which Gao called the "product of compromise" *(tuoxie de chanwu)*. However, despite playing down the provocative nature of these plays, the level of experimentation stimulated extensive controversy and invited all the labels Gao had scrupulously been trying to avoid.

In this context where artistic autonomy was beyond imagination, Gao had no choice but to compromise. There are two ways in which the extent of his compromises can be seen. One is by reading his retrospective confessions. The other is by closely comparing the printed dramatic texts and the performance texts. My discussion of Gao's plays has been based generally on the dramatic texts and the way in which the subtlety of the playwright's consciousness has been reflected in them. In this section, I will try to provide a brief description of the differences between the dramatic and performance texts, based on Gao's later accounts and the video recordings of *Alarm Signal* and *Wild Man*, so as to reveal some of the ideas that are not reflected in the dramatic texts.[8]

As noted, the plot construction and characterization of *Alarm Signal* generally follow a realist style. This was in keeping with the general trend of the time. For political reasons, the ending had to convey a sense of brightness in the future. An example of Gao's effort to produce a "product of compromise" is that, when the train robbery has been successfully prevented and Xiaohao starts blowing his trumpet, the stage direction reads: "It is a blast of brightness. Lights of different colors flash outside the train window. At center stage, lights of various colors are rotating and the sound of young men and women chatting, laughing, and dancing is heard. Xiaohao stands among them, blasting on his trumpet fervently" (Gao 1985a:80). Although sensitive issues such as crime and unemployment are discussed in the play, the ending of *Alarm Signal* suggests that all problems will be resolved, and a bright future is envisioned.

During the performance that was video recorded, Xiaohao did not blow his trumpet at all, let alone "fervently," nor was there the sound of "chatting, laughing, and dancing." When the Senior Train Guard flashed the safety signal, a trumpet solo began. The music was lyrical and melancholic. None of the characters appeared to be relieved or happy, but their expressions portrayed them as immersed in deep thought. The mood of the ending, in stark contrast with that stated in the dramatic text, was therefore one of uncertainty and confusion. Whereas the printed text portrays a bright future, the performance suggests that, while the present crisis is temporarily overcome, there are nevertheless more problems to be faced in the future.

For *The Bus Stop*, reading the dramatic text does not give a clear idea how the absurdity of the play is portrayed and enhanced on stage. According to the script, the seven characters gradually become more and more determined to start walking as the play progresses, and this suggests that individual willpower plays a vital role in taking action. However, one gets a rather different picture when one sees the actual performance. The following descriptions of scenes by director Lin Zhaohua are worth examining closely:

> Ten years have passed! [The characters] are all on the brink of collapse. They cry their hearts out: "We've been left behind by life!" "It's ridiculous! We've wasted our whole life waiting!" At this juncture, the Dolt is too bored, and he entertains himself by doing handstands. As his head is downward, he suddenly sees the Silent Man climbing [on the slope behind the audience seats] with difficulty. He shouts for the attention of the others, but they do not see anything. When he stands upright, he too cannot find him [the Silent Man]! As he does the handstand again, the Silent Man reappears! When he shouts for the others' attention, they still cannot see him.

> When they finally realize there is a notice saying service to the bus stop has been canceled, they give up waiting. They have no choice but to walk. I design the following scene: The actors form a large circle facing the audience. They speak one after another in a circular manner: "Go? Go! Go. . . ." It goes on and on, but they do not move at all. Looking at each other, they are waiting for someone to take the first step. (Lin 1989:236–238)

The performance suggests that all the characters are trapped in a circular situation of absurdity. At some moments, some of them may be engaged in a struggle to break away from the cycle of entrapment—sometimes their speech shows such initiative. However, the actions on stage are clearly portrayed to suggest that the situation is a circular one, and there is an endless repetition of wanting to go and hesitation. Individual willpower concedes to the absurdity of reality. When I asked Gao whether the characters leave in the end, he replied in a philosophical tone: "Until now, China is still the same. So is humankind" (Gao 1998a). The seemingly optimistic "bright ending" *(guangming de weiba)* presented in the text is visualized on stage as a pessimistic view of reality.

A "bright ending" is also provided in the dramatic text of *Wild Man*, and this too is subverted in the performance. In the final scene, the wild man is seen dancing with a boy in the latter's dream. In the first edition of the play, the stage direction notes:

> The music becomes louder. Their movements become slower, resembling slow motion in the movies. They are heading toward a higher level that, although in a misty atmosphere, is brightly lit, resembling the boy's bright dream. . . . Amidst the loud and boisterous music, the boy's voice is heard only vaguely [imitating the voice of the wild man in his attempt to communicate] in a cry of happiness, "Yaya, wuhu, yayayaya, wuhu, wuhu, wu—hu—." In a carnivalesque atmosphere, everyone is dancing and uttering, "Yaya, wuhu, yayayaya, wuhu, wuhu, wu—hu—." It is an echo of the communication between the boy and the wild man, or of that between human beings and nature.[9]

> (Gao 1985a:270–271)

In this printed edition, the final scene is a moment of celebration in which the future (represented by the boy) and the past (represented by the wild man) come together as a single unity. Coming in the midst of the gloom of environmental destruction, the ending signifies a sense of hope in the future. However, the images represented in the performance achieve the opposite effect. Gao recollects the final scene on stage:

> At the end, in the boy's dream, I wanted Lin Zhaohua to portray it in a bustling mood. Because it seemed to be bright. But it needed to be portrayed as very distressing and very bustling. When you looked at it, there were insects everywhere. Actors dressed as insects were all over the stage, and they were dancing. It seemed to be an ending full of brightness and bustling images. But it was very distressing. And very quiet. It was bustling when you looked at it, but you couldn't hear anything. (Gao 1998a)

In the performance, the audience could see that the boy and the wild man were trying to communicate without uttering a word. The dancers dressed as insects were dancing in ritualistic movements. All these actions were going on while the background music suggested solemnity and heaviness. It was quiet because no words were being uttered, even though the stage was full of performers. The silent interaction between the boy and the wild man set off a sense of emptiness and illusoriness. The bustling visual images appeared to have been extracted out of their real context. Through the striking contrast between the visual and aural effects, irony rather than harmony was portrayed. In the performance, far from being a "bright ending," the final scene served to continue the spirit of pessimism, rather than being a peripeteia leading to optimism.

From the very beginning of his career as a playwright, Gao fully understood the constraints of the Chinese context and consciously exercised self-censorship. The "compromise endings" in the printed texts and the implicit meanings conveyed during the performance, however, did not keep Gao from criticism. The pessimistic view portrayed in his works is essentially a result of such realization. In 1987, he left China and eventually made Paris his home. In 1991, he announced that he would never return to a "totalitarian China." In 1998, he became a citizen of France. He does not need to have any more "compromise endings" in his plays, and his deliberate effort to compromise with the Chinese political authorities has come to an end. When asked whether separation from his native soil would hinder his creative work, Gao asserted confidently, "Cultural traditions are within me."

—————————— PART II ——————————
Theater and Its Representation

Chapter 3
Space and Suppositionality

Liberating Theater by Liberating Space

First, Gao Xingjian discarded the idea of drama as exclusively an art of words and thus negated the conventional notion of spoken drama. Then, he demolished the fourth wall erected by the Chinese disciples of the Russian director Konstantin Stanislavsky. When this was done, he had a theater that was neither restricted by words nor bounded by walls. Gao was thus left with nothing more than empty space. This space was not, however, a theater of emptiness but one stripped of conventions and ready to be imbued with new vitality. After obliterating the old, Gao gave himself the mission of establishing the new.

The theater as an empty space, envisioned by Peter Brook (b. 1925), provides "the imaginative neutrality which allows the actor to move freely through the entire physical world and into subjective experience, not only presenting 'man simultaneously in all his aspects,' but also involving the audience collectively in a 'total experience'" (Innes 1993: 126). Gao may not have been influenced heavily by Brook. At least he does not mention any such influence, as he does dramatists such as Bertolt Brecht, Samuel Beckett, and Antonin Artaud. However, Brook, as well as Gao, uses Artaud's idea of representing intense physicality with powerful universal and primordial forces as a dominant component in his theater. Interestingly, if unsurprisingly, the vitality of theatrical space delineated by Brook is strikingly similar to that of Gao. Gao advocates "a return to the bare stage with sets and props reduced to a minimum" and "a return to acting itself, as the tension asserted by acting is the essence of drama." An actor's powerful performance, Gao contends, "is to mobilize the audience's unlimited imagination and transform the limited and restrained stage into a free space" (Gao 1996a:188).

It is apparent that in a theatrical space that has been set free, for both Gao and Brook, the main occupant of this space will be the actor. It is the actor who will inject life into the theater by maneuvering theatrical space and activating the audience's participation, both emotionally and intellectually. In fact, the revival of the active role of the actor has been the primary task of the many great directors of the twentieth century. Each does so in a different way. Brecht perceives objectivity on the part of his actor-narrator as the way to provoke the audience's intellectual involvement. The intensity of Artaudian theater is presented through physical language and movement of the actors. Jerzy Grotowski eliminates all music, scenery, lighting, and makeup, considering them external, and keeps only the fundamental spectator-actor relationship within the theater.

Gao's knowledge of such traditions and the history of modern Western theater has helped him achieve a high level of awareness of the possibilities of theatrical space and actors. Some of these Western playwrights are significant directors; Gao is one of the very few contemporary Chinese playwrights who can direct as well as write. For the productions of his three plays by the Beijing People's Art Theatre, he was a de facto codirector with Lin Zhaohua and also conducted actor-training workshops before rehearsals began.[1] After he left China, he was on several occasions invited to direct his own plays in Asian and European countries. Awareness of the theater as a three-dimensional space with actors generating live dynamism is something he is able to bring to fruition in the capacity of director and trainer of actors.

In this chapter, I shall examine Gao's works, with an emphasis on his postexile plays, from the perspective of his awareness of theatrical space and actor-spectator interactivities within such a space. In an article delineating the nature of his new theater, Gao sums up the first stage of his experimentation in an extensive definition of his ideal drama, which he calls "drama of the future" *(weilai de xiju):*

> Drama of the future is a kind of total drama. It is a kind of living drama that features enhanced interactions among actors, between actors and characters, among characters, and between actors and audience. It is different from the drama that is bottled and canned in the rehearsal room. It encourages spontaneous acting, which fills the theater with vibrancy. It is like playing communal games. It fully develops every potential of the art. It will not

be impoverished. It will collaborate with artists of spoken language and avoid degenerating into mime or musical. It is symphonic and multivisual. It will push the expressivity of language to its fullest capacity. It is an art that will not be replaced by another form of art. (Gao 1988b:86)

Three characteristics of his drama of the future can be extrapolated from this description. First is Gao's notion of total theater that, from its inception in *Wild Man*, developed into a unique and vibrant form of modern Chinese theater, also inheriting a sense of carnivalesqueness and ritualistic expressivity from traditional Chinese theater. The subjects and motifs of Gao's total theater usually derived from Chinese mythology and folk stories, especially those related to Daoist traditions. Second, this passage shows that the basis of Gao's theater is the suppositionality of theater *(juchang jiadingxing)* (the concept of suppositionality will be discussed below). The idea of theater as a suppositional space was discussed extensively in the debate stimulated by the notion of *xieyi* drama, which the veteran Shanghai director Huang Zuolin suggested in the 1980s. Suppositionality has its origins both in Chinese dramatic aesthetics and in the idea of stylized theater advocated in opposition to Stanislavsky's realist theater by Vsevolod Meyerhold at the beginning of the twentieth century. Third, Gao makes clear in this passage that the theater's suppositional nature revolutionizes the former actor-spectator relationship. With the rejection of theatrical illusions, actors are required to adopt a different approach to the representation of characters. In this process, they assume a new type of free capacity to establish direct interaction with the audience and hence transform passive receivers into active players within theatrical space.

Gao's indebtedness to Chinese traditional theater and culture is apparent. Suppositionality, the central idea of Gao's ideal theater, is, according to him, the basic characteristic of traditional Chinese theater. However, it is also unmistakably the fundamental feature of Meyerhold's theater, which he called "stylization." In their challenge to naturalism and realism, Meyerhold and Gao arrived at their own quite different ideal theaters that had similar features and were inspired by different sources. Meyerhold, a predecessor of many influential Western dramatists of the twentieth century, acted for Gao as a bridge from Stanislavsky to Brecht and Artaud in his early encounter with theater during the early 1960s.

Total Actors for Total Theater

Gao Xingjian's notion of total theater has two essential aspects. First, it is an ideal form of theater, which creatively appropriates elements from both modern Western and traditional Chinese theaters. Gao pursued this ideal throughout his career in the early and mid-1980s. *Wild Man* was the culmination of his idealism, which he called the "modern Eastern theater." His endeavor to realize total theater resumed with later, postexile works such as *The Nether City* and *The Story of Shanhaijing*, in which he returns to the form and subject matter of Chinese folk and traditional arts.[2] Second, total theater is a platform for the exploration and exploitation of actors' potentiality. The theater will, in Gao's view, only be able to achieve totality, that is, to express and present all possible forms of performance, if actors are well rounded. After the production of *Wild Man*, Gao started on his second stage of experimentation, in which he returned to what he perceived as the basis of performance, the actors, and began to place more emphasis on their training.

The Other Shore is Gao's first production reflecting this second stage of experimentation. The play was written after Gao returned from his visits to Berlin and Paris, with the specific objective of training student actors of the Beijing People's Art Theatre. Gao and his long-term working partner Lin Zhaohua planned to set up an Experimental Theatre Workshop, where actors would receive training different from the conventional Stanislavskian method practiced at the Beijing People's Art Theatre and generally throughout China (Gao 1996a:166).[3]

One of Gao's primary concerns during this period was to release drama from the restrictive notion of the art of words. He envisaged "resuming all functions of drama" and, for that purpose, adopting a new concept of acting for the effective presentation of his modern drama. Gao often made an analogy between this concept and the actors of traditional *xiqu*, who are able to call on reciting, singing, acting, and acrobatic skills. In the postscript to *The Other Shore*, Gao proclaims that the ultimate actor is capable of assuming roles in the drama of "Shakespeare, Ibsen, Chekov, Aristophanes, Racine, Lao She, Cao Yu, Guo Moruo, Goethe, Brecht, Pirandello, Beckett, and even mime and musical" (Gao 1995a:64). Gao's ideal actor therefore possesses, besides well-rounded performing skills, great versatility that will enable him or her creatively to construct a unique theatrical experience. The training Gao envisioned was intended to awaken the actor's capabilities so that he or she would not be confined to a single school of performing techniques. How can such an actor be fostered? How is Gao's training different from conventional methods? *The Other Shore*, the only play written by Gao specifically for such purposes, provides some answers.

The initial setting of *The Other Shore* is ambiguous. It is stated at the beginning of the script that the time "cannot be defined or stated precisely," while the place is "from the real world to the nonexistent other shore" (Gao 1999a:1). Without any specific delineation of time and place, Gao presents the theater as an empty space; he requires the actors to establish the temporal and spatial specificities in their performances. The performers also appear on stage in their capacity as actors rather than as characters. They are supposed to display to the audience the process by which actors are transformed into characters. Far from imposing an illusory scene on the audience, Gao deliberately and overtly presents to them an experience of the theater as it is being created. The play begins with an actor playing with ropes and leading a group of actors in a procession resembling a preperformance warm-up exercise. The lead actor sets the contextual situation with his words, and the ensemble follows his instructions by responding physically to what the former says. The lead actor begins:

> Here's a rope. Let's play a game, but we've got to be serious, as if we're children playing their game. Our play starts with a game.
>
> Okay, I want you to take hold of this end of the rope. You see, this way a relationship is established between us. Before that you were you and I was I, but with this rope between us we're tied to each other and it becomes you and I.
>
> . . .
>
> If I were to pull the rope real hard towards me, then we'd have to see who's stronger. The stronger one pulls and the weaker is being pulled. It becomes a tug-of-war, a competition of strength, and there'll be a winner and a loser, victory and defeat.
>
> Now if I carry this rope on my back like this and pull even harder, you'll be like a dead dog; likewise if you manage to gain control of

this rope, I'll be like a horse or a cow, and you'll be able to drive me around like cattle. In other words, you'll be running the show. So you see, our relationship is not at all constant, it's not at all unchanging.

(Gao 1999a:3)

With the lead actor's narration as a general guide, the ensemble is required to actualize the concept of the relationship and present it in terms of physical action. It is a process of improvisation, which Viola Spolin defines as "setting out to solve a problem with no preconception as to how you will do it" and "permitting everything in the environment (animate or inanimate) to work for you in solving the problem" (1973: 383). In such a process, the participants have to stretch their imaginations as well as be highly aware of their physical environment in order to present those concepts set out by the leader in a creative manner with their physical actions and movements. Physicalization, as it is "a visible means of making a subjective communication" (ibid. 1973:387), will ultimately lead to the integration of the actors' subjectivity into the theatrical space.

As the actors warm up and the audience becomes used to such imaginative representation, the ensemble starts to display more abstract concepts, such as conflicts, intimacy, exclusion, entanglement, abandonment, emulation, evasion, repulsion, pursuit, encirclement, congregation, and fragmentation (Gao 1999a:5). The gestures and movements of the actors become more sophisticated and portray stronger symbolism. The physical display of these concepts demands greater intricacy of interaction between the actors—two or more. At this juncture, one of the actors declares: "Now there is a river in front of us, not a piece of rope. Let's cross the river and try to reach the other shore" (ibid.:9). A real object, in this instance, is transformed into a symbolic one. The interaction with fellow actors is thus extended to incorporate the physical, albeit imaginary, space. As the audience's imagination has been stimulated and its members are guided into the space suppositionally constructed by the actors' performance, philosophical motifs begin to be revealed.

In the process of crossing the imaginary river, the actors narrate various feelings and situations such as:

Look at the water spray, how it sparkles in the sunshine!
What fun, just like a waterfall.

A dam, a river flowing gently down the dam. . . .
I've got some fish wriggling between my legs. . . .
The current is very strong, tread in the shallows, try going up
    stream! . . .
Can you feel it? We're drifting in the river.
Like corks on a string.
And like water weed. . . .
No oasis, and no light.
In total darkness.

(Gao 1999a:6–7)

While they narrate, they are again supposed to display these situations using physical actions. By this time, the smaller independent groups of actors have been transformed into an integrated ensemble. Each actor, in this instance, has to be aware of the interplay between him or her and all the other actors. Gao describes how different elements of performance work together to achieve a unity: "An ideal performance should be a unity of somatics, language, and psychology. Our play is an attempt to pursue this unified artistic expression and to assist the actors to achieve this goal. In other words, we should allow the actors the chance for linguistic expression in their search for suitable somatics movements, so that language and somatics are able to evoke psychological process at the same time" (Gao 1999a:42). The fact that a performance is a combination of these three elements—somatics, language, and psychology—is not new. The three are essentially the basic components cited in different schools of acting. The critical point is how these three are integrated into a workable formula for different dramatists. It is necessary to conceptualize Gao's idea of performance unity in order to compare his approach to those of his predecessors.

In acting, somatics and verbal language constitute the external components of performance readily perceivable by the audience. The psychological process is, on the contrary, experienced internally by the actor and only perceivable through the actor's physical actions and spoken words. Stanislavsky suggested that the psychological preparation of the actor is the key to the success of his or her performance. To him, the fundamentals are "the work of grasping the true nature of each emotion through one's own power of observation, of developing one's attention for such a task, and of consciously mastering the art of entering the creative circle" (Stanislavsky 1967:92). The basic approach for an actor in Stanislavsky's system is therefore to begin with internal creation, although some say that in the early stage of his career as an actor Stanislavsky worked successfully in the reverse way, that is, "from the body to the mind by copying models for his characters" (Mitter 1992:23).

Whereas the Stanislavskian method focuses on the actor and the actor's creation of a role by either immersing himself or herself in the psychological aspects of a character or by imitating the character's external features, Gao suggests that the starting point in acting should be an understanding of theatrical space through actions and words. The setting in the theater is therefore not constructed according to what is already physically present on stage but consciously established by the actors' suppositional and suggestive delineation. In this process, the actors are in control of both their actions and their words as well as the definition of that theatrical space. In the case of *The Other Shore*, the place where the audience gathers does not present itself as a theater until the actors gradually lay out the details that define it as a theatrical space rather than some other locale. When the actor declares that the rope is a river, he has elevated the physical and visible space into an imaginary and invisible one. When the ensemble has crossed over the river and reached the other shore, they have accomplished the transformation of a rehearsal venue into a symbolic dimension, which now becomes the specific attribute of that theater.

In opposition to the Stanislavskian method of acting, Meyerhold proposes the employment of "plastic movement." Plasticity, according to Meyerhold, is the actor's physicalized presentation of movements and poses "which enables the spectator not only to hear the spoken dialogue but to penetrate through to the *inner* dialogue." Together with the presentation of speech, plastic movement supersedes naturalistic scenery as the sole focus of attention in the theater. In order to capture this attention, Meyerhold proposes an iconic style of scenery and even suggests that scenery be "abolished altogether" (Meyerhold 1998:56-57). However, Meyerhold's actor is not supposed to be confined within the enclosed imaginary circle of public solitude required by Stanislavsky. On the contrary, he or she has to acquire flexibility of presentation: "We might see the dramatic theatre transformed into a kind of revue in which the actor appears now as a dramatic artist, now as an opera singer, now as a dancer, now as an equilibrist, now as a gymnast, now as a clown. Thus, by employing elements of the other arts the theatre can make the performance more diverting and deepen the spectator's comprehension of it" (ibid.:254). It is apparent that Meyerhold, as a director, places his emphasis on the training of actors with respect to the exploration of theatrical space. Two essential characteristics of his actors are, first, that they are highly aware of the way they portray their actions and words as well as the different combinations and, second, that they are equipped with various skills of presentation. This flexibility enables them to extend their relationship with the theatrical space.

Gao's notion of ideal acting has, apparently, developed in this direction. *The Other Shore* effectively presents a situation in which it is clearly discernible how the training of actors takes its course. Everything starts from scratch. Both the ensemble and the audience are guided through the process of the formation of a theatrical experience. The actor who plays with the rope, in this instance, is both a facilitator of improvisation training as well as a narrator who explains to the audience. With the rope as a medium, actors explore relationships and abstract concepts.

The act of exploration with actions and words helps to define the suppositional setting of the play with the establishment of what Gao calls the "psychological field" *(xinli chang)*. Gao defines his idea of the psychological field with respect to theatrical space as follows:

> The flexibility of the theatrical space is in fact immense. If the actors are able to create a psychological field with their performance, the presentation of the director and designers can only be more variegated and versatile. For example, by imagining the relation of two characters or that of characters and audience placed within an eggshell, or dispersing the characters' internal experience among the entire theater, there will be a lot of new possibilities. . . .
>
> The theatrical space is physically fixed while the psychological field created by performance is strong. The establishment of dramatic space relies primarily on the latter. In this way, a dead space becomes alive. (Gao 1996a:246)

Like a gravitational field or a magnetic field, the psychological field is defined by the force exerted within a region, with the actors as the initiators of this energy. The actors are not only required to portray the characters they are playing, but they are also supposed to be aware of and to maximize the potentiality of theatrical space. The theater will be lifeless without the actors' awareness of the psychological field. As the construction of such a theatrical space determines the theatrical experience to which Gao aspires, it is important to train actors who are capable of accomplishing such a task.

Another important quality necessary for the actors in their exploration of theatrical space is spontaneity. While he advocates learning from *xiqu* actors, Gao repeatedly cautions against the formalized acting found in *xiqu*. Formalization is the primary cause of the lack or the loss of spontaneity in *xiqu*, because every detail of performance is fixed and rigidified as it becomes formalized. Gao therefore suggests that in his rejuvenated theater "the actor should enter into a state of competitiveness similar to that of an athlete before a game, or of a cock preparing to slug it out in a cock-fight, ready to provoke as well as to receive his partners' reactions. Thus the performance must be fresh, regenerating, and improvisational, which is essentially different from gymnastic or musical performances" (Gao 1999a:44). With alertness and spontaneity, the newly trained actor thus acquires the ability to interact with fellow ensemble members. And he or she is also able to react to unexpected circumstances and dramatic surprises.

In Gao's view, the theater is a space filled with spontaneity. The space is therefore not cut off from reality but rather resembles reality. By contrast, while conventional realist theater manifests itself as a representation of the verisimilitude of real life, it paradoxically excludes spontaneity, an essential aspect of reality. Gao realized this quite early—during the rehearsals of his first staged play, *Alarm Signal*. Lin Liankun, a veteran actor who played the Senior Train Guard in *Alarm Signal*, came to the rehearsal with a preconceived character in his mind. Gao had to convince him to let go of everything he had prepared and to start again with the other actors (Gao 1998a). In this case, Stanislavsky's "circle of attention" seems to have squelched spontaneity as much as formalized *xiqu* acting.

As the most vital factor in the process of improvisation, spontaneity works together with intuitiveness. The latter, according to Spolin, is the ability to respond at unexpected moments. The person reacting with this intuition is able to "transcend the limitation of the familiar, courageously enter the area of the unknown, and release momentary genius within himself" (Spolin 1973:3–4). The actor's intuitiveness thus enables him or her to exercise spontaneity not only as a passive means to deal with unforeseen circumstances but on an active level to enhance interaction with other actors and the audience. A group of actors carrying out improvisation experience a process of what Brook calls "ensemble creation," in which unexpected situations lead to the emergence of something new. This process does not stop as the rehearsals come to an end before the actual performance but continues during the performance. Opposing the view implicit in Stanislavsky's book title *Building a Character,* Brook argues that "a character isn't a static thing and it can't be built like a wall" (1990:128). The actor must continue to be spontaneous in the theatrical space where he or she has to react to and interact with those present in the same space, including the audience, the members of which are totally new in every performance.

Spontaneity is brought into play at two stages: first during rehearsals and later during performance. The way spontaneity works at each of these stages is quite different. In contrast to Grotowski's training method, which Gao perceives as "helping the actor to discover himself or herself and to release its potential," Gao suggests: "Our play's performance helps the actor to ascertain his own self through the process of discovering his partners. If the actor, without being obsessed with his own self, is consistently able to find a partner to communicate with him, his performance will always be positive and lively, and he will be able to gain a real sense of his own self, which has been awakened by action, and which is alert and capable of self-observation" (1999a:43). In other words, an actor's understanding of the character he or she is playing does not arise solely from interpretation and creation. Instead, the actor has to make use of his or her senses to capture how his or her partners perceive the character and react to it. Then the actor has to react to those partners. In the course of this interaction, the alertness of the actors and their power of self-observation will be challenged. What is presented is thus not individualized performances but integrated acting by the ensemble as a whole. The scenes of actors representing abstract concepts and performing the crossing of river in *The Other Shore* in particular demonstrate such an "ensemble creation." Gao's theater is therefore an interactive theater. The interactiveness begins at the first rehearsal, long before the play becomes a performance that is presented in the presence of an audience.

Within the theatrical space, interaction extends to the relationship between actors and the audience. With the demolition of the fourth wall, the two spheres, on stage and off stage, that were previously separated, have merged into one. In his plays, Gao continually and deliberately attempts to maximize the potential of such interactivity. The direct revelation of internal emotions in *Alarm Signal* is only an initial attempt. The multivocality in *The Bus Stop* and *Wild Man* creates a multifocal and multidirectional situation where interaction with the audience illuminates the structural sophistication of the plays. Gao's extensive employment of a narrator, who first appears as the actor who plays the Ecologist in *Wild Man*, is further evidence of his effort to promote such interactivity (the complicated relations among actor, narrator, and character will be discussed in chapter 4). While Gao's narrator may have been influenced by Brecht, his use of narration is more akin to the Chinese tradition.

Whereas Brecht's narrator is a means to achieve the effect of alienation, Gao's narrator aspires to get the audience emotionally involved in theatrical activity resembling a carnival. In *The Story of Shanhaijing*, the narrator does not double as a character, as is normal for Gao's plays, but appears in his original capacity as a *shuochang yiren* (a performer of storytelling and ballad singing). A *shuochang yiren* is different from the more commonly known *shuoshu ren* (storyteller) in that he or she is not only able to recite stories from history and *yanyi* (historical romances), and to portray the characters dramatically in those stories, but is also able to produce a more sophisticated art form that combines singing and often playing a musical instrument as well as telling a story. More significant, he or she is highly responsive to the reception of the play by the audience and makes changes in performance spontaneously in accord with the situation. In the *shuochang yiren*, Gao has found a way to make interactivity work for his theater.

Gao's total theater requires actors who are equipped with an extensive spectrum of performing skills and, at the same time, have retained a high measure of intuitive spontaneity. Through their somatics and language, the theatrical space is established, and this occurs primarily through interactivity that takes place among the actors and with the audience. The physical space is less significant in such theater as the theatrical space is defined by the actors' performance rather than by its fixed physical dimensions. Emancipated from the restrictions of conventional perceptions of space and time, the actors have much greater freedom than in the conventional theater to create a theatrical experience by activating the audience's imagination. It is through suppositional and suggestive delineation that the audience is able to perceive and understand what is represented in the theater. Gao envisions such a theater founded on suppositionality and unbound imagination.

The Art of Suppositionality

Opposing the representation of reality, Gao Xingjian attempts to present his theater as an aesthetic experience that becomes established within the theatrical space. The most important characteristic of this theater is its suppositionality. The idea of suppositionality suggests that every element in the theater is artistically represented, subjectively imagined, and thus fundamentally unreal. Gao does not want his audience to perceive what is performed in the theater as a reflection of the real but to participate in the creation of the theatrical experience. Although, in proposing a theater of suppositionality, Gao has reiterated some significant ideas of the Soviet director Vsevolod Meyerhold and traditional *xiqu*, he consciously avoids advocating the utilitarian employment of suppositionality to represent reality or to profess ideology. Instead, he wants to develop it into an autonomous mode of artistic representation.

Before discussing the notion of suppositionality *(jiadingxing)*, I would like to visit two key concepts, namely, *xijuxing* (dramaticality) and *juchangxing* (theatricality), which Gao mapped out in his first articles on drama, published as a series in 1983. Fundamentally, Gao suggests, drama is an art of actions. Different types of drama, such as realist, naturalist, Brechtian, and *xiqu*, are established through dramatists' individual interpretations and practice of their arts. Each one emphasizes different aspects of action, which he or she perceives as of primary importance. Actions, Gao further contends, can be expressed in the form of spoken language, physicality, narration of events, psychological activities, and progression of discovery. More important, there are endless possibilities of form, as new means of presenting actions will always be created. It is essentially in the process of performing these actions that dramaticality is defined within the theater (Gao 1988b:15–21).

What makes drama a unique form of art, in Gao's view, is the direct interaction between performers and the audience. His idea of theatricality is illustrated with respect to this particular characteristic. First, in order to facilitate communication with the audience, dramatists experiment with different arrangements of the physical space of the theater. Spectators are placed at two or three sides of the performance area, surrounding it or even within it. Although this physical space can, to a certain extent, be manipulated, its dimensions are invariably fixed. Second, and more significant, it is a psychological space (which Gao, in his later articles, defines with respect to what he calls the "psychological field") created from the interaction among the performers and the audience, which provides the energy and life within the theater. Presenting illusions of reality restricts the establishment of such a space. However, energy is created when imagination is evolved through the performance of actions. The notion of theatricality hence turns on the way in which this particular space is maneuvered (Gao 1988b:8–14).

Two fundamental and related components in Gao's theater are actions and imagination. He starts from the proposition that a theatrical performance should not attempt to achieve verisimilitude but should take what is delineated within its boundaries as suppositional. But as I will go on to show, Gao deviates from the conventional notion of representing reality with theatrical suppositionality and treats suppositionality as the subject of his theatre.

The notion of suppositionality was widely discussed in China in the 1980s after Huang Zuolin's idea of *xieyi* drama, first advocated in 1962, resurfaced in 1982. Although Huang did not use the term *"jiadingxing"* in his seminal article, it is apparent that *xieyi* drama is accomplished through nonrealistic representation rather by mimicking reality. One critic summarizes this situation by saying that Huang's *xieyi* drama "fully demonstrates the fascination of dramatic suppositionality and extensively develops the formal representation of the theater's spatial and temporal dimensions" (Zhou Jie 1990:9). While the idea of suppositionality in modern Chinese theater may have emerged with Huang's advocacy of *xieyi* drama, it becomes a principal issue in the larger search for new modes of representation during the 1980s. As part of the discourse, Chinese dramatists and critics trace the idea of suppositionality to both Western and Chinese sources.

The first systematic introduction of Meyerhold took place in 1981. In an article titled "The Contributions of Meyerhold," the Chinese scholar Tong Daoming expounds on the life of the Soviet dramatist and his innovations as a director. Tong suggests that Meyerhold's concept of suppositionality was inspired by Chinese theater (1981:83). Although Meyerhold mentions Chinese theater as a source for the training of his actors well before 1935, when he watched Mei Lanfang perform,[4] he explicitly states that the primary inspiration for his concept of theater was from his European predecessors, the Belgian playwright Maurice Maeterlinck (1862–1949) and the Russian poet-director Valery Bryusov (1873–1924). He discusses their ideas extensively on several occasions (Meyerhold 1998:33, 35–39, 49).

The term for Meyerhold's concept, which the Chinese translated as "*jiadingxing*," is translated in English by Edward Braun as "stylization." Meyerhold explains his use of the term:

> With the word "stylization" I do not imply the exact reproduction of the style of a certain period or of a certain phenomenon, such as a photographer might achieve. In my opinion the concept of "stylization" is indivisibly tied up with the idea of convention, generalization and symbol. To "stylize" a given period or phenomenon means to employ every possible means of expression in order to reveal the inner synthesis of that period or phenomenon, to bring out those hidden features which are to be found deeply embedded in the style of any work of art. (Meyerhold 1998:43)

As Meyerhold emphatically declares, "Stylization is opposed to the techniques of illusion" (1998:63). He perceives his attempt to establish a stylized theater as a "campaign against naturalism" (ibid.:34). By breaking away from the restrictions of stage properties and technical devices, he envisions creating a "three-dimensional area" in which "the creative powers of the actor" are prominently restored. He also stresses that the spectator is a "fourth *creator* in addition to the author, the director and the actor," who "is compelled to employ his imagination *creatively* in order to *fill in* those details *suggested* by the stage action." Quoting from a letter from the Russian dramatist Leonid Andreev (1871–1919), he says, "The spectator should not forget for a moment that an actor is *performing* before him, and the actor should never forget that he is performing before an audience." "The more obvious the artifice," he stresses, "the more powerful the impression of life" (ibid.:62–63; italics in original).

Meyerhold's notion of stylization, advocated in the first decade of the twentieth century, is similar in many respects to the *jiadingxing* vehemently embraced by many Chinese dramatists of the 1980s. First, the targets were similar—that is, realist representation. Second, both Meyerhold and the Chinese dramatists encouraged the involvement of the audience in a combined effort to create a theatrical experience. Third and most important, they envisioned a theater that clearly reveals that it is not a mechanical reflection of reality but aspires to invoke the audience's imagination with its formal representation.

I prefer not to adopt Meyerhold's term "stylization" in my discussion of the Chinese concept of *jiadingxing*. Instead, I use the term "suppositionality," first because any aesthetic notion, be it *jiadingxing* or stylization, has its own etymological and epistemological significance. Although, for the convenience of discussion, one term could be used for another similar concept, the meaning of the latter would not be illustrated fully by that term, and the terminology would suggest spurious relations. Second, despite its resemblance to the Western concept, the Chinese notion of *jiadingxing* has its deepest roots in indigenous cultural and aesthetic traditions.

Discussions of the traditional concept of suppositionality can be carried out from two perspectives, the practical and the theoretical. Note, however, that the term "*jiadingxing*" does not occur in discussions of *xiqu* performance or in traditional dramatic aesthetics. It is a contemporary term adopted to explain a traditional Chinese concept. The traditional *xiqu* stage does not attempt to hide the fact that it is a venue for acting. A classic illustration is the common stage setting consisting simply of a table and two chairs. Different arrangements of these simple stage properties signify different localities, from the room of an ordinary family to a palace hall. They can also symbolize something other than furniture, such as a bridge or a hill. The actors dress in lavishly decorated costumes; speak stylized language, singing rather than talking; and express their emotions with formalized actions and movements. None of these conventions resembles real life. *Xiqu* is therefore a theater founded on an elaborated system of conventions with which all members of the audience are well acquainted. The art of *xiqu*, as the famous *jingju* actor of the Republican era Gai Jiaotian (1888–1970) proclaims, "has to be unreal: it won't be real if it isn't unreal; it won't be beautiful if it isn't unreal" (Hu 1988:75). In other words, *xiqu* is a performance of symbolic artifice. On the *xiqu* stage, it is always explicitly indicated that all that is represented is unreal. Contemporary dramatists have taken this acceptance of the unreal from *xiqu* and have further developed the notion of suppositionality, realizing that it provides a great deal of freedom for expression in theatrical art.

Within the discourse of traditional dramatic aesthetics, the dichotomy of the real and the unreal, expressed in different ways, is often adopted to evaluate the merits of dramatic works and performance. The late Ming drama scholar Wang Jide (1557?–1623) points out, "The way of drama is that the best work is founded on the real *(shi)* and expressed through the unreal *(xu)*." In the view of the contemporary writer Yao Wenfang, that which is depicted should be based on real life, while the vehicle of its depiction should express what is in the artist's imagination. Hence what is portrayed should both contrast with and be distant from reality (Yao 1997:47). Li Yu (1611–1680), a prominent aesthetician and playwright of the early Qing, asserts: "The behavior in life is completely natural *(ziran)*; the behavior on stage should be intentional [*mianqiang*, literally, to do with an effort]. Although intentional, it appears natural." Performance on stage, as Li suggests, should not be an imitation of reality, which is natural, but should represent it with artificial means (ibid.: 99–100). Both premodern dramatists espoused theories that are closely akin to suppositionality and that see portrayal of this kind as a higher realm of art. By transcending reality such a performance attains a greater sense of freedom and subjectivity.

Portrayal of reality in theater does not only mean representing its physical appearance but also expressing its spirit, that is, its *shen*, a term in traditional Chinese aesthetics. The idea of *shen* in the discussion of theatrical representation differs from what is conventionally translated into English as (internal) "spirit," as opposed to (external) attributes *(xing)*, although the term has been at the center of Chinese aesthetic discourse in this connotation. *Shen* is, as Yao suggests, a unique idea in classical Chinese aesthetics, that is roughly equivalent to the contemporary notion of imagination. With respect to formal structuration, Yao further asserts, *shen* facilitates the search for innovation, uniqueness, and exquisiteness. The effect created by *shen* is intrinsically rich and yet leaves much room for pondering (Yao 1997:335).

Representation is seldom treated independently in dramatic practice or theory. Traditional *xiqu* has often been used consciously by the authorities as a powerful didactic medium for the inculcation of political and moral values (Mackerras and Wichmann 1983:4–5). Aside from such uses, moral didacticism has been conventionalized and internalized in the stories of *xiqu*. The contrast of the real and the unreal in classical dramatic aesthetics reveals that the subject of artistic representation remains the effective portrayal of reality. Such an intrinsic relation between content and form continues to prevail in the contemporary era among those who are attempting to search for new theatrical forms. In her study of Huang Zuolin, Faye Fei summarizes Huang's concept of the theater as "sociopolitically realistic while technically non-*xieshi* (non-realist) but *xieyi*" (1991:192). Her statement neatly sums up contemporary Chinese dramatists' endeavor at formal innovation. While dramatists discover the freedom that suppositionality brings, they still maintain that realism is the essence of dramatic works. The Western dramatists that are most celebrated by the Chinese dramatists possess similar characteristics. Meyerhold is a Marxist searching for new forms with which to reveal the course of historical progression (Schmidt 1981:xvi). Brecht is also a Marxist, who has subverted the conventions of realist theater to effect his didacticism (Willet 1977:211). In other words, for these dramatists, Chinese and Western alike, artistic representation has never really gained full autonomy from the greater ideological structure.

Gao Xingjian differs from these dramatists in that his search for artistic representation is not burdened by ideological baggage. He scarcely professes ideology of any kind, although he unabashedly champions the concept of "no ism" as manifested in a collection of his critical essays titled *Meiyou zhuyi* (No ism, 1996). In an article published in 1983, he suggests that "the realness in dramatic art is established on suppositionality" (Gao 1983c:97). Interestingly enough, this line was deleted in the collected edition of Gao's essays (Gao 1988b:33). The deletion may not be sufficient to prove that Gao has departed from a view of the theater as a simplistic dichotomy of the real and the unreal. However, it has become apparent that the notion of suppositionality no longer merely represents "the realness in dramatic arts" to Gao but possesses a more complex significance.

Gao suggests that the knowledge of suppositionality has led to the understanding of drama as a game (Gao 1988b:65). Semantically, the Chinese word "*xi*" means both "drama" and "game," in a way corresponding to the English word "play," which refers to a dramatic piece for the stage as well as the playing of a game. As Xu Weisen, a Qing dynasty critic, once put it, "Drama *(xi)* is all a game *(xi)*, because it is unreal *(fei zhen)*" (Yao 1997:262). Underlining the awareness that what is on stage is an act of performance, Gao asserts that the objective of the theater is to make both the performers and the audience believe that it is suppositional and to join in playing the game (Gao 1988b:66). Gao does not propose that suppositionality is a means to the ultimate end of creating an impression of reality or, in his earlier words, the "realness in dramatic arts." On the contrary, he wants the audience to know and accept that the nature of theater is suppositional and to enjoy the artifice of suppositionality.

The issue, then, is how suppositionality is to be achieved. Here Gao's emphasis on the training of well-rounded actors displays its relevance:

> At a time when the contemporary theater is flooded with sounds, lights, colors, and properties, I propose to return to a bare stage and redefine suppositionality, the innate characteristic of the theater, with the actor's performance. Sets and props should be reduced to the minimum. Furthermore, not to create realness should be regarded as the highest mission. In contrast, the employment of sounds, lights, colors, and properties is only meaningful if they become the support for, and extension of, the performance. (Gao 1996a:247–248)

Whereas many dramatists who acknowledge the idea of suppositionality attempt to use various theatrical means to achieve effective representation, Gao perceives them as secondary and even unnecessary. The theatrical experience, therefore, is stripped of everything except two basic components, the actors and the audience. Such a conception was earlier advocated by the Polish director Grotowski in his notion of Poor Theater, which he defines as "what takes place between spectator and actor," stressing that "all other things are supplementary" (Grotowski 1969:32). For Grotowski, as Shomit Mitter asserts, "the actor becomes the sole vehicle of truth in the theatre" (1992:100). Gao's special focus on the actors' performance, in this context, differentiates him from Meyerhold and Brecht, and reveals his kinship to Grotowski.

While he regards "the personal and scenic technique of the actor as the core of theatre art" (Grotowski 1969:15), Grotowski requires his actors to "play their characters by playing themselves" and "express as fact the fiction of their narratives" (Mitter 1992:79). In contrast, Gao not only explicitly reveals that what happens in the theater is a conscious performance by the actors, but he also wants the entire process of performing to be watched and appreciated by the audience (Gao 1996a:249). The representation of reality, in this instance, is a nonissue. Suppositionality, as Gao conceives of it, is the subject, rather than the means, of representation. As the basic component of Gao's theater, his actors have to possess the fullest ability to exhibit the richness and fascination of suppositionality.

Gao's training of actors, as discussed earlier, is intended to evoke their spontaneity and to nurture comprehensive acting skills. In the theater, this well-rounded training is actualized in the actors' multifaceted and multilayered performance. The three performers in *Alarm Signal* portray distinctive aspects of the youthful characters in reality, imagination, and the recollection of the past. The actor who plays the Ecologist in *Wild Man* assumes three different personae as narrator, observer, and character. Whereas in these plays the adoption of different roles by the actors is an integral part of the plays' narrative structure, in *The Other Shore*, the change of roles becomes part of the performance per se. Initially, the ensemble performs the process of improvisation in the capacity of actors. When they reach the opposite shore of the river, the function of theater as a rehearsal room has terminated and a suppositional theatrical space is established. As the play progresses, the actors take on new roles, and each time they do this a different spatial and temporal dimension is being defined.

Besides their physically perceivable performances of various roles, the actors also portray abstract concepts and invisible objects through their speech and movements. For instance, the river that the actors attempt to cross does not physically exist, but the idea of the river is portrayed by the actors and accepted by the audience. Suppositionality is also achieved in a more intrinsic way, as illustrated in a scene toward the end of *The Other Shore:*

Crowd: *(Suddenly.)* Here he comes!
            Talk of the devil.
            Make way.

(Shadow backs in as the Crowd step aside to make way for him.)

Man: *(Weakly.)* Who are you?

Shadow: Your heart.

(As the Crowd watch the drooping, blind, and deaf Heart slouching past them, Shadow quietly drags Man away. The Crowd slowly follow behind the Heart which is extremely old and actually invisible. All exit.)

(Gao 1999a:40)

In this instance, it is not only the existence of an invisible object (the Heart) but also the features of the object (drooping, blind, deaf, slouching, extremely old) that need to be specified by acting. Furthermore, the performance also presents a process, from the Crowd's expectation of the Heart's arrival to its appearance and, finally, its departure. In this example of suppositionality, several aspects are to be noted. First, speech is minimal. Only the arrival and the object itself are briefly mentioned in words. Second, movement is also minimal. There is no exaggerated movement except for the Crowd walking off stage. Third, the invisible object is presented as if it is a character. Its features to be portrayed are not physically seen even though the object has a life of its own. Fourth, as the process unfolds, not only spatial but also temporal dimensions are involved. The other closely related factor, imagination, plays a vital part in the successful presentation of this scene.

By isolating this scene from the rest of the play, it becomes impossible to portray the complex image of the Heart as delineated in the written text. Movement and speech, in this instance, have their limitations. But imagination will work if the image is evoked earlier. This is established in the preceding context, in which the theatrical space is being defined, and extended later. Before this scene, the Man has arduously gone through a futile search for the significance of his being. In the process, as his alter ego, the Shadow, points out mercilessly that he is losing trust in others, his heart is becoming tired and feeble, and he is unable to love any more. When the Heart finally comes on stage, despite its invisibility, the audience will have no difficulty exercising the intercontextual referentiality of their imagination. The crux is therefore that they have got themselves fully involved in the game, that is, the activity in the theater, and accepted the rule of the game, that is, the suppositionality of the theatrical space. In the game of theater, as suppositionality is its nature, imagination is indispensable.

From this perspective, there are similarities between Gao's theater and traditional *xiqu*. First, they are both arts of suppositionality. They do not attempt to portray reality but focus on the artistic representation of suppositionality. Second, in the artistic world of both genres, imagination is an essential element in the process of creating and appreciating the theatrical experience. Third, didacticism is not the primary concern of either of these types of theater. Although traditional *xiqu* usually has moral messages, the artist's foremost interest is in displaying his or her skills in singing, reciting, acting, and acrobatics. Hence, these two genres of theater appeal more to the aesthetic sense than to the intellect. However, the two are not alike in that *xiqu*'s art of suppositionality is primarily founded on conventionalism, while Gao's is founded on spontaneity. Clearly, Gao envisions his theater to be a representation of art in its own right rather than a representation of reality or of ideology.

Re-creating the Carnival

In his theater of suppositionality, Gao Xingjian uses various means to help the actors and the audience achieve an aesthetic experience. The creation of a carnival mood in the drama and the employment of clown characters, both inspired by traditional Chinese theater, are the two most significant attempts. On the one hand, the carnival mood helps to create an environment that encourages the audience's emotional participation. On the other hand, the clown characters complicate the relationship between the real and the unreal, and stimulate the audience to adopt a different perspective from that represented in the play. These two seemingly contradictory aspects of Gao's theater are in fact integrated to present theater as a suppositional space in which the real and the unreal are interrelated, and art and life coexist.

Although Gao opposes didacticism in theater, his earlier plays have not been totally void of messages of one kind or another. *Alarm Signal* depicts the frustrations of Chinese youth at a juncture of social transformation. *The Bus Stop* portrays collective anxiety about moving forward. *Wild Man* is an epic of paradoxes arising from the conflicts of tradition and modernization. Beginning with *The Other Shore*, however, Gao is less interested in theater as a medium for didactic purposes than in theater as art itself. The transformation of theater from an instructional means to an artistic mode of representation inevitably involves a recontemplation of its intrinsic qualities. Gao has assimilated the spirit of Chinese traditional theater and has also proposed that actors should learn from the well-rounded training of *xiqu* performers. In the course of appropriation, however, he has always been careful to avoid adopting *xiqu*'s formalized conventions, which, in his view, caused *xiqu* to become a "dead art." By the same token, Gao has also borrowed some modes from traditional and folk arts to enrich his modern theater. One of them is the carnivalesque *(youyi)* form. This form has also influenced the content of his theater.

In *Wild Man*, Gao, for the first time, proposes to "create a cordial and lively atmosphere within the theater and let the audience be involved in an enjoyable performance, as if attending a festive celebration. They will be delightfully entertained, both physically and spiritually" (Gao

1985a:272). There are lively moments, such as a wedding scene where the performers are playing blaring percussion music and singing joyous nuptial songs. These carnivalesque elements are, however, juxtaposed against tree-felling motions of the lumberjacks upstage and loud sounds of falling timber filling the theater (ibid.:262–265). The supposedly joyous scene in actual effect suggests an ironic situation in which the audience experiences intellectual alienation rather than emotional involvement. The motifs of *Wild Man* prove to be too heavy for the evocation of a lively, festive atmosphere. The many social issues earnestly raised in Gao's earlier plays impede his attempt to incorporate the carnivalesque form in his modern theater.

In his later plays, Gao attempts to present a carnivalesque mood in a different way. Instead of having scenes of festive celebration with song and dance, he employs clown characters to create a carnival effect. Such a character first appears in *The Other Shore* as a "Dogskin" Plaster Seller. Before the Plaster Seller's appearance, the protagonist, in memory-like scenes, witnesses three particular occasions from his past: his first encounter with a girl; his oppressive relationship with his father; and an instance in which, being curious about what is happening on the other side of a wall, he trades a gift from his mother to an old woman who is collecting an entrance toll, only to see the girl he desires being raped. These are all perceivable as turning points in the protagonist's life. Before these scenes begin and in between them, there is chanting and reciting of Buddhist scriptures, creating a solemn, religious atmosphere that serves as a key to the main scene.

In such a context, the Plaster Seller enters. "With bare chest and tightened waist, he hits the gong while walking around the stage,"[5] hawking his dog-skin plaster, which he boasts is a panacea to all illnesses:

Plaster Seller: Dogskin Plasters! Dogskin Plasters! Thirteen generations in the family. Give me internal wounds, external wounds, fractures, strains and contusions, give me rabies, heart-attacks, infant convulsions, geriatric strokes, love-sick young men and women, unspeakable depravity and the possessed, stick one on and you'll be as good as new. The first don't work, the second will. . . . Dogskin Plasters! Dogskin Plasters! Taken junky home remedy? Swallowed the wrong drug? No problem! Infertile women, impotent men, sinners and delinquents? Sure thing! Oh yes, and the stutterers, the crooked mouthed, jealous women, avenging men, fathers who love not the mothers, sons who listen not to their old men, pock-marked faces, tinea feet, one plaster cures all. The first don't work, the second will. Satisfaction guaranteed or your money gladly refunded. . . . Dogskin Plasters! Come and get the miracle Dogskin Plasters! Don't miss this golden opportunity! Your chance in a life time!

(Gao 1999a:28)

At first sight, the brief appearance of the Plaster Seller seems to have little relevance to the scene. In the context of somber reflection on the protagonist's past, the hawking of the Plaster Seller seems strange and awkward. Because of the character's brief appearance, one critic has conveniently ignored his significance and focused his analysis merely on the memory-like scenes, which appear to accord with the general theme of the play (Zou 1994:156–158). Another critic speaks of Gao's philosophical dimension, suggesting that Dogskin Plaster is possibly a secular substitution for the failure of religious expiation (Huang Meixu 2000:300). However, he has not elaborated on his argument, nor has he looked at the character's formal significance.

From the Song dynasty if not earlier, festive carnivals and theater have been closely connected in the living sphere of the Chinese, especially in rural regions. In the predominantly agricultural society of premodern China, festivals and the slack seasons are the time when people rest and enjoy entertainment. During this time away from work, *xiqu* performances are among the principal forms of entertainment. One Chinese scholar has pointed out three important characteristics of *xiqu* in relation to the joyous nature of collective activity. First, as *xiqu* is enjoyed during a time of relaxation, most of its repertoire is filled with joyfulness and excitement. Even if the story begins with sorrowful incidents, it will usually end with a happy reunion. Second, being a form of entertainment whose audience is largely made up of illiterate peasants, the stories and dramatic lines tend to be straightforward and easily understandable. Third, as it is the main attraction at the carnival ground, the audience expects it to provide a lively atmosphere that members can enjoy and in which they can participate. Hence, a *xiqu* performance usually has elements such as buoyant music and acrobatics (Zheng 1990:24–30). Viewed from this perspective, the desire for a festive atmosphere not only has influenced certain aspects of *xiqu,* but *xiqu* has also become an integral part of the festive carnival. To a great extent, the traditional (folk) theater and the carnival are inseparable and even interdependent. Hence, the liveliness of the traditional (folk) theater fundamentally accords with the liveliness of the carnival ground.

Both the carnivalesque mood and the use of the clown character in Gao's plays further suggest connections with Mikhail Bakhtin's notion of "carnival laughter." Although Gao seems not to have been influenced by Bakhtin, directly or otherwise, it is useful to observe how Bakhtin's interpretation of European folk culture and Renaissance literature is relevant to the present study.[6] It should be noted, however, that Bakhtin's notion, with a different historical and cultural context, should be used only as a reference but not as a yardstick in the interpretation of Gao's works. My objective in adopting the Bakhtinian notion of carnival laughter as a point of comparison with Gao is to demonstrate the way in which Gao's employment of the carnivalesque form has defined a new theatrical space. I shall argue that Gao's carnivalesqueness is in fact more akin to the *choujue* (clown role) of Chinese traditional theater.

Carnival festivities, comic spectacles, and ritual, according to Bakhtin, constituted an important part of the life of ancient and medieval people. Before the Middle Ages, both serious and comic aspects of the world had an equally sacred and official status. However, this equilibrium changed as a result of the canonization of serious ecclesiastical and political ceremonials. Carnival laughter and comic ritual were transformed to a nonofficial level, although people of all classes still participated. Bakhtin summarizes the significance of carnival in everyday life as follows:

> Carnival does not know footlights, in the sense that it does not acknowledge any distinction between actors and spectators. Footlights would destroy a carnival, as the absence of footlights would destroy a theatrical performance. Carnival is not a spectacle seen by the people; they live in it, and everyone participates because its very idea embraces all the people. . . . It has a universal spirit; it is a special condition of the entire world, of the world's revival and renewal, in which all take part. (Bakhtin 1984:7)

In the world of the carnival, social rank and status disappear, and all people are considered equal. The carnival experience is therefore a unique situation, as it unites the utopian ideal and the realistic (Bakhtin 1984:10). By adopting the carnival spirit, works of Renaissance literature, such as those of Rabelais, portray a distinct aesthetic concept that Bakhtin called "grotesque realism." The principle of grotesque realism, Bakhtin asserts, is degradation, in which all that is high, spiritual, ideal, and abstract is lowered and demoted "to the material level, to the sphere of earth and body in their indissoluble unity" (ibid.:19–20). Such a process reveals "the people's unofficial truth" by overcoming the serious aspects of official and authoritarian culture: violence, prohibitions, limitations, fear, and intimidation, and hence it "clarified man's consciousness and gave him a new outlook on life" (ibid.:90–91).

When he first introduces ritual and festive scenes in *Wild Man*, Gao requires his audience to become totally involved in the joyous mood. Members of the audience become participants in that performance. Perceived in the context of conventional Chinese realist theater, it is apparent that Gao's objective is to create a new theatrical space in which the performers and the audience do not remain completely separate as two distinct and incommunicable communities. The presence of footlights, as Bakhtin argues, characterizes theatrical performances, but only conventional ones. Gao's removal of the footlights, in contrast, signifies a return from the enclosed space of realist theater to the carnival ground of antiquity. Although he was not successful in his initial attempt to create a carnival mood in *Wild Man*, the significance of carnival should not be disregarded.

First, from a formal aspect, although *Wild Man* was written to be performed on a proscenium stage, the incorporation of carnival scenes in modern theater is a vital step toward the adaptation of artistic forms from folk culture. The carnival is not artistically or artificially represented in the modern theater. Gao attempts to present events with a carnival mood in the original forms of carnival, albeit often in fragmentary state. In so doing, Gao intends to introduce the mood and spirit of carnival as an entirety without distorting it with modern consciousness. Second, from an ideological point of view, as the carnival compels total and equal participation of both the performers and the audience, it transforms their existing relationship. It subverts the conventional status of the audience at the lower, receiving end, as the group that is to be educated and instructed. The audience is given the freedom to express its sense of participation, both emotionally and intellectually. It furthermore acquires a higher status in the performer-spectator relationship, which gives it not only a different level of participation but also an entirely different role within the theatrical space.

From this perspective, the employment of a clown character in *The Other Shore* can be perceived as an extension of the same intention. Clowns, Bakhtin suggests, are not "actors playing their parts on a stage" but "representatives of the carnival spirit in everyday life" (1984:8). The carnival laughter generated by such characters involves all the people and is directed at everyone. In addition, it has an ambivalent nature; "it is gay, triumphant, and at the same time mocking, deriding." As such, it expresses both the real and the ideal point of view of the world. In Bakhtin's words, "he who is laughing also belongs to it [that he is laughing at]" (ibid.:12).

If the festive scenes in *Wild Man* are used to get the audience involved in a carnival atmosphere, the attempt is made in a passive way. The stage and the audience are separated, and the decision to participate remains predominantly with the latter. In *The Other Shore*, by contrast, the Plaster Seller, as a character, takes the initiative in such a process. He takes on an aggressive role, breaking through the boundary between performer and spectator by assuming a status lower than that of the audience. The stereotyped image of a mountebank, with his contradictory and nonsensical utterances, confers a higher status on the audience. The change of status, as Keith Johnstone explains in terms of improvisation, facilitates the flow of space: high-status players will allow their space to flow into that of low-status players (1989:58–59).

The Plaster Seller portrays himself initially as an object of ridicule. The audience laughs at him and his claims about the dog-skin plaster. When he says that the plaster cures all kinds of wounds, illnesses, and injuries, the audience despises him as they would any mountebank in the realistic world. When he boasts that it cures infant convulsions, heart attacks, and geriatric strokes, the audience is amused by his bragging. At this stage, the exchange of status between the performer and spectators is completed. However, the Plaster Seller in *The Other Shore* does not stop at this point; he continues to propound the dog-skin plaster's effectiveness against lovesickness, jealousy, and vengeance, all of which far exceed the curative powers expected in any medicine. Hence these are claims that go beyond normal rationality. By transforming a comic situation into one of farcical absurdity, Gao puts a final twist on the performer-spectator relationship. The audience is thus led to scrutinize reality in the context of absurdity.

To a certain extent, the above-mentioned scene in *The Other Shore* reminds one of a similar dramatic effect achieved by the situational absurdity in *The Bus Stop*. Whereas the latter scene is more concerned with the revelation of the dramatic characters' individual subjectivity, the Plaster Seller and his comic and absurd utterances present a dramatic juxtaposition of forms that extends the theatrical space to include the audience as participants in the entire experience. Within the larger context of the reflection of one's past, the presence of the Plaster Seller establishes a stark contrast with the solemn religious atmosphere and the protagonist's self-indulgence. In the process of juxtaposing reality and laughter, the Plaster Seller guides the audience toward a deeper participation in the search for the meaning of life.

The ability of carnival laughter in Gao's theater to revive and renew the spirit of the audience works in a different way for Gao than it does for Bakhtin. Whereas Bakhtinian carnival laughter is an effect that literary works produce, for Gao, carnivalesqueness is a technique to create an extended theatrical experience. When he creates a carnival mood and uses clown characters in his theater, Gao does not conceal the fact that within a common sphere, the theatrical space, reality and laughter coexist. It is exactly the juxtaposition of the real and the unreal that provides a different approach to reception and interpretation.

Interestingly, this approach is not unfamiliar to readers of traditional Chinese novels. The narrative structure of *Honglou meng* (The dream of the red chamber) is in fact founded on the ambivalence of the real *(zhen)* and the unreal *(jia)*. In the introductory chapter, Zhen Shiyin, who is almost at a dead end in his life, meets a seemingly crazy and erratic Daoist priest. After listening to the priest's *Hao liao ge* (Song of worthiness and dissipation), a song that depicts poignant reality in a jocular tone, Zhen is suddenly enlightened with an understanding of the mortal world and insouciantly follows the priest, leaving all his secular possessions behind. Both the song and Zhen's encounter with the priest are appropriate footnotes to the thematic verse "Reality becomes fiction when the fiction appears to be real; possession becomes emptiness when the emptiness appears to be possessed" *(jia zuo zhen shi zhen yi jia, wu wei you chu you huan wu)*.[7] In the aesthetic world of traditional Chinese novels, the real and the unreal are often interrepresented so as to present a more ambivalent and sophisticated cosmic view. The traditional jocular representation of the unreal emerges in Gao's theater in the form of carnivalesqueness. Significantly, carnivalesqueness becomes one of the fundamental elements in Gao's attempt to establish a theater that integrates the real and the unreal.

Apart from its affinity to Bakhtinian carnival laughter and the jocularity that appears in traditional novels, Gao's clown character, as a form of representation, closely resembles the role of the *chou* (clown) of traditional Chinese theater. Among the four primary role categories of traditional theater, the *chou* has the most flexibility in performance style.[8] First, as the *chou* appears in virtually every play and is usually the supporting role to the *sheng, dan,* or *jing,* he is required to be familiar with their performing styles and skills. Traditionally, other than his own role, the *chou* is also trained extensively to perform other roles. Second, the *chou* plays a wide range of characters, from government officials to poor scholars, from hooligans to old women. He has to speak in *jingbai* (the local vernacular language of Beijing) as well as various other dialects. He also needs a good command of acrobatic skills. Third, the *chou* is free to improvise his own lines on the spot in response to the audience's reaction to the play or to comment on current affairs not at all related to the play. In summary, as A. C. Scott puts it, the *chou* is "sanctioned to use colloquial speech, indulge in personal or topical allusions, and identify himself with the crowd out in front" (1983:126).

Although the performance of the *chou* is no less formalized than that of the other three conventional role types, the fact that its antecedents are the public storyteller and the fairground entertainer (Scott 1983: 125) indicates that it has its roots in popular entertainment closely connected with the people's everyday lives. Remarkably similar to the Bakhtinian clown, the *chou* is not only close to the audience, but he also "serves a catalytic function" by satirically depicting negative characters such as corrupt or stupid officials or petty criminals (ibid.). With this understanding of the characteristics of the *chou,* it becomes apparent that Gao is most interested in the *chou* among all four role categories and presents it in different variations in his modern theater because of its potentiality to establish an experience of total participation.

Variations on the clown character are adopted more extensively in *The Nether City* and *The Story of Shanhaijing,* the only two plays by Gao that are based primarily on Chinese classics. *The Nether City* is adapted from *Da pi guan* (Smash the coffin), a title from the traditional *xiqu* repertoire. First written as a dance drama and later reworked into a full-length play, the play is about Zhuang Zhou (Zhuangzi), who disguises himself as a handsome young man to lure his wife and test her chastity. *The Story of Shanhaijing* is based on pre-Qin records of primeval mythology. It depicts the genesis of the world as well as the ancient gods resentment of each other. With these plays Gao attempts to bring a new perspective to the conventional reception of Chinese folk stories and mythology as well as to carry out more extensive experimentation with the forms of traditional Chinese theater.

Most of the ghost characters in *The Nether City* bear the characteristics of the *chou* role. At the end of the first part, when Zhuang Zhou's wife realizes that her husband is not dead and the young man who has seduced her is in fact Zhuang Zhou in disguise, she becomes horrified and is frightened literally to death. The second part of the play depicts the experience of Zhuang Zhou's wife in the nether city and especially of her judgment. Two ghostly runners escort her to the nether city. They argue and fight with each other and sneer at her. In a later scene, the black and white ghosts *(hei bai wuchang)* and a crowd of female evil spirits *(mu yecha)* sing, dance, and ridicule each other in a carnivalesque manner. The performance of these characters, Gao indicates, should be "exaggerated to the utmost extent," with bustling percussion music, heavy makeup, and variety and magic tricks, "to achieve the entertaining and recreational effects that have previously been missing from the modern theater" (Gao 1995c:68).

In *The Story of Shanhaijing,* many of the gods are also portrayed in a farcical and jocular manner. Mythical emperors such as Huangdi, Yandi, and Dijun appear with worldly lust and sentiment. Subordinate gods such as Wucainiao, Chiyou, Shentu, and Yulei, who resemble jesters, often surround them. The heavenly gods are depicted as clowns. The heavenly palaces are transformed into carnival grounds. Again, Gao proposes that the play be performed in a "recreational style" so as to create a lively atmosphere comparable to that of a carnival during a temple festival *(miaohui)* (Gao 1995d:108). Gao suggests two methods for attaining the carnivalesque effect. First, performing techniques of traditional *xiqu* can be employed, such as the use of painted faces and masks, the brandishing of swords and spears, stilt walking, playing with dragon lanterns, somersaults, high-wire walking, and so on. Second, activities that go on off stage during the temple carnival, such as hawking, selling dog-skin plaster, monkey shows, acrobatics, puppet shows, and selling candies, are also incorporated (ibid.:108). Significantly, Gao attempts to employ elements from the traditional *xiqu* stage as well as elements from off stage. He is trying to create not only a theater within the carnival but one embodying the entire carnival event. The boundary between performance and the audience disappears as does that between art and life.[9]

In theory, Gao's theater has expanded beyond the performance sphere of traditional *xiqu*. Whereas *xiqu* continually renews itself by incorporating elements from other artistic genres such as folk dance and music, Gao boldly attempts to incorporate elements that are not conventionally considered artistic. He aspires to a theater that offers an experience larger than art, that is, one that involves audience participation on a par with their participation in life. This experience of integrating art and life has its roots, apparently, much earlier than the emergence of theatrical performance proper. In this respect, Gao's theater resembles religious rituals of ancient times, *xiqu* performances on carnival grounds during a festival, or what Bakhtin called the "ritual spectacles" of folk carnival (1984:5), in which everyone is a participant.

In practice, such an experience depends on two conditions. First, there should be virtually no physical distinction between the performers and the audience. That is to say, they must be thoroughly mixed in a communal space. Second, the audience should not be expecting to watch a performance but should be mentally prepared to participate in the process, either as part of a performance or of a carnival. In a modern urban theatrical space, Gao's ambition may not be easily achievable. However, he has introduced a freer and more flexible spatial dimension than is found in most theater. In this suppositional space set free from restrictions, the adoption of carnival forms and clown characters not only enriches Gao's artistic representation, but also suggests a reevaluation of the traditional notion of the real versus the unreal.

The Ambivalence of the Real and the Unreal

Suppositionality, as previously discussed, has not only provided Gao Xingjian with flexibility for artistic representation but has also become the subject of his theater. The employment of suppositionality as a form has given rise to the establishment of a new mode of theatrical aesthetics, which is opposed to the conventional way of representing reality. The employment of suppositionality has also, unavoidably, resulted in the intervention of suppositionality in the narrative structure of the plays. I suggested earlier that the carnivalesque aspect of Gao's theater might be connected to the traditional notion of the real and the unreal in *The Dream of the Red Chamber*. In the following discussion, I intend to illustrate further how suppositionality constitutes an integral part of Gao's narrative and is intrinsically involved in the subject of his plays.

The Dream of the Red Chamber was probably the first Chinese novel to employ the idea of the real and the unreal as a form of fictional structuration.[10] Yu Pingbo, one of the early-twentieth-century scholars who established the new textual criticism of The Dream of the Red Chamber, points out that the unique representational mode of the novel was suggested from the very beginning: the real incidents were hidden away (zhenshi yinqu) and represented by mendacious speech (jiayu cunyan) (Yu 1988:635). The intention of the writer Cao Xueqin, Yu argues, was to present the unreal in an explicit manner and the real as the hidden truth. Giving the Mirror of Lust (Fengyue baojian) as an example, he suggests that the image of the beautiful lady Jia Rui saw in the obverse side of the Mirror of Lust is actually the unreal, while the skeleton in the reverse side is the real. Extending the metaphor to the structuration of the entire novel, Yu concludes, the obverse represents the unreal, as portrayed in prosperity and lustfulness, and, in contrast, the reverse represents the real, as suggested by hidden darkness (ibid.:811). Many scholars have adopted this interpretation of the novel and further elaborated on it. Although the mode of interrepresentation in The Dream of the Red Chamber exhibits some sense of ambiguity, the writer's cosmic view apparently identifies a subjective truth. The writer has attempted to present this truth in a manner resembling a mirror reflection, through a spectrum of delusive images of reality.[11]

In Gao Xingjian's plays, the idea of the real and the unreal is articulated in different ways. Significantly, the representation of the unreal is intrinsically intertwined with the theatrical form of suppositionality. Looking at the Plaster Seller in The Other Shore, one can see that the unreal is presented at several levels. First, the Plaster Seller, as a character, and his dog-skin plaster signify falseness, although there is a certain sense of realness, as there are such things in real life. Second, his boasting that the plaster is effective in curing all kinds of illness further dramatizes this characteristic of falseness. Third, as part of his jocular and exaggerated utterances, the Plaster Seller also enumerates human weaknesses and villainies in a way that defies rationality; hence an additional level of unreality is suggested. In the process, the impression of unreality is gradually constructed and enhanced. However, in the most unreal and unbelievable instance, Gao reveals the deepest truth, that what needs to be cured is not any kind of physical illness but the viciousness of human nature itself. Such a revelation emerges from an intertextual reading with reference to the protagonist's reflection on the past and the religious chanting.

An awareness of suppositionality is established from the very beginning: the audience should be conscious that everything represented is suppositional and unreal, and that it is being led to perceive the incident in a detached and objective manner.

Suppositionality, in this sense, provides an additional perspective on reality and unreality in the play. Where Gao's play is similar to *The Dream of the Red Chamber* is in his suggestion that reality is not to be perceived in a straightforward manner but that there is an ambivalent nature within it. His theater differs from this great novel in that the play's ambivalence is made more complicated by its unique form. Rather than a single mirror that provides a particular reflection, suppositionality serves as another mirror, so there are in fact two parallel mirrors facing each other, creating infinite images. Therefore, the seeming truth suggested in the play is not the absolute truth but only one of the many appearances of truth. As truth is represented in the theater by means of suppositionality, it loses its status of absoluteness. Truth is only a representation, and, by this logic, there can be different representations of the truth. The underlying message, then, is that the reader or audience should not be deceived by any appearance, even if it is that of the truth, because there are many aspects of reality that are not and cannot be fully represented.

This ambivalence runs through the entire play. *The Other Shore* begins with the ensemble, in the capacity of real-life actors, explicitly presenting the process of constructing a theatrical experience with suppositionality. In so doing, it is suggesting that the actors are real, while that which is represented is unreal. The represented includes the relationships and abstract concepts portrayed at the beginning and also the entire world of the other shore signified later. These are all suppositional and established with the effective operation of imagination. However, in this suppositional world of the other shore, the playwright presents incidents that strike a chord with the audience's real life experience. When the actors cross over to the other shore, they assume fictional characters, which are members of the crowd. At this moment, a woman appears and teaches them to speak and to express the feelings of love. After they have gained the ability to express feelings, they begin to create their own malicious expressions and use them on the woman. As the crowd becomes more excited, they, as a collective, lose their moral and intellectual judgment and kill the woman (Gao 1999a:8–12).

In another scene, a card player is leading a game with the crowd. One rule of the game is that whoever loses has to stick a piece of paper on his or her face. As the game goes on, nobody wins but the card player. A man begins to suspect that the card player is playing a trick and warns the crowd not to submit to it. But the crowd, manipulated by the card player, continues to reject the man's accusation. Under increasing pressure from the collective, the man finally gives in and submits to the game of deception (Gao 1999a:17–23). These incidents instinctively remind one of the Cultural Revolution and thus are starkly real to the audience. Yet because they appear on the suppositional other shore represented in a suppositional space in the theater, there exists a distance, deliberately created by the playwright, in perceiving these incidents. In this instance, moreover, the nature of the real and the unreal is blurred, which accords with the fact that the miseries of the past, despite its recentness, have become nebulous and even illusory.

Toward the end of the play, as all the stories of the other shore have been told, the characters resume their initial capacity as actors. The actors talk about things totally irrelevant to the previous scenes:

We set off before dawn. The morning dew was thick, and in the dark we heard the cows breathing while they were chewing grass on a small hill nearby. . . .

I dreamed that there's a piece of ivory in my stomach, it scared me to death!

Have you thought of becoming a bird? . . .

Faulkner.

I like "Roses for Emily." . . .

How are you going back?

It's so bad, what kind of stupid play is this anyway?

Are you doing anything tomorrow? Shall we have dinner together?

(Gao 1999a:40–41)

As casual as they may seem, these comments by the actors gradually depart from any relation with the play and its themes, and become closer to their everyday lives as well as the audience's. The play ends with all sorts of sounds being heard, as stated in the final stage direction: "Sounds of a baby crying, a car engine starting and running, bicycle bells and the trickle of running water from a tap, and in the distance, the siren of an ambulance" (Gao 1999a:41). These sounds, along with the actors' prattle, signify a return to reality and remind the audience that what they have just seen is only a fictional representation. The process of the construction of suppositionality is thus completed with the deconstruction of it. If there is any suggestion that the other shore is the only truth amidst all the unreality of life, the ending relentlessly breaks this illusion. In a theater of suppositionality, what is seen as the real in one instance may turn out to be the unreal in another. The many appearances of the real do not necessarily combine to form the truth. On the contrary, to borrow and modify the verse in *The Dream of the Red Chamber,* "Reality becomes unreal when the *truth* appears to be real."

This notion of the unreality of the real reemerges and intensifies in *The Nether City.* The real and the unreal are further intertwined as suppositionality intervenes deeper. Gao adapts the story presented in the *jingju* title *Smash the Coffin* and, with his unique mode of suppositionality, presents some new perspectives on the familiar story. In *The Nether City,* the actor who plays Zhuang Zhou performs several roles. Initially, he appears on stage as an actor who has no relation to the character, and directly addressing to the audience, he gives a synopsis of the story:

Actor: It happened once upon a time. It is an extremely outmoded story. It is a story about the ancient sage Zhuang Zhou who has played a prank on his wife, which is ridiculous, foolish, and irremediable. That's why we have this play: utterly unbelievable, thoroughly outrageous and awfully disastrous. It has even astounded the gods and the ghosts. Of course, it has absolutely nothing to do with the people of today.

(Gao 1995c:6)

As accomplished by the storytelling and singing in *The Story of Shanhaijing,* the actor makes it explicitly known to the audience that what follows is fictional and unreal. Moreover, by alienating the audience from the temporal and spatial locality of the story, commenting in an exaggerated manner, and reminding the audience of the story's irrelevance to the present, the actor has repeatedly instilled in the audience the suppositional nature of what is being represented.

The actor then puts on his cloth hat *(jin)* and assumes the role of Zhuang Zhou.[12] When he is playing the role, he does not fully enter the character:

Zhuang Zhou: This man is Zhuang Zhou. He has been away from home for years. . . . He doesn't trust his wife, who is alone at home. An idea comes swiftly across his mind. He bribes the shaman and pretends to be dead. With some men carrying a coffin and playing mourning tunes, here he comes to relay the bad news.

(Gao 1995c:6)

Although he is already in the role, he also maintains the capacity of an actor to introduce the character. When the troupe arrives at Zhuang Zhou's home, Zhuang Zhou disguises himself as a resplendently dressed young man, the Prince of Chu.

Zhuang Zhou: How grievous! How distressing!

(Gao 1995c:11)

He laments to Zhuang Zhou's wife in his role as the Prince of Chu, whom he is impersonating. He has already assumed the role of the Prince of Chu, leaving his former role of Zhuang Zhou. Then he starts to seduce Zhuang Zhou's wife:

Zhuang Zhou: *(Aside.)* This Zhuang Zhou is so wicked. He is seducing his own wife.

(To the wife.) Madam, you are so pretty!

(Gao 1995c:12)

From the above examples, one can see that the actor has four roles: as a narrator, as Zhuang Zhou, as the Prince of Chu, and as a commentator while playing the role of Zhuang Zhou.

There are several levels on which one can see the representation of the real and the unreal in this play. In the context of the story, Zhuang Zhou is the real person, while the Prince of Chu is impersonated and therefore unreal. Zhuang Zhou's purpose in doing this impersonation is to find out whether his wife is truly honest to him. His pursuit of truth is embedded in untruthfulness. Thus, before his quest for truth actually begins, the truth has already been subverted by his untruthful act. As Zhuang Zhou's wife gradually submits to the Prince of Chu's seduction, she perceives the unreal as the real. What she sees and believes is a superficial appearance, which had concealed the truth. It is thus inevitable that she eat her own bitter fruit when the hidden truth is unveiled. The tragedy is therefore the result of the subjective misapprehension of the real and the unreal by both Zhuang Zhou and his wife.

As suppositionality comes into play, the relations between the real and the unreal appear in a different light. The straightforward moral in the original story is deflected, and a new angle of perception is offered. First, the actor's swift interchangeability between different capacities makes it plain that it is a story being acted out, and it continually reminds the audience of the theater's suppositional nature. Nothing is to be perceived as real, not even the character of Zhuang Zhou. Second, the notion of unreality is enhanced by the actor's alienating himself from the character in order to comment on it. In so doing, he is resuming the capacity of a person in real life, a coinhabitant of the same world as the audience. Moreover, he stands with the audience on the one hand and establishes a distance between himself and the audience on the other hand, when he says that the story "has absolutely nothing to do with the people of today." Once again, Gao Xingjian suggests that all the characters and incidents that appear to be real in the play, in fact, have a certain connotation of unreality. In Zhuang Zhou's final words: "Living is like death; death is like living. Life and death, no one ever knows [the truth]" (Gao 1995c:64). With the employment of suppositionality in the representation of his dramatic subjects, Gao does away with all possible illusions within the theater as he eliminates all elements suggesting realness and reality.

Chapter 4
Performance in Alienated Voices

The Neutral Actor

"I am," says the Stanislavskian actor as he or she prepares to take up a role. The ideal relation between the actor and the character for Konstantin Stanislavsky is for the two to become completely merged, suggesting a "condensed and almost absolute truth on the stage" (Stanislavsky 1967:52). When actors transform themselves into their characters, there exists on stage one and only one truth—the truth of the character's world —while the actors disappear and lose their own identities.

Many dramatists, Western and Chinese alike, have worked within the artistic paradigm established in Stanislavsky's method of performance. The Stanislavskian paradigm is not only concerned with representing reality on stage; it constitutes an entire system, both technical and ideological, of how this reality is to be represented. Although the system's primary concern is performance, it has also greatly influenced playwriting in the twentieth century. To break away from this paradigm, some dramatists such as Bertolt Brecht, Samuel Beckett, and Jerzy Grotowski have constructed different theatrical sign systems. In the case of contemporary Chinese dramatists, Gao Xingjian is the rare exception to the rule of the Stanislavskian paradigm. Gao joins the ranks of Brecht and others who have consciously attempted to search for a new relationship between the actor and the character and to experiment with unique forms of narrative.

Although Gao is renowned as a playwright, he stands out from other contemporary Chinese playwrights in also being an experienced theater director. Since his first production in 1982, he has been a de facto codirector of all three of his plays staged in China. Since moving to France in 1987, he has also been invited to direct his own plays on many occasions. As such, a look at how performance theories inform his play-writing provides some interesting perspectives. In this chapter, I focus on Gao's unique mode of narrative (expressed through the characters' voices) and his experimentation with language, showing his creative effort in establishing a dramaturgy that is different from that of his contemporaries.

One of Gao's key explorations involves the concept of the actor's identity. "Identity" *(shenfen)* is a term used by Gao to describe the three distinct qualities that an actor might possess. These qualities are the actor in real life, the actor who has transformed into his or her role, and the neutral actor who is in an intermediate stage between the first two identities (Gao 1996a:257). In his search for a more comprehensive and flexible identity for the actor, Gao begins, in *Alarm Signal*, to allow his characters to speak in three different spatial modes: reality, memory, and imagination. In the memory and imagination modes, characters are able to express their sentiments more freely than in the reality mode. While they change swiftly between modes, the actors always maintain their identities as characters in the dramatic context. In this respect, *Alarm Signal* still fits the Stanislavskian paradigm of realistic representation, a characteristic many critics have observed.

It is quite different in *The Bus Stop*. Toward the end of the play, the actors detach themselves from their dramatis personae and resume their capacities as actors, commenting on the issues and characters presented earlier in the play. In *The Bus Stop*, actors have taken on two roles: that of the actor and that of the character. *Wild Man* is a much more ambitious production that experiments with new forms integrating Eastern and Western theatrical arts and explores issues beyond immediate social concerns, such as nature conservation and the marginalization of alternative cultures. The dual capacities assumed by the actors thus enable them to present the issues with greater flexibility. In addition to his dramatic role as the Ecologist, the lead actor also assumes the roles of a narrator and an observer. As an actor adopts different roles, he or she views and presents the object of representation from different perspectives. In so doing, Gao's actor is able to demonstrate several points of view as compared to the single view of the Stanislavskian actor. From these earlier experiments, Gao began to develop his performance theory on the identities of actors and to employ the theory in the writing of his plays.

The use of the narrator in *Wild Man* suggests Brecht's influence on Gao's exploration of the actor's capacity to adopt various roles. The play begins with an actor (who later plays the Ecologist) explaining the dramatic situation to the audience. As the drama unfolds, the same actor, on several occasions, detaches himself from the character he plays to provide observations and comments on dramatic incidents. Gao's Ecologist reminds one of the Brechtian character Shen Teh in *The Good Person of Szechwan*, who directly addresses the audience in two separate modes: in prose when she acts in the role of the narrator and in verse in the role of the observer. Brecht's intention is to imbue his theater with various points of view beyond that of the conventional single perspective of the central figure (Brecht 1974:70–71).

In addition to acknowledging the political connotations of Brechtian theater, Raymond Williams examines its formal significance and observes that Brecht's conventions of exposition and commentary offer an "open sequence of scenes" in which "a movement corresponding to a flow of action" is presented as a process but not a product (1993:288–289). The use of such conventions creates an open structure of representation. The audience is deliberately and consistently invited to exercise its reflection on the events and on the actors' self-reflection. Although Brecht does not require the audience's physical participation, unlike Augusto Boal (b. 1931) and his Forum Theater,[1] the intellectual and emotional involvement of its members nevertheless constitutes an important part of the performance process and is an essential element of the dramatist's concern.

Brecht's intention is to demonstrate the dialectic relationships that exist between individuals and the historical process. He has created a form that allows the objective examination of such relationships, and he does this by alienating the actors, and hence the audience, from the dramatic situation. His ultimate concern, however, is to focus on the sociopolitical situation in which individuals are trapped and to indicate the alternatives that are available to people within historical reality. In Mitter's words, Stanislavsky wants the audience to believe in absolute reality, whereas Brecht wants them to believe in relative reality (Mitter 1992: 60–61). Thus, a primary function of the Brechtian narrator involves the revelation of different aspects of reality in a specific historical context. Gao Xingjian's use of the narrator in *Wild Man* seems to exhibit an ideological interest in environmental issues and the dilemma of human existence. However, the unique narrative developed in his later plays effectively shows that his ambition transcends immediate social concerns.

The actor speaking aside in a capacity alienated from his or her dramatis persona, which Gao frequently adopts, is also a common convention of traditional Chinese theater. The spontaneous changes between several dramatic roles by the actors in *The Other Shore* indicate that Gao is more interested in experimenting with the different capacities that an actor can assume in his or her performance than in adopting such a narrative mode as a novel technique. Gao stresses the flexibility of role changing beyond the limitations of spatial and temporal conditions. A Brechtian narrator may be helpful in releasing the actor from the Stanislavskian immersion in the character, but such a narrator also restricts the actor to just another role. Gao is searching for a narrative that allows his actors flexibility in the playing of different dramatic roles.

In an attempt to free the actor from specific roles, Gao critiques the conventional two-dimensional relationship between the actor and the character. When an actor takes up a role as a character, Gao observes, he or she experiences a transitional state between an identity in real life and that of the character. The conventional duality of actor and character seems to neglect this in-between state, which is especially discernible in a *xiqu* actor. In discovering this identity, what Gao calls the "neutral actor" *(zhongxing yanyuan)*, Gao proposes a "tripartite of performance" *(biaoyan de sanchongxing)* to open up a new sphere of possibilities (Gao 1996a: 257). He observes:

> As a well-trained and experienced *xiqu* actor prepares to put on his makeup, he begins to undergo a process of self-purification. He detaches himself from his personal daily life, entering the state of a neutral actor. When he has completed his face painting and dressed in his costume, his posture, tone, and mien will be totally different from that of his usual being. As the gong and drum sound, ready in rapt attention and full energy, he goes onto the stage to perform his character. This process of transformation is more apparent when a male actor is taking up a female role, such as that of the *dan* in *jingju* or the *onnagata* in Kabuki. (Gao 1996a:238)

This state of transition exists only for a short time, so brief that even the actor may not be aware of it, as he is normally intensely occupied with the task of entering his character. Gao further analyzes this process:

> A man has his experience, character, mentality, behavior, and expression as a man. When he plays a female role, he has first to purge himself of his own gender and character, taking up the identity of a neutral actor. He may be a

youth, or a sixty-year-old man like Mei Lanfang, but with the help of physical and vocal training, he enters such a state of preparation. The costume and makeup will also cover up his male identity. Once he is on stage, he will instantly assume his role, be it a fishing girl or an imperial concubine. (Gao 1996a:238)

Gao's focus is on the psychological transition that the actor experiences. With his conscious attempt to represent it, such a transitional state, which is usually brief, is prolonged and enlarged. In his representation, it seems that Gao is more interested in the psychological significance than the physical existence of the state.

In this transition, the actor has to leave his or her personal world to enter the character's world. The conventional concept of the duality of performance recognizes the existence of these two worlds as well as the ways in which an actor can successfully achieve the transformation. In proposing the neutral state, Gao wishes to do more than simply accomplish such a transformation. As the objective of a conventional actor is to enter the character's world fully, the state of neutrality is only a means to an end; once the actor has achieved the transformation, the means is no longer necessary. Even for a Brechtian actor, although the way he or she plays the character is important, the ultimate emphasis is on the actor's perception of his or her own historical situation. By contrast, in prolonging the state of neutrality Gao wants his actor to maintain the consciousness of being in such a state throughout the performance. In so doing, the actor is not only able to enter as many roles as is required, but also to maintain a substantial amount of objectivity in interpreting characters. The actor thus acquires the ability to interact with both the character he or she is playing and the audience.

Such flexibility is clearly illustrated in *The Other Shore* and *The Nether City*. *The Other Shore* is a play for actors' training. It does not have a linear plot, but there are many different roles to be taken up by members of the ensemble. As an ensemble, the performers begin as neutral actors who, following the lead actor's instructions, demonstrate the process of role-playing. They appear to possess no specific temperament or personality. Gradually, as they go through different dramatic situations requiring increased sophistication, they become fully developed characters. As all the dramatic settings are hypothetical, the world of absolute truth is non-existent. Moreover, actors transform into a different character in each instance and must maintain the ability to change roles quickly. The fundamental element at work is the actors' subjective control over their imagination and performance. It is their identity as neutral actors that enables them to maintain autonomy from their dramatis personae.

The Nether City is based on Smash the Coffin from the jingju repertoire. Gao turns around the traditional narrative of the young scholar testing his wife's chastity by seducing her by providing a woman's point of view. Notably, the way in which the actor playing Zhuang Zhou presents his character displays a mode of narrative that Gao had never used before. The actor, in "neutral" mode, first recounts Zhuang Zhou's story. In this capacity, he functions as a narrator who relates the dramatic situation to the audience, while he himself is getting ready to assume the character of Zhuang Zhou. Although in the role of Zhuang Zhou, the actor does not fully enter the character's world but maintains a sense of flexibility that allows him to shift between three capacities, as Zhuang Zhou, as the Prince of Chu (who is Zhuang Zhou in disguise), and as a commentator (who observes and remarks on Zhuang Zhou's actions and utterances). In many instances the actor delivers only one or two lines in one capacity before swiftly assuming another. He is able to make this shift only if he always remains neutral, ready to take up any dramatic role. In this neutral capacity, in which he maintains a certain degree of objectivity, the actor is, in addition, accorded the autonomy to reflect and comment on the character he plays.

As different capacities exist at once in the same character, the words uttered call for an interreferential reading. Zhuang Zhou does not remain a simple integrated self in his own capacity, as in the original xiqu story of Smash the Coffin. Hence, the singular truth of the original character's world is deconstructed and replaced by a multiplicity of personae. Zhuang Zhou's testing his wife is the focus of observation, but each of the four personae provides a different angle from which this focal point is viewed, and all together form an integrated totality. What the audience sees, however, is not a single Zhuang Zhou but four voices. In coming from the same physical being, these voices are interrelated and interreferential.

Gao's idea of the neutral actor functions on the premise of a suppositional theater. The state of neutrality that the actor acquires keeps him or her in an intermediary position between and separate from the two other worlds of reality, that is, the actor's selfhood and the character's identity. Such an actor must be clearly aware that the theater is a suppositional space in which the character's reality is at once experienced and performed. A suppositional theater requires the actor's imagination to fulfill its utmost creative potential. To play various dramatic roles as a neutral actor demands a similar quality of imagination. The basic concern is thus not the object of representation but the process of representing. If Gao's theater is accorded unlimited potential by its suppositionality, its representation of characters is also enriched by the performance of the neutral actor.

Gao is a playwright who understands theatrical space. With his knowledge of theatrical practice, he deliberately takes new discoveries and adopts them as subjects for subsequent plays. In the following sections, I shall discuss Gao's employment of the state of neutrality in relation to the motifs in his plays in order to elaborate its significance for a new mode of dramatic narrative.

Speaking in the Voices of Others

In *The Nether City*, four different capacities work to portray a character. The interreferentiality of the form essentially externalizes the psychological aspect of the character. This aspect is conventionally represented through the character's utterances in Gao's earlier plays. In his later plays, Gao presents a dialogic contrast by using different voices spoken by a neutral actor. In a number of plays, the actor adopts a third- or second-person narrative to create a dramatic tension. A peculiar contrapuntal effect is sometimes achieved in a dialogue between third- and second-person narratives. By adopting different personae, Gao's neutral actor displays both subjective and objective aspects of the character's psychological world.

Between Life and Death is about the life of a woman. Largely comprising an extensive monologue by a single female actor, the play presents a woman's personal experience at different stages of her life, her encounters with various people, and her physical and emotional struggle as a woman. (There is also a male actor in the play who remains silent throughout, performing only with physical movements.) In her performance the female actor appears in a neutral identity adopting, interchangeably, two different personae: the narrator and the Woman. Differing from the Ecologist in *Wild Man* or Zhuang Zhou in *The Nether City*, the actor does not speak in the capacity of her character. While the Ecologist and Zhuang Zhou deliver lines in first-person voice, the actor in *Between Life and Death* always speaks in the third person even when she takes up the role of the Woman. Throughout the play, she consistently maintains a neutral identity, giving her a sense of alienation from all the personae she plays.

Gao's technique of alienation in this play marks a step beyond Brecht. First, although Brecht demands that his actor should not "become completely transformed on the stage into the character he is portraying," the ultimate aim of his alienation effect is "to make the spectator adopt an attitude of inquiry and criticism in his approach to the [dramatic] incident" (Brecht 1974:136). By contrast, Gao seeks to achieve alienation from the psychological contradictions of a character. The inquiring attitude that the audience develops toward the dramatic events is just a by-product of the revelation of the character's psychological contradictions. Second, Brecht occasionally instructed his actors to deliver their lines in the third person and in the past tense, but these practices were carried out only during rehearsals for the practice of "adopting the right attitude of detachment" (ibid.:138), and he did not extend this peculiar mode of narrative to actual performance. Gao, however, writes third-person narrative into his scripts. In so doing, the narrative is not just a means to achieve the alienation effect, but becomes the *theme* of alienation itself.

As is true with most of Gao's recent plays, *Between Life and Death* opens with an empty stage. In a cold, desolate mood suggested by dim lighting, monochromic costume, and pale makeup, the Woman and the Man appear,

Woman: *(She wants to say something but stops. Eventually she cannot hold back and speaks in an indifferent voice.)* She says she's had enough, she can't take it any more!

(Man raises his hand slightly.)

Woman: *(Cannot control her outburst.)* She says she can't understand how she's managed to endure it, to put up with it for so long until now. Him and her, she says she's talking about him and her, their relationship just can't go on like this, it's not living or dying, and it's been so difficult, so enervating, so uncommunicative, so muddled, and so entangled. It's so sickly and so tense that her nerves are going to snap at any time. She's talking about her spiritual being, the spirit and the nerves are all but the same thing, there's no need to be so picky about words!

(Man shrugs his shoulders.)

(Gao 1999a:47)

The use of the third-person narrative persists throughout the play. The story the woman is telling initially appears to be that of another woman, but the audience soon comes to realize that she is actually talking about herself.

Simply reading the text one can observe an interesting tension engendered by the actor's utterances—a tension between her words and her suggested emotional expressions. As the actor refers to the character that she is playing in the third person, the character's inner world is exposed, in the process of narration, by an implied observer. When such a third-person narrative is used, as opposed to a first-person narrative, the character's utterances are alienated from their speaker and appear to be less precise than if presented in direct speech. In this process of speech transformation, the original emotional characteristics ascribed to the character undergo a certain degree of variation. Seen through a filter of the subjectivity of an other, the character's utterance may appear distorted, diluted, or exaggerated. A psychological distance is therefore always observable between the speech in the third person and the character's inner truth.

The stage directions in Gao's dramatic text suggest that he is further probing this relationship. The stage directions indicate that the actor, using third-person narrative, is to speak in a way that expresses the emotions (e.g., she wants to say something but stops or she cannot control her outburst) of her character. Contrary to the nature of the adopted narrative as it may seem, the actor is required to represent her character's truth as a text but not an act. In conventional theater, as the actor enters his or her character, this task is easily accomplished. The coexistence of the third-person narrative and the required emotional engagement, however, induces a seemingly irresolvable tension in the performance of the neutral actor. In other words, as she maintains the state of neutrality, she shifts freely between the objectivity of the narrative and the subjectivity of the character's world, and the conflict between the two creates a dramatic tension.

Given this dramatic tension, *Between Life and Death* is not the monologue (although it is delivered by a single actor) it appears to be. In fact, it fulfills the requirements of a dialogue. A dialogue is a mode of speech exchange requiring the agency and involvement of at least two participants who communicate through the medium of language (Herman 1998:1). Although not a conventional dialogue carried out by two characters, Gao's narrative form is a dialogic discourse with the duality of interactive speech.

Even if an utterance is not presented as two or more voices speaking within a character, it can display an intrinsic dialogic nature. This sense of dialogism points to a meditation on the nature of self. Selfhood, in Bakhtin's view, is essentially novelistic, constructed by inner dialogues and the processes that shape them over time into a personality. Such an utterance is therefore more appropriately conceived of as one or more performed acts rather than as a text. Quoting autobiography as an example, Bakhtin argues that an utterance, even if it is one's own story, told by oneself, is most often not a recounting of direct experience or memory but a narration with an imagined other's values and intonations. Bakhtin's notion of the self can therefore be imagined "as a conversation, often a struggle, of discrepant voices with each other, voices (and words) speaking from different positions and invested with different degrees and kinds of authority" (Morson and Emerson 1990:216–218).

From this perspective, what Gao has done with his neutral actor is to formalize and hence externalize this dialogic characteristic of an utterance. The intrinsic relationship between the self and its other is transformed into a dramatic tension. The self is no longer seen as an integrated, self-contained entity, as its world of truth has been subjected to interference by the external other. This tension has in turn determined the nature of the character's existence. The sense of alienation between the narrator's objectivity and the character's subjectivity is therefore expressed in two dimensions. The presence of such alienation, on the one hand, determines the conflicting nature of the relationship and, on the other, represents a psychological split within the self that is effectuated by the discrepancy of the two voices. The tension does not always remain at a static level but fluctuates as the degree of alienation changes. At the beginning, while the neutral actor is narrating her character's recollection of her relationship with her man, a strong sense of alienation emerges from the contemplative nature of the narration. As the actor gradually becomes more involved in her character's inner world, her objectivity as a narrator diminishes, and she is more deeply engaged with the character. Although she continues to use the third person, the tension in the relationship between the two personae is relaxed as her distance from the character is compressed:

Woman: *(Shouts.)* She doesn't want to hear it! She doesn't want to hear the lies! Save them for the bobby-soxers! His sugary talk has been a fraud from beginning to end. She'll never again believe that there's true love in the world, don't talk to her about loving or not loving!

(Gao 1999a:50)

Two characteristics of her speech here are distinct from her previous utterances. First, the actor omits the phrase "she says" before her lines, resulting in the third-person voice fading away. Second, on certain occasions, she slips into direct speech, revealing the extent to which she is entangled with the character's emotions. In this instance, the character almost supersedes the narrator as the dominant persona.

There are also moments when the narrator dominates. The actor's narration about the relationship between the Woman and her man comes to an end as her actions suggest that she kills him. The female actor starts to pack the clothes left by the male actor, signifying the man's final departure from her life. Then, the phrase "she says" disappears from her utterance again:

Woman: *(She kneels on the ground before a pile of folded clothing. In front of the clothing lies a pair of men's shoes; on top of the shoes is a man's hat. Next to her is a leather jewellery box.)* She says she's never, ever in her life thought that it would end like this, that she would actually kill her man, her darling, her treasure, her little zebra, her sika deer, her sweetheart, her life and destiny.

(While speaking, she takes down her ring, bracelet, and earrings and puts them into the jewellery box one by one.) What a real nightmare! She's just woken up from it, she feels a bit cold.

(Wraps the shawl tightly around herself.) The cold rain and autumn wind raging outside the window, when will they ever end?

(Listens.) There'll be no more telephone rings in the middle of the night, its endless ringing scares her and makes her heart jump, she wants to answer it but she wouldn't dare, but then if she didn't she'd feel guilty.

(Sighs.) There'll be no more sweet-nothing whispers, the whispers with so many pauses in between. Neither of them was willing to hang up the phone, even when they were too drowsy to talk any more.

(Gao 1999a:54–55)

This time, the absence of "she says" from the second paragraph onward suggests that it is no longer necessary to use the phrase to stress the presence of alienation. The persona of the character has departed from the neutral actor, and tension no longer exists. The actor speaks only in the voice of the narrator, observing the character in full objectivity. The stage directions indicating actions such as "listens" and "sighs" should not be seen as actions of the character but of the detached narrator lamenting the sorrow of the Woman.

These extreme cases occur only on a few occasions in the play. When they do, dialogic contrast is reduced to the minimum. When the neutral actor is dominated by her character's persona, she becomes entrapped in the agony of the character's past experience, unable to reflect effectively on her situation. Mostly, though, she is untouched by the character, displaying a strong sense of detachment in her attitude and coldness in her temperament. In her neutral identity, her performance largely remains in the middle parts of the performative spectrum. Because dialogue is maintained between the two personae, alienation is effectively demonstrated.

A different voice—the second person—is adopted by the neutral actor in *The Nocturnal Wanderer*. This play is set in two contrasting worlds: reality and the dream world. Apart from providing a referential context at the beginning of the play, the world of reality reappears only briefly at the end of each of the three acts. In the play, the main protagonist, the Sleepwalker, experiences dreamlike encounters with people from all walks of life. Although he is physically not alone, his sense of isolation increases every time he fails in his attempted interaction with other characters, resulting in his retreat to an enclosed inner world. The dream seems more like a nightmare, ending with the Sleepwalker killing himself.

All the actors use the first person when they are in the world of reality and, with the exception of the Sleepwalker, in the dream world. The Sleepwalker is played by a neutral actor who speaks in the second person in two capacities: as a narrator and in his encounters with other characters. As the realistic setting transforms into a dream, the actor begins to speak in a unique voice:

Sleepwalker: You can hear your own footsteps, you can hear your own breathing. When you take a deep breath and the air rushes in from the tip of your nose to your lungs, you feel cold all over. . . . Only your feet are heated and warm. When a man's feet are warm, he feels snug and comfortable.

(Gao 1999a:142–143)

The speech is delivered in the manner of an omniscient narrator observing both the physical and psychological beings of the Sleepwalker. The use of "you" in the speech inherently sets up a dialogue between the narrator and the character. As the Sleepwalker comes across other characters, scenes like the following take place:

Tramp: What the hell is going on? *(Sticking his neck out from the box.)*

Sleepwalker: You say you didn't see . . .

Tramp: Look, this is a huge cardboard box, not a dinky needle. There's no way you could've missed it.

Sleepwalker: Sorry.

Tramp: Sorry my ass!

Sleepwalker: You say you weren't looking, and you thought that this late at night only the garbage waiting to be picked up would be stored in the cardboard boxes discarded in the street. You didn't think that you'd be resting inside. Therefore you offer an apology.[2]

(Gao 1999a:143–144)

The Sleepwalker's utterances when in dialogue with another character usually begin with the phrase "you say." In contrast to the use of "she says" by the Woman in *Between Life and Death*, this phrase does not suggest internal alienation within the psychological world of the protagonist. Rather, it indicates the existence of a state of alienation between him and the entire external world.

In her survey of second-person narrative, Monika Fludernik suggests that the narrator, as the teller of the story, and the protagonist (you), as the listener of his or her own story, are frequently engaged at an "explicit communicative level" in an interaction of the latter's past and present personae. A second-person text is open, particularly "on the scale between narration and interior monologue, where the text's address function can frequently be read as an instance of self-address" (Fludernik 1994:288–289). Fludernik's analysis seems most relevant to those instances when the Sleepwalker speaks exclusively as a narrator. Two characteristics of these utterances stand out. On the one hand, as the use of "you" is more personal than "he" or "she" (Bal 1997:47–48), the utterance can be seen as self-addressing and hence self-referential, in nature more akin to the use of "I." On the other hand, the presence of the narrator indicates a dialogic characteristic of the utterance in which a reflective point of view is imposed on the protagonist's self. In this sense, the narrator speaking in the second person, as Helmut Bonheim suggests, provokes greater initial empathy with the character (in Fludernik 1994:286).

As the Sleepwalker meets other characters, a peculiar situation arises. He continues to speak in the second-person voice, while the others use the conventional first person. Whereas the Woman in *Between Life and Death* is fundamentally isolated within an exclusive world made up of only herself, the Sleepwalker enters a world in which he is compelled to interact and communicate with others. By adopting second-person narrative, the protagonist is immediately differentiated from the world of the other characters. That world is external to him, and the characters appear unable to communicate with him. He is enclosed in his own world, defined by the second person's self-address and its self-referentiality. Thus, the sense of alienation in *The Nocturnal Wanderer* is not so much within the psychological world of the protagonist as between an isolated individual and the estranged external world.

The use of second-person narrative has an interesting effect when it is used in the theater. The pronoun "you," Gao suggests, can refer to both the protagonist and the audience. Hence, Gao raises some essential questions: "Is the actor supposed to play the role of 'you'? Or is he or she searching for an angle with which the audience can identify? In other words, is [the purpose of the second-person narrative] to transfer the position of the audience onto the stage? Or is it to let the audience assume the psychological status of 'you'?" (Gao 1996a:263). When an actor speaks to the audience using "you," the latter has little difficulty in identifying with the implied addressee. This method is conventionally employed to facilitate effective interaction and to break the invisible "fourth wall," and it is also used by the Brechtian narrator. In *The Nocturnal Wanderer*, however, the nature of "you" as a double-addressee introduces an ambiguity that provides a larger space for interpretation and performance. It not only intensifies Gao's dramatic world, but also proposes a new actor-spectator relationship within the theatrical space. Once psychologically mobilized to identify with the protagonist's predicament, members of the audience will be estranged from relationships with the other members of the cast and enter a similar state of isolation.

The isolation of the characters is further polarized in *Dialogue and Rebuttal.* A play without conventional plot, it focuses on representing the relationship between a man and a girl with conversations written in a style resembling Chan *gongan*. At the beginning of the play, the Man and the Girl talk to each other in the first person, suggesting an attempt to communicate. Halfway through the second half, their respective modes of narration change abruptly:

> *(The two sit quietly back to back.)*

Girl: *(Persistently.)* She asks, what did you say?

Man: *(Wearily.)* You say, you didn't say anything.

> *(The two sit in kneeling position. Girl's face moves closer to Man's head.)* [3]

Girl: She says she clearly heard you say something.

Man: *(Without looking at her.)* You ask what did she hear you say?

Girl: She says would she ask you if she knew?

Man: You say that means you didn't say anything.

Girl: Then she says, Oh. *(Turns to face the audience.)*

(Gao 1999a:123–124)

Speaking in the third person, the Girl detaches herself from the dialogue, demonstrating a strong sense of skepticism toward the Man, while the latter, speaking in the second person, recedes into an isolated world, withdrawing from any further attempt to communicate.

Instantly, the conversation is transformed from a dialogue into a rebuttal, as suggested in the title of the play. Both characters in their own ways have abandoned dialogue. Although their initial conversation shows an intent to communicate, even if that communication is insubstantial, their later use of third- and second-person narrative modes indicates that both the Girl and the Man have given up on such an intent. Talking in different spheres of consciousness, they are both psychologically cocooned within their own subjectivities, each unable to reach out to the other. Resembling the predicament of the Sleepwalker in *The Nocturnal Wanderer*, both the Girl and the Man experience a state of alienation, each entrapped in his or her own isolation. The dichotomy of self and other has undergone a fundamental transformation. The alienation in *Dialogue and Rebuttal* suggests a world constituted of various isolated, enclosed "selves" for whom neither dialogue nor communication is possible.

Alienation: The Irony of Subjectivity

Gao Xingjian's protagonists exist in a state of solitude as a result of their alienation, either forced or self-imposed, from the external world. Their ability to interact and communicate is nullified as they enter a space that contains nothing other than their subjective consciousness. This situation reminds one of what Marshall Berman calls the third phase of modernity, during which the public "shatters into a multitude of fragments, speaking incommensurable languages." In the third phase of modernity— the twentieth century—the process of modernization has expanded to envelop the whole world. This phase is characterized by fragmentation, loss of meaning in life, and discontinuity with traditions (Berman 1983: 16–17). The idea of a Chinese modernity has been widely discussed since the 1980s, especially in the 1990s, for instance, by Rey Chow (1991), Lydia Liu (1995), Leo Lee (1996), Xudong Zhang (1997), and David Wang (1997). However, the context of Gao's postexile plays is nonspecific, and it is thus perhaps not inappropriate to examine them without regard to the boundaries set by the present scholarly discourse on Chinese modernity.

Gao has, with his later plays, demonstrated the predicament of humanity in the modern age. References to the Chinese sociocultural context have almost completely faded from his settings and characters. The plays appear to be thematically universal and formally innovative, and yet his themes are all discussed and represented with reference to various cultural traditions. Self and other, being and existence, alienation and solitariness, all of which have been represented in Gao's plays, are also some of the recurring themes in the works of Western writers, particularly the Existentialists.

Alienation is a common state of existence in modern times. In his etymological account of the term "alienation," Raymond Williams delineates three broad senses. First, it is the action of estranging or the state of estrangement. In the theological sense, it means cutting off or being cut off from God. In a more philosophical sense, originated by Jean-Jacques Rousseau, human beings are seen as cut off or estranged from their original nature. Second, Williams discusses the socioeconomic sense, where alienation is the action of transferring the ownership of something to another, a notion Marx developed in his discussion of the struggle of an alienated labor force in a class society. Third is the psychological sense, referring to a loss of connection with one's own deepest feelings and needs, usually in the context of a modern society (Williams 1988:33–36). Although it can be discussed in these various contexts, alienation has as a primary concern the sociopsychological state of an individual with respect to his or her physical and mental environments. This state of existence is especially related to the overwhelming solitariness experienced by modern human beings, recognized as a fundamental cause for such a predicament.

In his examination of the notion of alienation from a structural sociological perspective, John Torrance proposes distinguishing between "alienation" in the sense of loss or relinquishment and "estrangement" in the sense of strangeness or hostility. However, these two concepts can be interrelated. If the alienation involving loss is caused by an unfamiliar other, it is then also estrangement. Alienation in general may occur in two ways. First, alienation may arise through an intrinsic incomprehensibility or threat of an other. Second, if the other is a stranger or enemy, alienation may also be caused by an extrinsic unfamiliarity (Torrance 1981: 69–72). Torrance's argument defines alienation in both subjective and objective senses. In what he calls "alienation," on the one hand, the alienated person subjectively isolates himself or herself from others. In what he calls "estrangement," on the other hand, he or she is forced to retreat into isolation, either by the threat of the other or because he or she has failed to communicate to the other.

With these views and definitions of the complex idea of alienation as a background, it is clear that, with his unique third- and second-person narratives, and the extensive representation of alienation in his later plays, Gao has joined the ranks of writers dealing with the perennial issue of human existence in modern times. The sense of alienation in his later plays is quite different from that in his earlier plays. In *Bus Stop*, the intense frustration of the characters arises from the discrepancy between the characters' aspirations and the disappointment of reality. The predicament faced by the Ecologist in *Wild Man* is engendered from the anxiety of losing one's traditions. The playwright demonstrates an earnest concern for society and culture, not without a sense of emotional engagement. Although Gao does not avoid contemplating social and cultural issues entirely in the plays to be discussed in this section, his interest is primarily in the more universal problems of alienation.

The monologic utterances of the Woman in *Between Life and Death* suggest that she is enclosed in an alienated world, cut off from any involvement with people or matters in the external world. The voice of the narrator, albeit presenting an objective point of view, is not external in origin but is engendered by her inner being and offers a clear picture of her subjectivity from a detached perspective. Everything seen, heard, or represented on stage is an explicit revelation of the Woman's subjective world. It is in this state of physical alienation that the Woman begins to unravel the intense sense of alienation that is deeply rooted in her psychological being.

First to be placed under the Woman's subjective scrutiny is her relationship with a man. The emotion-ridden recollection—and her reflection in the narrator's voice—of the past relationship points to a sense of alienation, which arises from the presence of verbal incommunicability. The Woman's feeling of being estranged from communication leads her to a state of intense agony and frustration, which in turn aggravates her hostility toward the man. The man's actions and words appear to originate beneath a façade of deceptiveness, which essentially deepens her sense of estrangement.

In her alienated world, notions of truth and falsehood are dominated by her subjectivity. The only truth to her is her complete possession of the man and his love:

Woman: She says if she wanted to possess she'd possess everything, if she wanted to love she'd love with all her heart, she wouldn't allow even the tiniest bit of untruth, otherwise, she'd rather have nothing at all. She wanted to possess him, to possess all their feelings together, even if they should be darkness personified, all the sounds and movements of darkness. But she'd already known that there was no way she could possess this man completely. The darkness, the whispers, suffocation, tolerance, agony and happiness they shared together, he also shared them with other women in the same way. She's not the only one, she might as well sever their relationship and leave him once and for all.

(Gao 1999a:50)

Despite her stifling possessiveness, or perhaps because of it, the external world remains out of her reach. Alienation is in fact a consequence of her failure to claim her truth. This in turn provokes her perception of the external world as full of falsities:

Woman: (Starts muttering.) She says she doesn't understand how there could be so much disloyalty and betrayal, so much indifference among people and between men and women, it's so frustrating, so disheartening, and so unbearable. The dating games, trendy clothing, genuine and fake jewellery, woman's vanity and man's attention are all deceptions. Movies, pop stars, dancing parties, theatre-going, and even taking a trip together are nothing but excuses to flirt and make out, what follows is either contraception or litigation. The disapproval on a man's face and a woman's tantrums, they don't mean anything to her any more, all she wants to do is to cry her heart out, just like a small child—

(Gao 1999a:50–51)

Here the Woman is experiencing a double alienation. First, she is alienated by the man's deception. Then, she is alienated by her rejection of any truth in the external world other than her own. After that, she enters a state of absolute solitude.

The Woman's existence, at this stage of retreat, is still filled with ironies. She rejects the external world, on the one hand, perceiving it as completely false and deceptive, and, on the other hand, continues to aspire toward a fulfillment of her emotional expectations. This does not suggest that she has surrendered her subjectivity. On the contrary, the seemingly softened tone and sense of entreaty are ways of consoling her defeated subjectivity. After expressing her regrets to the man, who is facing away from her, she turns him around and realizes with a shock that he has turned into a piece of clothing hanging on the rack (Gao 1999a: 54). Ironically, the man's symbolic final departure occurs just when the Woman tries to retrieve the relationship. It is, however, exactly her unrelenting, self-indulgent subjectivity that causes the reification of the man.

In a mixture of disillusionment, disappointment, and astonishment, the Woman is "totally down on herself, she doesn't have a desire for sex any more, she even finds her own body repulsive" (Gao 1999a: 55). Far from being without desire and affection, she confronts her own being in the coldness of her solitude. As a projection of her alienation from her physical being, the Woman, in deep shock, discovers that her arms and legs have turned to wood and fallen off. With this self-reification, she is led relentlessly to the realization of her existence in the face of death:

Woman: *(Panting.)* No . . . *(Beginning to feel terrified.)* she wants to know if her fear is real. Maybe she only thinks she's afraid but actually she's not? She must experience death once to find out what death is and to feel its pain, in other words, a living experience of death, then, and only then can she prove that she is still alive, and then she'll know if life is worth living, if it's really necessary. She's too hurt to free herself from suffering now, but she still keeps on analyzing herself in desperate pursuit of her true self, to find out for sure if she's real or just a body without a soul.

(Gao 1999a:56–57)

The agony of mortality, however, has not resulted in a sober understanding of her existence, as she is still deeply absorbed in her subjectivity. Totally entrapped in her isolation, witnessing the reification of her own body, the fear of death—the final stage of existence—eventually directs her toward total despair with regard to her present physical existence. She then begins to look to her past in search of some significance for her life.

Through the progression of these stages in her alienation, the Woman's predicament is that she cannot escape her subjectivity. Although she may initially have been disturbed by the man's indifference, it is her continuous process of self-alienation that has led her into a state of absolute solitude. Temporarily detached from the agony of the present, she realizes that "in this vast world, it is not the other person who is truly lonely but precisely the one who is watching the other's loneliness" (Gao 1995e:18).[4] However, this realization is not some sober reflection of her present predicament or a recollection of her distant past. It will soon be revealed that the "other" mentioned here does not refer to an external other but to her very own self. The Woman's past exists as an illusion: "she doesn't know if it's a dream or reality" (Gao 1999a:65). The dream—a recurring metaphor in Gao's plays and one that becomes the subject of *The Nocturnal Wanderer*—is essentially a projection of the Woman's inner self. The dreamlike instances in her memory exist entirely in the sphere of her subjectivity and are dominated by it. The incidents that she recalls are moments of unhappiness and pain that only intensify her agony and lead her to become even more deeply immersed in her subjectivity.

After revisiting her past, the Woman is again trapped in an existence filled with lust and emotion. Neither the reflections on her relationships nor the recollection of her past have resulted in a better understanding of her being, as she had hoped. Unable to achieve self-salvation, she "prays in a whisper, pleading [for] the merciful Bodhisattva to look after her, to help her to sever her ties with the mortal world" (Gao 1999a:71). At this moment, a nun appears sitting on a futon with her legs crossed. To the Woman's surprise, the nun suddenly thrusts a pair of scissors into her own abdomen, pulls out her internal organs, and begins to knead them. Observing what the nun is doing, the woman says:

Woman: *(Gets up on her knees.)* She says she must cleanse the intestines, this big mess of filth and blood.

(Leans forward and watches attentively.) How can they be cleansed? After all, they are so bloody and filthy!

(Takes one step forward and listens.) She says she must cleanse them whether they can or can't be cleansed.

(Pressing.) She knows there's no way she can make them clean, but why does she still insist on cleansing them?

(Gao 1999a:72)

The third person, used throughout the play, generally refers to the Woman herself; in the context of this utterance, however, the Woman's referent is clearly the nun. This deliberate confusion results in the unification of the identities of the Woman and the nun, suggesting that it is the Woman herself who is trying to cleanse her physical being.

The image of the nun cleansing her organs is a powerful one, which one might perceive as religious. The Taiwanese scholar Hu Yaoheng suggests that it symbolizes the severity of religious practices; he further argues that the Woman "cannot and will not accept such strict religious regulations and hence does not have any karmic affinity for religion" (1995:50). The Woman may have missed a chance to be spiritually expiated, but this scene can also be perceived as another unavoidable failure in her effort to extricate herself from her subjectivity. Huang Meixu may be right when he points out that Gao "is only interested in the image" rather than the significance of the religious story (2000:307). The image of the nun may refer more metaphorically than realistically to religious redemption. The Woman's eventual refusal to identify with the nun signifies that even the supposedly omnipotent deity has been unable to lead her to religious truth.

The Woman's final encounter in the play is with a headless woman holding an eye in her palm. Shocked, the Woman wonders if her own soul has left her body:

Woman: *(Staring.)* She can even see her own eyes! In these eyes she sees her own naked body again.

(Gao 1999a:75)

The headless woman, despite the appearance of being external to the Woman, is not an other but another subjective projection of her own self. This time, with the extra eye, she is able to see herself from her other self. The eye is at once physically external to the Woman and subjectively an intrinsic extension of herself. She remains alienated but thoroughly scrutinized. This scene is essentially a physicalization of what the Woman has spoken of before as "not the other person who is truly lonely but precisely the one who is watching the other's loneliness." As the grim scrutiny becomes unendurable, she becomes resentful and attempts to exterminate the headless woman. Soon she realizes that the body has turned into a floating shirt (Gao 1999a:76). In the all-encompassing state of alienation, the Woman has still not been able to find her way to freedom but continues to be trapped in an illusory world. In this play Gao coldly illustrates the irony of subjectivity in the midst of self-alienation.

The process of understanding the conditions of one's existence in *The Nocturnal Wanderer* is demonstrated in quite a different manner. Here, the protagonist starts his journey as an imperturbable individual, seemingly alienated from the rest of the world. From the second scene onward, he realizes that he is unable to transcend the entrapment of his subjectivity and alienation from his own self. At the beginning of the play, there is a brief scene set in a train car representing the world of reality. While all the other passengers are on the train without valid tickets, the Traveler lawfully and obligingly pays both the fine and the fare; the Traveler exists in a different world from the others, and there is a stark psychological distance between them. With this as a background, the Sleepwalker—doubled by the actor previously playing the Traveler, signifying that the former is a reflection of the latter—begins his adventures in the dream world.

The Sleepwalker appears in the dream world as a loner, seemingly possessing absolute freedom. Confidently and consciously, he alienates himself from the external world:

Sleepwalker: Finally you're free of all responsibilities, free of all troubles. You know, man asks for troubles himself. Everyone has to have either this or that problem, if he can't find any problem, he loses all reason for living. But at this moment in time you have absolutely no problems at all. *(Thinking.)* No problem whatsoever, nothing, really nothing! It's hard to say if it's lucky for a man not to have any problems. In the final analysis, you should congratulate yourself somewhat. And because everyone has problems and you don't, you can't help but tell it to the world. But the street is empty, so you can only tell it to yourself: Hear! Hear! You're the only person without any problem in this huge metropolis!

(Gao 1999a:143)

He sees himself without any relation to the external world, shows no concern for it, and hence alienates himself from the others, appearing to be free from human perplexities. However, his utterance betrays the intrinsic nature of his existence. He considers himself to have "absolutely no problems at all," while paradoxically he cannot control himself from wanting to announce his freedom to others. He is therefore not fully divorced from the external world, because he still expects others to provide confirmation of his existence. Hence, his freedom is essentially projected from and conditioned by his subjectivity. Similar to the Woman in *Between Life and Death*, the Sleepwalker, in a state of solitude rather than freedom, is unable to escape the agony that has been engendered by his self-alienation.

Dominated by his alienated consciousness, the Sleepwalker constantly strives to cast off any external threats to his freedom. In response to the Sleepwalker's uncertainty as to his direction, the Tramp says: "Just follow the street and go straight. If something hits your nose, make a turn!" This arbitrary remark ignites the Sleepwalker's defensiveness about his supposedly autonomous being: "Everybody wants to control you, everybody wants to be God. You only want to take a leisurely stroll, without purpose and without destination" (Gao 1999a:145). In a self-imposed manner, the external world continues to have an effect on the Sleepwalker's existence. His apathy toward others is a conscious choice, but it is instantly transformed into hostility when his subjectivity is presumably under threat.

The protagonist's indulgence in his own subjectivity is demonstrated by his deep immersion in his thoughts. The notion of "thoughts" is indeed a recurring motif in the play. In an instance of self-contemplation, the Sleepwalker expresses his uncertain feelings:

Sleepwalker: You know that right now you're sleepwalking, living in a world between dream and reality, and you can't be sure whether the reality you're in is merely your memory or imagination. You don't even have the courage to disturb your dream, is it because such a disturbance would mean the death of your self? There's no way to detect whether you, your self, are real or fictitious.

(Gao 1999a:173–174)

The anxious uncertainties reveal the protagonist's stark awareness of his existence, which is determined by his thoughts. Ultimate freedom remains unreachable as he continues to wander between dream and reality, and the dream world is essentially a projection of his subjectivity. His reluctance to depart from the dream world suggests that his self-proclaimed freedom only exists in his subjectivity.

Later in the play, the Man brings on stage a head in a suitcase. He calls it "thinking" and warns the others that it is "too hot to handle" as "it tends to roll all over the place" (Gao 1999a:179). Later, another character, the Prostitute, takes the head, which bears an extreme likeness to the Sleepwalker, out from the suitcase and rolls it on the floor. The Sleepwalker stamps on the head and squashes it, symbolically destroying his own subjectivity, which has continuously thwarted his attempt to attain freedom (Gao 1999a:184). However, it soon becomes clear that what the Sleepwalker squashes is merely an illusion.

Toward the end of the play, as dawn approaches, the Sleepwalker prepares to go home, hoping that the nightmare will end when he stops sleepwalking and gets back to sleep. At this moment, a masked man, wearing an undershirt similar to the Sleepwalker's, comes on stage and blocks his way:

Sleepwalker: Who are you? What do you want? You want you to step aside and let you pass! You ask what in the world do you want? You want you—to let you—pass—!

(Neither of them is willing to yield, and they grapple with each other in silence. . . .)

(Gao 1999a:188)

In the Sleepwalker's utterance, the speaker himself and the addressee are both referred to as "you" ("*ni*" is used for both parties; the respectful pronoun "*nin*" used earlier with reference to the addressee is not used in this instance) and hence merge into one. The second-person narrative ingeniously presents an ambiguity in the character's identity. A similar technique with the third-person narrative was demonstrated above in the scene with the nun in *Between Life and Death*. The present instance is more powerful, as the pronoun "you" has a direct and personal referentiality and evokes a closer link between the two referents. The utterance signifies that the masked man is an alter ego of the Sleepwalker, another illusory image projected by his subjective self. The conflict is not between the

Sleepwalker and an other from the external world, but an other within his own subjective being.

Consciously wishing to alienate himself from the external world, the Sleepwalker is self-deceptive from the very beginning. He may have alienated himself from the world of reality, but, psychologically, he continues to show concerns about how he is being perceived by others. The dream world he has entered, similar to the dreamlike memory of the Woman in *Between Life and Death,* is essentially an illusory world created by his imagination. The Sleepwalker, aspiring to a life of freedom, has ironically ended up in a situation in which he is more deeply entangled not with any external elements, but with his own self. Alienation may have begun with hostility toward others; it concludes with an internal hostility. The Sleepwalker has always been a nocturnal wanderer. He exists in the dark side of the world, incessantly wandering, unable to achieve ultimate freedom.

Alienation is the norm for characters in both *Between Life and Death* and *The Nocturnal Wanderer.* Through the representation of their estrangement and lack of communication, a kaleidoscope of their psychological world is also exposed. The characters' subjectivity dominates their respective alienated beings, and in several instances transforms a self or an other into inanimate objects. In *Between Life and Death,* reification of the human occurs when the Woman's subjectivity is overwhelmed by agony arising from her alienation.[5] The man with whom she has had a relationship is first reified when she appears afraid of accepting the grim truth that their relationship is irretrievable (Gao 1999a:54). Next, parts of her body are reified as she finds herself hating her own body (ibid.:56). Then, the headless female body with an eye in the palm of its hand—the Woman's alter ego—is reified as she, in despair, tries to kill her own spiritual being (ibid.:76). In these instances, reification symbolizes further alienation, that is, the irreversible disconnection with the different aspects of the Woman's being. The play ends with a scene described as follows: "Woman, still lying down, looks like a pile of abandoned clothing in the faint light" (ibid.:79). The final reification of the Woman marks a conclusion to the gradual process of her alienation. In a progression from external to internal, the final object of reification is inevitably the Woman herself. By suggesting reification results from alienation, Gao has displayed a fundamentally pessimistic view of human existence.

Reification also appears in a different form. In *The Nocturnal Wan-*

derer, human beings are metaphorically compared to worms that "squirm all over the world" (Gao 1999a:182). In *Dialogue and Rebuttal,* the alienation demonstrated by the two characters is essentially a process of metamorphosis. Speaking in the second- and third-person voices respectively, the Man and the Woman converse with each other but without real communication. Enclosed within their subjective isolation, their actions become more and more weird and unhuman. They crawl around on the stage and giggle to themselves. Their utterances become indecipherable. Gradually, the speed of their speech increases while their motion slows down. In the end, "their bodies become more contorted, like two strange crawling reptiles" (ibid.:133).

Their metamorphosis naturally recalls similar examples in the Western literary tradition, but it has a different significance. In Apuleius' *The Golden Ass,* the metamorphosis happens when, in moments of crisis, an individual is transformed for the purpose of a rebirth (Bakhtin 1981: 114–115). In Franz Kafka's *The Metamorphosis,* the monstrous vermin is seen as an alien body that imprisons the sober consciousness of the protagonist (Sweeney 1996:140–141). In these instances, metamorphoses are ongoing searches for personal identity. In Gao's plays, however, these metamorphoses result from the protagonists' failure to free themselves from their own subjectivity. In this sense, metamorphosis is not dissimilar to reification. The Woman in *Between Life and Death* has been reified into a lifeless being while the characters in *Dialogue and Rebuttal* have metamorphosed into monstrous creatures. In both cases, nothing recognizably human remains.

Questioning the Existence of the Self

Moving from alienation to reification and metamorphosis, Gao Xingjian suggests that the search for freedom is inevitably pointless if one is to hold on to his or her physical being and psychological self. What then is the ultimate freedom Gao envisions? The answer is vaguely suggested, at the end of *Between Life and Death,* through the Woman's voice in the capacity of the narrator. In a somber mood, she speaks as if she is singing:

Woman: Is this about him, about you, about me, about her who is that girl, about her but not her, not about you, not about me, and not about you or all of you, just as what you all see is not her, not me, and not you, it's merely the self, but the me you all see is not me, not her, it's only that so-called self looking at her, looking at me, what more can you or I say?

. . . What is self? Besides these words, these empty, hollow words about nothing, what else is left?

(Gao 1999a:78)

In these concluding sentences, two issues of profound philosophical implication are put forward directly to the audience. First, the meaning of one's existence is usually defined by one's subjectivity. However, one can also be entrapped if unable to overcome self-indulgent consciousness. Second, words are essential in the construction of the self. However, whether words are effective in achieving such an objective is another question to be challenged. The final issue is in fact an ironic assertion. The implicit message is that without the burden of words one can rid oneself of subjectivity and attain a state of freedom. Although the question of "what else is left behind" remains open, one might come up with the answer "nothingness."

"Nothingness" is a notion that recalls the Existentialist writers whose ideas Gao mentions in his essays. A key concept of the French Existentialist Jean-Paul Sartre, nothingness, according to Roseline Intrater, refers to an emptiness that "provides both the space for being and the vacuum force to draw it into endless successions of existences." Intrater further summarizes the three implied conditions of nothingness. First, being always at a distance from oneself, with a degree of objectivity, one's present choices are not determined by those of the past. Second, being a presence to oneself and not simply a self implies the ability to regard oneself as an object rather than becoming lost in one's subjectivity. Third, being transcendent, one is able to overcome the end of life and realize oneself in terms of one's ultimate existence (Intrater 1988:38).

"Nothingness" also reminds one of the Daoist thinkers, one of whom Gao represents as a protagonist in one of his plays.[6] The ideal state of existence, as manifested by Zhuangzi, is expressed in three ideal models: "The superior man has no self, the heavenly man has no deeds, the sagacious man has no name" (Zhuangzi 1983:14). One will only achieve the ideal when one has released oneself from both external and internal circumscription. The prisons of deeds and names are easier to cast off.

Ultimately, however, one has to break out of the yoke of inner conscious-ness, which is the most difficult task. Without these constraints, one is able to interact freely with Nature.

In the concepts of nothingness of both Sartre and Zhuangzi, sub-jectivity is seen as the primary obstacle to an existence of complete free-dom. The Woman in *Between Life and Death* has gone through a strenu-ous process to search for such freedom even though she is not sure of finding it. She continues to wander, physically, at the edge of life and death—as suggested by the Chinese title—or, metaphorically, at the edge of existence and extinction. But she never goes beyond the border. The Woman, who has been alienated first by the external world and then by her own self, finally submits to her subjectivity, relinquishing any further attempt to search for the significance of existence.

By contrast, the Sleepwalker in *The Nocturnal Wanderer* may be aware of preserving himself from the interference of others, but he does not seem to be aware of the domination exerted by his own subjectivity. In a state of alienation, he aspires to an absolute freedom:

Sleepwalker: You're all by yourself, you're talking to yourself. What are you thinking about? It doesn't matter. What's important is that you're still thinking, that you still have your own thoughts. Never mind if they seem totally worthless in other people's eyes.

Other people are nothing to you. They're their own busi-ness; you are you, and only you. You are a human being, or maybe a worm, a butterfly, or an ant. Why should you worry about what you look like in other people's eyes? Happiness is only when you're contemplating things by yourself.

You contemplate and you wander without any worries, between heaven and earth, in your own private world, and in this way you acquire supreme freedom—

(Gao 1999a:149–150)

An existence unimpeded by the perception of others, in which one breaks away from spatial and temporal circumscription and achieves ultimate freedom, is an ideal to which philosophers of all times, including the

Western Existentialists and the Chinese Daoists, have aspired. Gao's ideal state of existence, as manifested in the Sleepwalker's utterance, suggests a relation to Zhuangzi's notion of "free wanderings" *(xiaoyao you)*.

Zhuangzi praises Song Rongzi for his inattention to secular names and glories. Song Rongzi differs from many people, because he neither becomes excited over eulogies nor becomes depressed over criticism. He is also capable of recognizing the distinction between the internal self and the external world, and that between honor and disgrace. However, Zhuangzi's ideal is beyond that displayed by Song Rongzi: "If one follows the rules of Nature and masters the variation in the universe's vitality, he will then be able to wander freely in infinity. What boundary could enclose him?" (Zhuangzi 1983:14–18). Zhuangzi's ideal being breaks away from self-centeredness and attains freedom in merging with the spirit of the universe. What the Sleepwalker proclaims—Gao puts it as an irony rather than an assertion—is an ideal existence resembling Zhuang-zi's freedom, but the Sleepwalker does not realize that he is unable to achieve it. He is limited by his deep immersion in his subjectivity, represented by his "thoughts." In this sense, the Sleepwalker is not enlightened enough even to join ranks with Song Rongzi and thus is obviously far away from Zhuangzi's ideal.

In his observation—and through his representation—of human existence, Gao Xingjian adopts a more detached position than Zhuangzi. The first story told by Zhuangzi is about two birds, the *peng* and the *xue-jiu*. The *peng* is a gigantic bird whose back measures a few thousand *li* and whose extended wings resemble a cloud. It waits for a strong wind and then travels ninety thousand *li* to the south seas. In the eyes of the little *xuejiu*, this effort is ridiculously unnecessary. It stops flying when it hits branches and lands when it cannot reach the treetop (Zhuangzi 1983:1–10). In Gao's plays, the protagonists appear to be in a situation somewhat similar to that of the *xuejiu*. Both indulge in their subjective perceptions of others and of themselves. Whereas the ignorance and narrow-mindedness of the *xuejiu* confines it to an enclosed but self-contented sphere, Gao's protagonists attempt to acquire a freer existence but fail, as they are helplessly entrapped within their own minds. The *xue-jiu* remains what it is despite its inability to understand others. In contrast, human beings possess an ability to engage in self-reflection but are unwillingly or unconsciously reified or metamorphosed, ironically, in the very process of self-reflection. This is because self-reflection is only made possible by subjectivity.

Gao seems neither emotionally nor personally engaged in the dramatic world of his protagonists and gives the impression of being an observer of all the subjective revelations and transformations in his plays. This detachment is effectively maintained through his narrators, who all speak in alienated voices. Uninvolved in the subjectivity of the protagonist, the narrator—played by the same actor in a state of neutrality—is able to scrutinize the protagonist's existence, as well as his or her utterances. From this perspective, I would suggest that the voice of the neutral actor might be perceived as that of the playwright. Gao displays not only a sober attitude toward his dramatic objects but also a serious interest in the way in which these objects are being represented. As an observer of human existence, he not only fundamentally questions the significance of being, but also critically probes a related issue: the meaningfulness or meaninglessness of words.

This issue is repeatedly elaborated through the various protagonists. The protagonists usually demonstrate a skeptical attitude toward the meaningfulness of words when they come to realize that they are unable to find freedom from their subjective isolation. *Between Life and Death* offers the following passage:

Woman: She says she doesn't know what she was saying, she doesn't know what she really wants to say, maybe she didn't say anything, if what she said is useless, then she might as well not say it, she says she doesn't know what she ought to say, and what else she has not said. But what more can she say?

(Gao 1999a:74)

In a state of confusion and misery, the Woman realizes that the means for expressing her feelings—language—is unreliable and without meaning. Her conscious rejection of words shows her loss of faith in the meaningfulness of utterances. In *The Nocturnal Wanderer*, this loss of faith is proclaimed more explicitly and in a more assertive tone:

Sleepwalker: [You say] a word is a word. Originally it has no meaning, but it could be given countless meanings. It's all up to you depending on how you want to explain it. But in the final analysis, a word is still a word, it has no meaning. Take for instance black, white, eat, make love, saviour, suffering, and baloney, no matter how you mix these words, using combination as the principle or process, or dismantle them and mess them up again before regrouping them once more, the resulting eloquence is still only a repetition of nonsense.[7]

(Gao 1999a:183)

Here Gao has subverted, in a rational manner, the conventional relation between words and meaning. However, he has attempted to reconstruct a closer link between meaning and subjective consciousness. This attempt becomes clearer when the Sleepwalker later claims:

Sleepwalker: Whether nonsense or not, it's not important. The important thing is that you're still saying them. You are you only because you can still say the words.

(Gao 1999a:183)

In this statement, an utterance and its meaning are exclusively dominated by one's subjectivity. A similar notion emerges in *Dialogue and Rebuttal:*

Man: Actually you don't know what you're talking about, you talk only because you want to. . . .

You can't understand the meaning of your own words, you're just the slave of language, but you can't stop yourself from talking endlessly—

(Gao 1999a:131–132)

It is finally revealed to the audience that when speaking of human being and utterance, the manipulator is actually not the former but the latter. The Man wants to be the master of his utterance but, ironically, ends up a slave to it. The Woman in *Between Life and Death* expresses her agony and despair. The Sleepwalker in *The Nocturnal Wanderer* appears to be arrogant but pitiable. The Man in *Dialogue and Rebuttal* exudes helplessness and powerlessness. Presented through intense emotions, the meaninglessness of utterance is connected to the insignificance of existence.

The protagonists' negation of the meaningfulness of language has its roots in their state of subjective alienation. These characters, deeply immersed in a self-constructed isolation, all experience Berman's modern predicament where the public "shatters into a multitude of fragments, speaking incommensurable languages" (1983:17). Every individual in this world remains physically related to each other but, at the same time, spiritually disconnected. Among other subjects, Gao Xingjian has chosen repeatedly to represent this grievous aspect of human existence and thus reveals his modernist pessimism. When Gao left China and obtained freedom from political oppression, he was free to establish a theater without ideological restriction and aesthetic limitation. However, he is now absorbed by the sense of futility that has perplexed many other writers who contemplate the nature of human existence.

Conclusion
The Playwright as an Intellectual

The Chinese Context and Beyond

When Gao Xingjian's first production, *Alarm Signal,* appeared in a provisionally converted studio theater in 1982, it began cautiously as an internal trial performance. The playwright and his team as well as the Chinese critics were uncertain of what the audience's response would be to a play that aesthetically departed from the deep-rooted realist traditions of the Beijing People's Art Theatre. To everyone's surprise, the play was enthusiastically received and went on to more than a hundred shows. Theaters across the country soon restaged it. A significant number of articles, mostly acclaiming the play's experimental spirit and relevant themes, were published in journals and newspapers. The authors of these articles were excited by a new theatrical form that provided a refreshing experience and explored contemporary issues that they were able to relate to.

With the production of *The Bus Stop* and *Wild Man,* Gao became the most daring figure in Chinese experimental theater, in the eyes of both Chinese and Western critics. Since then, Gao's name has been featured in most accounts of the history of contemporary Chinese drama. While Chinese critics have hailed him as an "outstanding representative of experimental theatre" (Wang Xinmin 1997:333), Western critics perceived him as a "new force in world theatre" (Roubicek 1990:190).

However, when I visited Beijing in May 1999, a year and a half before Gao was awarded the Nobel Prize in Literature, I was given a very different impression by some scholars whom I interviewed. It appeared that most students of drama were unfamiliar with Gao's name. They were also unaware of his avant-garde experimentation, which was at the center of controversy during the 1980s. According to Lu Min, a professor specializing in contemporary Chinese drama with Beijing's Central Academy of Drama, the Chinese people's ignorance of Gao was due to his absence from the Chinese stage since his departure from China in 1987. Since then, many other exciting works had emerged, and, despite the earlier controversy, it was inevitable that Gao would gradually fade from the Chinese drama scene.

Lin Kehuan, president of China's National Youth Theatre, agrees that, although Gao received widespread attention, his position in the history of contemporary Chinese drama may be less significant. In an interview, Lin suggested that the issues Gao represents in his plays, especially *The Bus Stop* and *Wild Man*, go beyond the immediate social concerns of the Chinese audience. Instead of dealing with contemporary themes directly related to China's present, Gao probes universal issues that are detached from the Chinese sociocultural context and may only be faced in a remote future. In addition, Lin contends that, in terms of both formal experimentation and thematic exploration, *Wild Man* is the pinnacle of Gao's works. Gao's later plays, in Lin's view, do not display the power and depth of *Wild Man*, as the playwright has lost contact with Chinese society—the soil of his creativity.

Both Lu and Lin perceive Gao with regard to the Chinese context. In their eyes, Gao's position is to be weighed against the relevance of his works in representing the social and psychological states of the Chinese in a specific temporal and spatial framework. During the period between the end of the Cultural Revolution in 1976 and the Tiananmen Incident in 1989, the foremost task of most Chinese writers was to search for and remold a Chinese identity that had been distorted and lost over the previous decade or more. From the corpus of works of the literature of the wounded, the literature of self-reflection, and the literature of root-searching to the fervent call for a literature of humanism, the expression of self, as Jing Wang suggests, is usually closely related to the dramatic changes and contradictions that took place in the cultural, economic, and sociopolitical sectors (Wang 1996:32). The problematics of self in this extensive process of identity searching is thus intrinsically inseparable from an understanding of the problematics of the era.

In the field of drama, early plays such as *Hot Spring Outside* (1979) portray a heroic image of an individual who displays patriotic spirit and takes pride in sacrificing his life for the advancement of his country. Although the protagonist in this play is no longer a class hero as in revolutionary literature, the worthiness of the individual hero remains dependent on his attitude toward the collective. Later plays such as *Father Dog-*

gie Nirvana (1986) by Liu Jinyun and *The Chronicle of Mulberry Village* (Sangshuping jishi, 1988) by Chen Zidu, Yang Jian, and Zhu Xiaoping, are perceived as representative works of the 1980s for their profound depiction of peasants' struggle in the process of modernization. In both plays, peasants are portrayed as a collective within the context of their fate vis-à-vis overwhelming social and economic transformations.

Issues presented in *Alarm Signal*, such as anxiety about unemployment and the hope for a better future, show Gao exhibiting similar concerns in constructing a forward-looking humanistic Chinese identity. However, one should not forget that Gao's first play was not *Alarm Signal*, which he described as a product of compromise, but *The Bus Stop*, which dealt with the revelation of the absurdity of Chinese society. In *Wild Man*, he further uses the metaphor of the death of the modern epic to illustrate his pessimism about China's future.

Beneath the veil of the many current social issues discussed in his plays, Gao's modernist consciousness and his perception of China's problems in a universalistic idiom—beyond the indulgence of immediate concerns—is clearly discernible. From this perspective, the subject of *The Bus Stop* is not the Chinese people's struggle to advance, but the human weaknesses obstructing their advancement. Similarly, the subject of *Wild Man* is neither the imperiled natural environment nor the dilemma of love and marriage, but the inevitable loss of humanity and cultural tradition in the process of heading forward. As such, at an early stage of his creative life, Gao had already transcended the burden of C. T. Hsia's "obsession with China," which dominated the consciousness of several generations of Chinese writers in the twentieth century.

While the prevailing dramatic discourse privileged the idea of modernization or the imagination of a Chinese modernity, Gao had already begun to reflect on the problems of a modernity that was still in the process of being constructed. In retrospect it is clear that he was proceeding on a different course than his contemporaries. However, Chinese critics either received his plays in a way that contradicted his original intentions or placed him inappropriately among other contemporary playwrights. For instance, both *The Bus Stop* and *Wild Man* were labeled as "philosophical plays" (*zheli ju*) with positive themes. The former was seen as "representing the human will in overcoming the restriction of old habits and determination in pursuing great ideals" and the latter as expressing "the power of life and eternity of history" (Tian Benxiang et al. 1996:171). Furthermore, the editor of a collection of experimental plays of the 1980s categorized *The Bus Stop, Hot Spring Outside,* and Wei Minglun's modern *chuanju* (Sichuan opera) *Pan Jinlian* under the subheading of "absurdist plays" *(huangdan ju)* (Tian Xuxiu 1988). In fact, the latter two do not resemble the Theater of the Absurd formally or ideologically. Their so-called absurdist characteristic comprises a nonrealist representation style with the appearance of a spirit as a protagonist and the coexistence of modern and ancient characters. In contrast, Gao's play displays some degree of awareness and appropriation of that Western tradition.

The remarks by Lu Min and Lin Kehuan only confirm Gao's poor fit in the discourse of Chinese drama history. Their comments are representative of the general perception of the playwright since the 1990s. In a drama history published in the late 1990s, Gao was described as a dramatist who advanced too fast, leaving his audience unable to catch up with him. His inability to understand the audience's level of appreciation was perceived to be a shortcoming (Wang Xinmin 1997:344). Hence, it is problematic to compare Gao with other playwrights in this way. Instead, a different set of criteria must be adopted when trying to determine Gao's significance.

Gao was undoubtedly a pioneer in formal experimentation in the 1980s. Staged in a performance space converted from a rehearsal studio, *Alarm Signal* discarded the conventional proscenium stage and demolished the fourth wall. It was generally perceived as the first "little theater" *(xiao juchang)* production that successfully challenged the Chinese realist tradition. With *The Bus Stop,* the barrier between the performers and the audience was further broken as members of the cast appeared occasionally among the audience. Direct communication was effectively enhanced, with the cast resuming their capacity as performers to address the audience. Gao's last play produced in China, *Wild Man,* led the audience into an overwhelming experience of total theater, which he designated as "multivocal theater." In it both thematic and formal representations were displayed in a comprehensively multilayered and interwoven manner.

Each time one of Gao's plays was staged, the Chinese audience and critics underwent a new and provocative theater experience. Although many other Chinese playwrights and directors had attempted to experiment with novelty in their plays, their works did not usually display a creativity as shocking and extensive as Gao's. Gao's knowledge of French language and literature expanded Gao's world and provided him with an advantage over his contemporaries, especially at a time when many were eagerly looking for inspiration from the modern West. He also had access to firsthand information regarding the most recent developments in the theater outside China when Chinese translation was still limited and restricted. In this respect, one other Chinese dramatist who was at center stage in advocating new dramatic concepts should not be forgotten. He was Huang Zuolin, who was well-versed in the English language and had received drama training in England. In the post–Cultural Revolution era, no dramatist has proved to be more provocative and inspiring than Huang and Gao. Huang's notion of *xieyi* drama and Gao's multivocal theater have both been debated enthusiastically and have been used to describe experimental works in general.

Another of Gao's strengths is that he is a writer knowledgeable in literary theory. He first evoked controversy by writing a series of articles on modernist techniques of fictional writing.[1] Then, while his first play was being staged, he published another series on the concepts of modern theater.[2] In his many essays, he critically discusses the ideas of influential Western dramatists such as Bertolt Brecht, Antonin Artaud, Samuel Beckett, and Jerzy Grotowski. The ideas of these masters together with Gao's knowledge of traditional Chinese theater have provided him with a concrete foundation to construct his own dramatic aesthetics. Furthermore, Gao is not a desktop playwright. His experience as a theater director allows him to write plays with a clear picture of how they will appear on the stage. His experimentation is therefore not confined to words and theories, but is also a direct challenge to theatrical conventions.

Since the late 1970s, China has entered an era in which theater performance is more powerful than dramatic text in the printed form. The creative involvement of directors has become more important, especially in breaking realist conventions. In this light, the success of Gao's experimentation is a result of his collaboration with director Lin Zhaohua. Gao and Lin established a uniquely close working relationship with their first production, *Alarm Signal*. Before Gao's scripts were finalized, they exchanged views on theater and discussed how the plays were to be staged (Gao 1992:1–2). Before their collaboration, no other playwright and director had worked in such a close and integrated way. Lin's open-mindedness and boldness complemented Gao's spirit of experimentation. Together, they became the most innovative and controversial team of the modern Chinese theater scene in the 1980s.

Most significant, Gao is different from his contemporaries in that he always displays a profound intellectual quality as a playwright. Admittedly, many Chinese writers exhibit intellectual awareness and reflection in their works; China has always had a rich literary tradition created by literati-writers. A recent, vivid example is the generation of May Fourth writers who willingly and painstakingly took for themselves the responsibility of constructing a new national character. Gao emerged as part of this tradition. While Gao was involved in such an enterprise in the early and mid-1980s, he unhesitatingly severed ties to that tradition afterwards. On the one hand, his continuing challenge to realist traditions was a conscious effort to break away from existing conventions in hopes of establishing an alternative aesthetic. It is through formal experimentation that Gao first contributed to the renewal of the Chinese theater. On the other hand, while he began with contemplation on contemporary sociocultural issues, he soon took up a more detached and sober position in dealing with Chinese issues and, later, broader issues of universal human existence in modern times. Gao's intellectual awareness has thus played a vital role in his selection of artistic elements originating in various Chinese and Western traditions as well as his proposal of a transcultural theater in a spirit of challenge to norms and conventions. Ironically, this consciousness has resulted in alienation from the Chinese context as he has been enthusiastically embraced in the international arena.

Imagining Alternatives

As he challenges orthodox modes of representation, Gao Xingjian also questions the adequacy of a dominant Confucian cultural tradition. Gao's inclination to Daoism, folk cultures of the various ethnic minorities, and the philosophies of Laozi and Zhuangzi has been demonstrated in many of his plays. In his view, these elements, which are normally at the periphery of Chinese cultural traditions, encompass a potent creativity as opposed to rigidified orthodox Confucianism. In his opposition to Confucianism, Gao has apparently inherited the spirit of the May Fourth intellectuals. In the contemporary discourse on revitalizing Chinese culture, Gao points to the rediscovery of alternative traditions rather than the rejuvenation of the orthodox culture. In-depth engagement of this issue is found in his novel, *Soul Mountain*, whereas it is less directly discussed but inherent in the artistic representation in his plays. Nevertheless, alternativeness is always at the center of his vision of Chineseness.

Although Gao has claimed that his contemplation of alternative cultures is independent of and predates the root-searching literature of the mid-1980s (he began research on alternative cultures in 1982 for *Soul Mountain*), it can also be seen in the broader context of the ongoing discourse about new understandings of Chinese cultural identity. Since the mid-1970s, new archaeological findings have shown that the northern central plains *(zhongyuan)* were not the only genesis of Chinese culture. The construct of a unilinear culture was superseded by the recognition that other cultures existed as early as and, more important, were the equals of the central plains culture. Among these previously marginalized cultures, Chu culture is especially celebrated (Friedman 1994:70–71, 80–81). In Han Shaogong's 1985 seminal article that unveiled the Root-Searching Fever (Xungen re) of the literary scene, Chu culture is presented as a symbolic subject of alternative imagination. Han further asserts that the search for roots is "neither cheap nostalgia nor provincialism" but a process of self-realization in the course of assimilating and digesting other cultural referential systems (1985:2–4). In the context of the Cultural Debate that emerged during a similar period, Gan Yang criticizes the notion that Confucian culture constitutes the complete system of Chinese culture. He proposes an open spirit in reconstructing Chinese cultural traditions with Confucianism as merely one of many possible contributing elements (Gan 1989:29–30). The process of reimagining a multiorigin and multifaceted Chinese culture with concrete scientific support from archaeological and anthropological excavation is a comprehensive project that involves academics, intellectuals, writers, and artists who have all come together in search of a new Chinese identity in a new era.

In contrast, the response from the drama circle was rather insignificant. While the intelligentsia was fervently involved in discussions on cultural identity, drama critics and theater practitioners were whole-heartedly engaged in expanding and redefining the concepts of drama that began to emerge in 1983. In their discussion, they have also dug into the cultural past. But their focus has been on alternative modes of representation rather than a search for alternative cultural identities. Interestingly, while the Chinese dramatists were enthusiastically producing Brecht's plays and appropriating Brechtian techniques, none of them mentioned or appeared to be inspired by the fact that Brecht was an admirer of Confucianism and Daoism. Within the context of such an emphasis on theatrical forms, Gao became a pioneer of formal innovation. In addition, with *Wild Man*, he became involved in the construction of cultural identity beyond the theatrical world. For the first time, an entire theater celebrated folk songs and dances of rural minority peoples. A desolate epic of southern origin was presented in relation to urban modernization and the literati consciousness.

However, Gao is not naively optimistic about the fate of the cultures he explores. Although these elements are presented as lively, vigorous, and vivacious, *Wild Man* concludes metaphorically with the inevitable disappearance of the epic *Song of the Dark*, when the only man who knows the epic dies. *Wild Man* is designated by the playwright as epic theater. In fact, it is a theater that demonstrates the woeful fate of the epic. On the one hand, Gao cherishes the creativity and freshness of alternative cultures and would have them inject vitality into the rigidified orthodox culture. On the other hand, he laments the continuous marginalization and eventual destruction of these cultures by both the rapid process of modernization and the hegemonic literati culture. In this respect, the play's message transcends social concerns of environmental destruction. It ends with the following prophecy on the destiny of Chinese culture: if alternative cultures are ignored and forsaken, the future will be gloomy and somber.

The alternative portrayed in *Wild Man* remains remote and even unreal. Vaguely reminiscent of the "imaginary nostalgia" that David Derwei Wang finds in Shen Congwen's lyrical stories and essays about West Hunan (Wang 1992:249–253), the alternative cultures in Gao's play are essentially a reimagination and re-creation in a modern urban theater environment. In fact, Gao's dramatized alternative cultures have a grimmer fate than Shen Congwen's literarized West Hunan. Gao's imagination of alternatives is detached from their original context, interpreted with a modern consciousness, and presented to an urban audience. As such, the literati consciousness that Gao vehemently rejects is inevitably and paradoxically an integral component in his perception and representation of these cultures. They are thus more imagined than real. They bear the function (or are given the task) of enriching Chinese culture at large rather than being preserved in their original forms. In addition, as they are expected to rejuvenate a rigidified culture, they also have to face the threat emerging from that new context. Gao's pessimism toward their fate is apparently a result of his placing them in the context of an extensive and unavoidable disturbance by modern living and modern consciousness. Like many modern writers, Gao is trapped in a paradox of both advocating and lamenting these alternative cultures.

Gao's imagination of a Chineseness with alternative cultural elements, in this respect, is a literati construction. Gao constructs his representation of alternative Chineseness with a strong sense of modern consciousness and integrates these elements into a theatrical form that is inspired by both traditional Chinese and modern Western theaters. Nostalgia continues to play a part, even since Gao left China in 1987. The outcome is *The Nether City* and *The Story of Shanhaijing*, both conceptualized while he was still in China and completed in Paris. Since then, he has written five other plays that seem to depart from such pursuits. However, his recent play, *August Snow*, a "modern *xiqu*" as he describes it, only proves that universal themes have not totally displaced his passion for an imagined Chineseness.

In *The Nether City* and *The Story of Shanhaijing*, elements from Chinese folk culture and religion of southern origins are extensively represented. The second part of *The Nether City* depicts the wife of Zhuang Zhou entering the underworld and undergoing judgment by the Nether King after her death. Gao stresses that the image of the nether world is derived from the primitive shamanism of the Han inhabitants of the Yangtze basin and the folk Daoist religion. He also suggests that the gods and ghosts should be portrayed as grotesque and jocular, because "that is their original image as represented in folklore" (Gao 1995c:68). Similarly, the models of the gods in *The Story of Shanhaijing* are to be based on those that appeared in "Shang dynasty bronzeware, lacquerware from the Chu tombs, silk painting of the Western Han dynasty, the stone carving of Han tablets, and mural paintings found in Yunnan and Guangxi provinces" (Gao 1995d:108–109). From his list of permissible sources of inspiration, it is apparent that Gao carefully chose to avoid cultures that are canonized and dominant. His choice of alienated cultures and even unearthed artifacts reflects his intention to enrich Chinese culture with alternatives that are unfamiliar and that serve as a powerful and effective counterbalance to the orthodox tradition's dominance.

The imagination of an alternative Chineseness is not a novel trend that began in the 1980s. While Zhou Zuoren (1885–1967) criticized the barbarism of shamanism (Zhou 1989b:200–202), he also perceived shamanistic mythologies as a valuable legacy of primitive people's imaginations (Zhou 1989a:50–52). Lu Xun (1881–1936) was not only fascinated by the fantastic world of *The Classic of Mountains and Seas* as a child (Lu Xun 1981:246–248), but he also represented ancient mythologies and legends with the eight tales in *Old Tales Retold* (Gushi xinbian), which Leo Lee describes as an effort to "recreate [the ancient past of Chinese culture] with the radical sensibilities of a modern novelist" (1987:32).

Shen Congwen's idealized world of West Hunan, which Jeffrey Kinkley describes as "the modern descendant of an ancient kingdom and state of mind called Chu" (1987:5), is the most vivid example of the construction of an alternative imagination among the May Fourth writers. Gao's creations are essentially part of an ongoing search for alternatives. The scope of his imagination is, however, much wider than that of his predecessors, as he probes all available sources of spatially and temporally remote cultures.

With *The Nether City* and *The Story of Shanhaijing*, Gao also attempts to remold the popularly accepted legendary images that, in his view, are secularized and Confucianized, and have thus lost their original humanity (Gao 1996a:243–244). The story of Zhuang Zhou testing his wife's chastity in *Smash the Coffin* stereotypically portrays the wife as a licentious and unfaithful woman. In the *jingju* story, the goddess Guanyin suggests to Zhuang Zhou that if he wishes to devote himself to the pursuit of the Dao, he has to set himself free from the mundane encumbrances of the marital relationship. He first makes his wife vow that she will remain chaste after his death. Later, while pretending to be dead, he disguises himself as a handsome young man to seduce her. The wife instantly falls for the man and proposes to him. When the man pretends to be critically ill and asks for Zhuang Zhou's brain as the remedy, the wife prepares to smash the coffin containing Zhuang Zhou's body without the slightest hesitation. Zhuang Zhou comes alive and upbraids his astonished wife as an evil woman. She is utterly remorseful and kills herself. Liberated from mundane worries, Zhuang Zhou then begins his journey to pursue the Dao.

Like the vast majority of traditional titles that have submitted, consciously or otherwise, to Confucian ideologies of moral teaching, *Smash the Coffin* demonstrates patriarchism and repression of women. The message is that an unfaithful woman deserves death. (Taking a closer look at how the story is told, however, the fundamental motivation for Zhuang Zhou's testing his wife is, oddly enough, to set himself free from worldly life in order to pursue a higher spiritual being. The wife's death, as it is represented, is not so much the outcome of her unfaithfulness as the result of Zhuang Zhou's selfish intention.)

In *The Nether City*, Gao retells the story from a patently modern perspective. In contrast to the traditional play that portrays Zhuang Zhou's wife as an evil and lustful woman, Gao presents Zhuang Zhou's attempt to test his wife as ridiculous, foolish, and wicked. The actor playing

Zhuang Zhou speaks aside to criticize the character, and there are cho-ruses of men and women who lament the wife's misfortune at being made to undergo such an unnecessary test. In Gao's play, the wife is the unfortunate victim, while Zhuang Zhou is the inhumane victimizer who will have to eat his own bitter fruit. With his attempt to reverse the repre-sentation of Zhuang Zhou's wife in the traditional play, Gao tries to break away from Confucian moral encumbrance, which traditionally prevails in Chinese theater. Similarly, humanity is restored to literary characters that have been distorted and suppressed in traditional representations.

The Story of Shanhaijing is a more ambitious project, which sees Gao extending his exploration into collective memories. As an essential con-stituent of a people's ethnic and historical past, Chinese mythologies have lost their primitive vitality in the course of rerepresentation. This is especially so when they are used for Confucian moral teachings. Gao asserts that his play is written according to ancient mythologies originally recorded in the ancient text of The Classic of Mountains and Seas, and he makes no reference to stories of later periods derived from the text. In so doing, Gao wishes to restore the "original features" of these mythologies, which he claims have been seriously misrepresented in later orthodox Confucian classics (Gao 1995d:107). Gao's ambition is to reconstruct a set of mythologies that can be shared and appreciated by contemporary Chinese. In other words, he is offering an alternative to a collective mem-ory that has been molded predominantly by Confucian ideology. In this play—which he calls "a Chinese Bible" (Gao 1998a), with reference to his ambition to represent all the ancient Chinese gods in one play—the gods and their deeds together with their relationships are stripped of the seri-ous and moralist images put up by Confucianists over centuries. In fact, they appear more like the gods in ancient Greek mythology who bear significant human characteristics. As such, Gao de-deifies the Chinese gods and restores their humanness.

To reconstruct a collective memory is often too big a task for a nation, let alone an individual. Even if The Story of Shanhaijing were to be produced and accepted by the Chinese audience, it would only be an alternative viewpoint for the perception of Chinese culture.[3] Yet Gao con-tinues to offer alternativeness in his August Snow. Departing from all his other plays, August Snow is not a play for a modern theater performed in the vernacular language, but a xiqu piece commissioned by Taiwan's Kuo-Kuang Theatre Company, which performs jingju.[4] In general, most tradi-tional xiqu depict heroic deeds (such as those from The Romance of the

Three Kingdoms [Sanguo yanyi]) or romantic encounters (such as those from *The Romance of the Western Chamber* [Xixiang ji]). Even if the characters are Daoist or Buddhist in origin (such as Zhuang Zhou in *Smash the Coffin*), they are usually Confucianized. When he was asked to write a modern *xiqu*, Gao chose to break away from the prevailing Confucian ideology by portraying Huineng, the Chan Buddhist patriarch, as his central character. The stories of Chan Buddhism, as depicted in *August Snow*, have provided *xiqu* with new content in the same spirit as Gao's call for the renewal of its forms.

Although *August Snow* is Gao's only play to date with Chan Buddhism as its main theme, his previous plays also display immense interest in the philosophies of Buddhism and Daoism. The title *The Other Shore* has Buddhist connotations, and the play's central theme involves human beings' mortal ordeal and psychological transformation without religious redemption. The dialogic form of *Dialogue and Rebuttal* reveals characteristics of Chan *gongan*. The image of a nun cleansing her internal organs in *Between Life and Death* is borrowed from Buddhist stories, and that of a man morphing into a butterfly in *The Nocturnal Wanderer* has its antecedent in the *Zhuangzi*. While Buddhist and Daoist philosophies inspired Gao to adopt an alternative perspective for understanding Chinese culture, they also provided him with a vast array of images that have evidently enriched his theatrical representation.

Gao is different from many of his predecessors in two ways. First, he demonstrates a direct and vigorous challenge to orthodox Confucianism. Similarly, he opposes cultural orthodoxy in the same manner he opposes artistic orthodoxy. Second, it is a conscious effort, rather than an arbitrary interest, that has led to the representation of Buddhism and Daoism as well as elements of folk and primitive cultures in Gao's theater. These elements are some of Gao's attempts to contribute to the construction of a new and vital Chinese culture that is not dominated by any orthodox ideology. In his own way as both a playwright and an intellectual, Gao continues the task of creatively imagining an alternative Chineseness.

Fleeing the Collective

Gao Xingjian's imagination of cultural alternatives reveals an unavoidable conflict between his individual consciousness and the mainstream ideology. At a deeper level, it reflects an essential problem faced by the playwright: the notion of the self versus the collective. Such a conflict will naturally emerge when a writer acquires a certain degree of freedom of explo-ration into his or her own self, producing a "literature of the unfettered self," which is "potentially seditious," suggests Mabel Lee in her discus-sion of *Soul Mountain*. Lee also claims that deep under the surface overlay of the conflict, which is the writer's immediate response to the collective's violence and repression, "there should remain an underlying stratum with relevance to broader human concerns" (1996:148). This is also true for Gao's plays, although it is sometimes represented with subtleness. For example, the Ecologist in *Wild Man* is portrayed as being trapped help-lessly in the collective aspiration for modernization. His despair over the destruction of the natural environment and the death of the Old Singer remains an individual agony that will never be consoled. In the card-playing scene of *The Other Shore,* facing the lie told in unison by a manip-ulated collective, the protagonist is forced to submit his individual belief to the collective mendacity. The anxiety that arises when the individual is swamped by the collective is a recurring theme that reflects Gao's intense revolt against the idea of the collective. In his advocacy of individual con-sciousness, he also opposes the notions of patriotism and what he calls the "modern myth of the nation" *(guojia de xiandai shenhua)*.

In this regard, Gao's paper titled "The Voice of an Individual" (Geren de shengyin), presented at a 1993 conference in Stockholm, is one instance when he publicly and comprehensively denounces the collec-tive. The paper begins with his forceful profession that "it is usually sus-picious to speak in the name of the collective. What I am more afraid of is that [an individual] will be silently killed in this name of the collec-tive" (Gao 1996a:88). Traditionally, Gao observes, the Chinese notion of individuality, despite its concern for personal character and spiritual being, displays more emphasis on moral achievement that is predomi-nantly defined by Confucian ethics. The modern Western notion of indi-viduality only emerged during the May Fourth era. It appeared foremost in terms of political activism and then as a personal pursuit of spiritual worth. The predicament of modern Chinese intellectuals is determined by the intertwined nature of their personal spiritual pursuit and their involvement in the political struggle to attain personal freedom. In this context, Gao questions: "Is it possible to achieve the independent self-worth of an individual without becoming either a savior or a victim?" The answer, as Gao suggests, is probably "no." Presented in the context of the collective interest of the nation or class, the individual self inflates into a consciousness of "greater self" *(dawo)*. As Chinese intellectuals claim to be representatives of their people, country, and class, their independent selves inevitably disappear in the collective consciousness (ibid.:88–90).

At issue, Gao argues, is not the inferiority of the general public, but the weakness of intellectuals, which has its roots in traditional culture. He claims:

> Chinese intellectuals who emerged from the culture of the traditional gentry class, despite the fact that they have, to a certain extent, embraced the Western notion of individualism, are not fully able to rid themselves of the influence of the traditional ethics of placing the society above the self. Such deep-rooted patriotism becomes Chinese intellectuals' biggest psychological obstacle in their effort to achieve an independent understanding of individual value. (Gao 1996a:90)

Gao calls this patriotism demonstrated by Chinese intellectuals the "China complex" *(Zhongguo qingjie)*, which effectually nullifies their ability to distinguish the concept of the nation and the consciousness of the individual self. As such, intellectuals are easily manipulated by politicians who use notions of the collective and patriotism in the service of their personal desire for power. Gao further contends:

> I believe that the responsibility of Chinese intellectuals today is to eradicate the modern myth of the nation. The realization of human rights, especially freedom of thought, is extraordinarily difficult because the burden of patriotism is too heavy for Chinese intellectuals. The collective consciousness imposed by state authority is a restriction to the individual. When it exceeds a certain degree and turns into an invasion of the individual's fundamental human rights, it becomes oppressive. (Gao 1996a:91)

In his contemplation of individuality and the self, Gao revisits the historical contexts of these notions and concludes that an individual consciousness dependent on the collective will not be able to realize its own significance.

Gao's claim for individuality appears somewhat akin to the individualism of the hermit or recluse, which is a significant characteristic of the traditional Chinese literati. The "public individualism" historically exemplified in the Confucian tradition "seeks to establish the place of the individual or self in relation to others, to secure his rights or status in some institutional framework or on the basis of widely declared and accepted principles." In contrast, the "personal individualism" exhibited by the hermit or recluse "has no effect on the status of other individuals," "makes no positive claim within society," and "establishes the right not so much to dissent from the group or reform society as to secede from them" (de Bary 1970:146–147). But the substance of Gao's individualism belongs to neither tradition. On the one hand, it is in opposition to public individualism, as it refuses to be defined by and confined to relations within society. On the other hand, it does not demonstrate a full retreat from society, as it always maintains its freedom and ability to express views and criticisms of reality. This position is clearly illustrated in Gao's attitude toward politics: "I do not intend to be involved in politics, but I also do not refuse to express my views on politics" (Gao 1996a:94).

This is why Gao agreed when he was invited to write a play on the Tiananmen Incident. When the play *Fleeing* was completed, however, the American theater that commissioned it wanted Gao to rewrite the play, as it did not portray a "heroic figure," which was normally expected by American theater goers (Gao 1998a). Gao's now famous response was straightforward and firm: "Not even the [Chinese] Communist Party could ask me to rewrite my play, let alone an American theater" (Gao 1996a:183). Gao is not a self-proclaimed representative of the people. Nor does he intend to become a voice for the collective, even a group he principally sympathizes with. Not only is a heroic figure absent among the characters, but the play begins with a character fleeing from the massacre and ends with a grim revelation of weaknesses in human nature.

Set in a dilapidated warehouse, *Fleeing* is about three characters who escape from the "square,"[5] where a demonstration is going on, as the armed forces begin to open fire on the demonstrators. Hysterical as she enters, the Girl appears to be frail and in a state of shock. She keeps asking the Young Man who fled with her if she is still alive, as she thinks that she is injured and will die soon (Gao 1995f:4–7). Later, the audience realizes that she is the broadcaster at the square who has bravely used her voice to move and arouse the crowd (ibid.:25). Among the agitated crowd, she appears as a heroine. However, when she is no longer in the square, she is only a feeble, insecure girl who badly needs comfort. Her seemingly heroic behavior is only a façade created in the escalating mood of the collective, which hides away the individual's real feelings.

The other two characters are no less unheroic than the Girl. The Young Man is equally immersed in fear and suspicion. His view on the demonstration of people's power is naïve and wishful. The Middle-Aged

Man is indifferent to and skeptical about the entire incident going on at the square. Through a debate between the two men, the playwright's voice is clearly heard:

Middle-Aged Man: . . . I'm sick of dirty politics. I've had enough.

Young Man: Is anyone forcing you?

Middle-Aged Man: Young man, you are not the only one who feels indignant. Everyone is; otherwise there wouldn't be so many people parading on the street supporting you. And there wouldn't be thousands of people being killed!

Young Man: Are you implying that the people's struggle for democracy and freedom is after all meaningless?

Middle-Aged Man: *(Becomes agitated.)* Don't tell me about the people, they are just the millions of residents of this city who are absolutely bare-handed. They have only bottles and bricks. But bricks are no match at all for machine guns and tanks! It is utterly obvious, this is only a courageous suicide. After all, people are just too naïve and stupid.

Young Man: And that includes you?

Middle-Aged Man: *(Bitterly.)* Yes.

Young Man: *(Advances.)* Are you sorry?

Middle-Aged Man: *(Coldly.)* It is too late to be sorry, young man. Aren't you sorry too?

Young Man: The people's struggle for freedom will achieve the final victory, even if the price is blood!

Middle-Aged Man: Why then have you run away from the tanks?

Young Man: I don't want to sacrifice unnecessarily.

Middle-Aged Man: You don't, fine, then is it for me to sacrifice? Don't tell me about the people, is it you or me? You are only yourself, you don't even know whether you are in control of your own self! And don't tell me about the final victory. If freedom will only bring death, such freedom is no different from suicide! When you are dead, what's the meaning of the final victory? The reality is that you and I have to flee!

(Gao 1995f:13–14)

In powerful and persuasive tones, severe criticism is directed at those who are taking part in the demonstration. While they do not genuinely understand their actions, under the Middle-Aged Man's scrutiny, they use the name of the collective—the people—to legitimize their deeds. Furthermore, their actions are regarded as a reflection of naïveté and stupidity, as they have overestimated the ability of the so-called people against the oppressor. In other words, in the name of patriotism, they claim to be the people's representatives without true knowledge of and a real relationship with the people. Their cowardice and selfishness are revealed when a life-threatening situation arises. The people rather than themselves are to be sacrificed for the demonstrators' unrealistic aspirations.

Gao has portrayed the ironic relationship between Chinese intellectuals—represented by the Girl and the Young Man—and the people. Although the intellectuals assume that they are fighting for the betterment of the people, they have only led the latter to a worse fate. Thus, not only have the intellectuals surrendered their independence in their attempt to represent the collective, they have in fact sacrificed the collective's fundamental interests in their ungrounded idealism. In the entire process in which the characters are claiming the right of representation, the notion of "the people," which has all along been vague and precarious, ironically slips away from the center of argument. A more direct criticism is pointed specifically at the intellectuals' actions with reference to the Tiananmen Incident:

Young Man: According to what you say, we shouldn't have started this democratic movement?

Middle-Aged Man: If the result is massacre, then it is not for the good.

Young Man: *(Stands up, advances.)* What do you mean?

Middle-Aged Man: What I mean is, if you only know how to start but not how to end, if you only know how to attack but not how to organize a retreat, then you shouldn't get involved in politics, because you will only be the one who is sacrificed in this game of chance. Young man, you are just too inexperienced to play politics.

(Gao 1995f:27)

The Middle-Aged Man seems to suggest that as the intellectuals are idealistic but overly simplistic in their actions, neither the so-called people's struggle for freedom and democracy nor the intellectuals' self-proclaimed representation has a chance at winning the battle. It is no wonder *Fleeing* has generated vigorous condemnation from some of the prodemocracy activists (Gao 1996a:183).

If not for his sympathy for the demonstrators, Gao would not have agreed to write a play "expressing support for the Tiananmen Incident" (Gao 1998a). However, his intellectual consciousness has prevented him from producing a blind eulogy of the student demonstrators. His usual pessimism has prevailed in his view of the incident. In an interview in France, Gao was able to predict the suppression of the demonstration a few days before June 4, 1989 (Gao 1998a). Gao is neither a prophet nor a political observer. What he says and writes about the incident simply reflects his contemplation on the relationship of the individual and the collective. In this respect, he is essentially a pessimist.

What then is the way out for the individual? The answer is suggested on several occasions in *Fleeing*, the most forceful instance being another debate on the development of the demonstration:

Young Man: We have news about the internal split within the army.

Middle-Aged Man: Are you still placing your hopes on this? On underhanded deals between the military and the politicians? Hasn't the student movement been a card in their hand for long enough?

Young Man: Aren't you a card too? Just an unimportant card!

Middle-Aged Man: In that you are right. It is exactly because I don't want to become a card in other people's game that I must maintain my own consciousness, independent consciousness. And that's why I have to flee!

Young Man:	*(Turns coldly, with hostility.)* So you evade us, and evade the democratic movement?
Middle-Aged Man:	I evade everything that has the name of so-called collective consciousness.
Young Man:	If everyone was like you, there would be no hope for the country.
Middle-Aged Man:	What is a country? Whose country? Has it been responsible for me? Why should I be responsible for it? I am only responsible for myself.
Young Man:	So, do you then look on the death of the nation without doing anything?
Middle-Aged Man:	I have only myself to save. If one day the nation is to perish, it deserves to perish! Don't you want me to say this? Have you got anything else to ask me? Have you finished your interrogation?
Young Man:	*(Helplessly.)* You are a . . .
Middle-Aged Man:	Individualist or nihilist? I will say, I am a man of no "ism," and I don't have to believe in any "ism." I'm only a living individual who can tolerate neither being slaughtered nor being forced to commit suicide.

(Gao 1995f:29–30)

The last speech of the Middle-Aged Man in the above quotation resonates with the playwright's manifestation of "No Ism" *(meiyou zhuyi)*, which is the title of his collection of critical essays as well as the title of the first essay in that collection (Gao 1996a). As suggested by the dramatic character, the best an individual can do in maintaining his or her independence is to alienate himself or herself from any connection with the collective. The individual neither attempts to manipulate the collective by claiming to represent it nor is such a person manipulated and sacrificed as a nameless, faceless member of the collective. Gao realizes, however, that such independence will never be achieved in a totalitarian country like China. Seemingly, the only way out is "to flee"—to leave one's country without hesitation or sentimental attachment. The Tiananmen Incident occurred while Gao was writing *Soul Mountain* in Paris. At that moment, his thought was to finish writing *Soul Mountain*, to clear his emotional debts to China, and to leave behind any nostalgia for China. In his words, "I wanted to start a new life altogether. . . . China is not my country any more" (Gao 1998a). Gao had already fled once between 1983 and 1984 when *The Bus Stop* was under apparent political attack. But then he fled within the geographical boundaries of China. In 1987, not only did he physically flee to a place far away from China, he was, as he claimed, determined to cut himself off emotionally from a place he once called home.

Fleeing, in this respect, is not essentially a play about the demonstrators of the Tiananmen Incident. Metaphorically, it reveals a psychological predicament deeply rooted in human nature. It is also a personal manifestation of the playwright's need to flee. Gao clearly advocates: "In the midst of power politics, public opinion, ethical and moral principles, party and collective interests, fashions and customs, if a person wishes to maintain his individual worth, personality, and spiritual independence, that is, so-called freedom, the only way out is to flee. Those who cannot even do this will perish" (Gao 1996a:21). Gao suggests that the individual's predicament is not restricted to political oppression. The notion of the collective is also related to social and cultural circumstances. To flee is therefore to break away from all physical and emotional confinement engendered through the interwoven relations of the individual and society.

Even a Chan patriarch like Huineng, who had attained spiritual transcendence, had to make a conscious effort to escape the oppression of the mundane world. In addition to its representations of Chan Buddhist philosophy, *August Snow* dwells significantly on Huineng's various acts of fleeing. After becoming the successor to the fifth Chan patriarch, Hongren, Huineng had to flee for the first time. Hongren advised him to flee, as the former felt that it was impossible to disseminate Buddhism in northern China, where people were occupied by the desire for mortal fame and profit. Huineng was pursued by other priests who were resentful about his surprise succession. He lived in an era when "it was hard for one to escape even if he had attained the dharma, as Buddha would find it difficult to live in this mundane world" (Gao 2000a:37). Hence, he spent most of his time hiding in the deserted mountains of southern China, seldom appearing in public to promulgate Buddhism. In the following years, Huineng had to flee for the last time. The emperor ordered him to preach in the royal court, and he firmly refused to submit to imperial power. Huineng soon passed away without naming a successor.

The life of Huineng is thus represented as a prolonged process of fleeing. Although he had attained spiritual freedom from the earthly world, he lived in a world in which it was impossible to be detached and isolated. As a result, he had to flee. The juxtaposition of Huineng's rejection of the imperial order and his passing is indeed a reflection of Gao's belief in the need to flee. Huineng's case displays, however, that a conscious and protracted course of fleeing might not keep one from all undesirable disturbances. More metaphorical than realistic, the message is that the final and only way to escape from the earthly world is through one's death. In this respect, death is essentially a form of fleeing. From a Buddhist perspective, this death is called nirvana.

There is apparently a price to pay for maintaining an independent individual existence. That price is a state of solitariness. Solitariness is the most striking theme in Gao's plays and is usually presented in terms of the character's spiritual detachment from the environment in which he or she is physically entrapped. The Ecologist in *Wild Man* is a typical example. During his fervent search for the wild man, as suggested at the beginning of the play, the Ecologist appears to be an isolated individual dealing with his personal concern for the natural environment. It is soon revealed that the issue is neither the environment nor the wild man, but the Ecologist's confused understanding of himself and his inability to communicate with others. The solitariness experienced by the Ecologist, however, is more a result of his inability to escape his physical environment and less a state of mind that is consciously attained. He is therefore destined to be filled with misery and loneliness.

In contrast, the Silent Man in *The Bus Stop* is portrayed as a loner who is not burdened by reality. He does not belong to the crowd that is at the same time procrastinating and aspiring to advance. As he disappears from the scene, one wonders if he has, as generally assumed, really gone in the direction that the other characters are headed but have failed to actualize. With the understanding of Gao's determination to flee both physical and spiritual confinement, the symbolism of the Silent Man demands a deeper level of interpretation. His departure may not point to advancement toward a better future. In fact, his destination remains ambiguous and open to interpretation. One thing that is sure, however, is that no one in the crowd fully comprehends his significance or understands his solitariness.

Compared to characters in other plays, the Silent Man is more symbolic than realistic. He is the ideal figure of a loner. He does not undergo an ordeal of physical alienation and psychological conflict. In short, he does not need to flee. Fleeing, as represented in Gao's plays, inevitably leads to facing and understanding one's self. He suggests: "I believe life is after all a process of fleeing. If not to escape from political oppression, then it is to escape from other people and to escape from one's self. As the self is awakened, one will have to face the fact that one cannot escape from this self. That is the tragedy of modern humanity" (Gao 1996a: 184). That is indeed the irony presented by Gao in most of his plays. Different characters in *The Other Shore, Between Life and Death,* and *The Nocturnal Wanderer* have all fled from the collective and entered their respective solitariness as they tried to understand their own selves. However, fleeing does not seem to be their way to nirvana. After revisiting their past experience and scrutinizing their present existence, they have fallen into deeper misery.

Although he suggests that fleeing is the only way to achieve salvation, Gao is apparently pessimistic about what fleeing will actually bring for the individual. *Fleeing* ends with the following scene: Hiding in the warehouse and waiting for the massacre at the square to end, the three characters are hoping for a chance to flee. They then hear a continuous loud banging on the door. "It sounds like the firing of machine guns. They keep still and sit quietly in pools of bloodlike muddy water" (Gao 1995f:68). There is no definite solution. The ironic consolation is probably that, by fleeing the collective, the individual will need only deal with problems of his or her own self.

Writing in Coldness

Like many Chinese writers and intellectuals of the 1980s—especially after the 1989 Tiananmen Incident—Gao Xingjian chose to flee his country and live in exile. He believed that exile was the only, and ultimate, option for him if he wanted to be freed from spiritual oppression. It would provide him with both the physical and the psychological space to maintain intellectual autonomy and to express his individuality freely. In a state of exile, Gao suggests, one is confronted with a distinct and unavoidable reality. "In your personal journey, there is nothing but yourself to depend on" (Gao 1996a:147). After all elements imposed on a person are stripped from one's existence, one is then be able to affirm one's own worth, including the value of "self-doubt" (ibid.:154).

Consciousness of exile emerged in Gao's earlier plays such as *The Bus Stop* (in which the Silent Man unhesitatingly left the crowd) and *Wild Man* (symbolically as the death of the Old Singer Zengbo), and later developed into a key, recurring theme after his exile. Although his earlier works have been analyzed in this study primarily with regard to the specific sociopolitical context of 1980s China, Gao's consciously self-imposed detachment from the social and political realities of China, often represented with a strong sense of irony, is starkly observable. Later, the physical state of exile further enables Gao to explore his ethnic-cultural position and to redefine his identity as a "Chinese" writer.

Gao's position as a writer-in-exile is similar to Western counterparts who are described by Anthony Coulson as "strangers to both self and other, embarked on a journey between 'we' and 'they,' between memory and hope" (1997:7). Gao's journey started early, when he was still in China. But it is in his later, physical exile that Gao explicitly expresses the complexities of detachment experienced by the Western writers in Coulson's study. These writers, Coulson observes, are cut off from the familiar and exposed to the hardship of their present exodus. Conversely, they also enjoy a new freedom offered by the detachment from their homelands. Being in an alien environment, they are able to "claim the impartial objectivity of the outsider" and "exercise a new degree of self-determination." As such, they reassess their past and present, which allows them to experience "a certain openness and principle of hope" (ibid.:7–8).

Coulson's descriptions generally fit the contemporary generation of exiled Chinese. However, an emerging Chinese nationalism—among Chinese both in China and in the diaspora—together with the immense growth in China's economic and political power in the global arena adds complexity to their willingness to detach themselves from their home-lands. Encompassed by a nostalgia evoked by nationalistic emotion, exiled Chinese are, on the one hand, agonized by their newly experienced unfamiliarity with the foreign social environment and alien cultural prac-tices and, on the other, remorseful about missing out on the chance to be involved in the construction of a Chinese economic, political, and cul-tural superpower.

Gao seems aware of such a possibility and has therefore manifested his unambiguously independent position, which may appear as indifferent. Gao's self-imposed exile places him in a locale that is temporally and spatially alienated from physical reality—be it China of the 1980s or the world beyond China in the post-1987 years. Although he writes about the notions of self and other (in *The Nocturnal Wanderer*), human beings and society (in *Fleeing*), and even collective memory (in *The Story of Shanhaijing*) with a strong sense of estrangement (in John Torrance's sense; see chapter 4), his concerns, as represented in his plays, are usually more sober than indulgent, more decontextualized than localized. This sense of estrangement is most strikingly represented in his treatment of issues relating to China and Chineseness, as he intentionally assumes a position that holds himself back from emotional involvement. Such an emotional detachment—building on his knowledge of various cultures—enables him to recontemplate the meanings of China and Chineseness from a transcultural perspective.

With an "impartial objectivity," Gao is also equipped to produce what he calls "cold literature" *(leng de wenxue)*, as he describes in his Nobel lecture: "Cold literature is literature that will flee in order to survive; it is literature that refuses to be strangled by society in its quest for spiritual salvation. If a race cannot accommodate this sort of nonutilitarian literature, it is not merely a misfortune for the writer but a tragedy for the race" (Gao 2000b). Always conscious of the relationship between literature and society, Gao defines his notion of "cold literature" with regard to that relationship:

> Literature, in fact, is unrelated to politics. It is merely a personal affair, a process of observation, a review of past experience, imagination, and feeling, a kind of emotional expression, and the satisfaction from reflective thinking. . . . A literature that regains its original nature can be called "cold literature" to distinguish it from the literature of moral teaching, of political criticism, of social engagement, and even that which expresses one's depression and aspiration. Such is cold literature. (Gao 1996a:18–19)

Gao is not only calling for writers to be honest with their personal thoughts and feelings, but also to possess intellectual integrity. The ideal position for a writer, Gao argues, is at the periphery of society. One is then able to write with sober observation and self reflection (Gao 1996a: 20). Such a position often translates into strong and distinct metaphorical representation in Gao's theater. Be it the Woman struggling between life and death or the Sleepwalker wandering in his dream world, many of Gao's characters are similarly posited at the periphery at which the playwright has chosen to stay. When he wrote *Alarm Signal, The Bus Stop,* and *Wild Man,* Gao was restricted by social and political circumstances. These works were thus produced with conscious compromise as a result of self-censorship. However, once in exile, he became free to express the severe criticisms contained in *Fleeing.* By detaching himself from contextual restraints and allowing himself to to reflect on human existence, he was able to produce works such as *Dialogue and Rebuttal* and *August Snow.*

It is not surprising, then, that Gao, on various occasions, has insisted on maintaining his right to comment on politics. Such an insistence can perhaps be read as a clear demarcation between himself and the politically tainted notion of China, which is an intellectually informed and reflective position. Gao's intellectual integrity is also exemplified by his Nobel lecture, in which he, on the one hand, professes that "literature transcends ideology, national boundaries, and racial consciousness" and, on the other hand, condemns the restrictions of politics, society, ethics, and customs, which "set out to tailor literature into decorations for their various frameworks" (Gao 2000b). While he enjoys his freedom of expression, both artistically and intellectually, Gao assumes an attitude that is at once detached and engaged toward himself, his past, and the present world. Without the burden of nostalgia or obsession that arises from Chinese nationalism, Gao is relieved of the need to compromise (not only with political reality but also with his desires), and he is hence able to write with coldness. The coldness in his literature is thus not an indifference toward the mundane world, but a peripheral position consciously adopted by Gao to engage society and to reflect on the problems faced by people in the modern era and, ultimately, the problems of humanity.

Notes

Introduction

1. I interviewed two drama specialists during my visit to Beijing in May 1999. The interviewees were Lin Kehuan, president of the National Youth Theatre and a prolific drama critic, and Lu Min, an associate professor specializing in contemporary Chinese drama at the Central Academy of Drama in Beijing.

2. After Gao left China and before he was awarded the Nobel prize, Chinese editions of all his major works, including two novels (Gao 1990a and 1999b) and an anthology of his dramatic works (Gao 1995a–f), were only published in Taiwan, while a collection of his critical essays (Gao 1996a) and two plays (Gao 1993 and 1996b) were published in Hong Kong.

3. Julia Lovell (2002a) has done in-depth research on China's perception and expectation of the Nobel Prize in Literature in her Ph.D. dissertation, "China's Search for a Nobel Prize in Literature: Literature, and National and Cultural Identity in Twentieth-Century China." See also Lovell 2002b.

4. Chan is a sect of Chinese Buddhism (more commonly known as Zen in Japanese) whose name derives from the Sanskrit term *"dhyana"* (meditation). Founded in the late fifth century by Bodhidharma, who came to China from India, Chinese Chan Buddhism became known for making its central tenet the practice of meditation rather than adherence to a particular scripture or doctrine.

5. In his Nobel lecture delivered at the prize award ceremony on December 7, 2000, Gao once again strongly denounced communist ideology and activism: "Using some scientific ism to explain history or interpreting it with a historical perspective based on pseudo-dialectics has failed to clarify human behavior. Now that the utopian fervor and continuing revolution of the past century have crumbled to dust, there is unavoidably a feeling of bitterness among those who have survived" (Gao 2000b). Gao's severe criticism of the Chinese communist regime was strongly refuted by the Chinese Association of Writers as a "malicious attack" that "revealed his true intentions" (*Yazhou zhoukan*, December 18–24, 2000).

6. The following account is primarily based on two sessions of personal interviews carried out with Gao at his residence in Bagnolet, Paris, on May 2 and 3,

1998. Each session lasted about four hours. These interviews are listed in the bibliography as Gao 1998a. Other major sources are his articles "Jinghua yetan" (Evening talks in Beijing) in Gao 1988b:152–241 and "Geri huanghua" (Yesterday's blossoms) in Gao 1996a:158–166, and the chronologies in Gao 1995f:86–106 and Yip 2001:311–339. Subsequent references to these sources in the following biographical account will not be itemized. All quotations in this chapter are from Gao 1998a.

7. A type of traditional Chinese theater, *jingju* is commonly translated as "Peking (Beijing) opera." Literally, *jingju* means "drama *(ju)* of the [Chinese] capital *(jing)*." Whether "opera," a term with essentially Western cultural connotation, is an appropriate translation is debatable. I will use the transliterated form of *jingju* and a few other terms (*xiqu* and *xieyi*), on which I will further elaborate later.

8. When *Alarm Signal* was first published in *Shiyue* 5 (1982) and later collected in Gao 1985a, Liu Huiyuan was listed as cowriter together with Gao. However, when the play was reprinted in Taipei (as part of a complete collection of his dramatic works) after Gao was awarded the Nobel prize (2001b), Liu's name was taken out. When I interviewed Gao in 1998, he revealed that while *Alarm Signal* was based on the brief story of a train robbery told by Liu, the latter was not involved in the actual writing process.

9. *The Other Shore* was later premiered by Taiwan's National Institute of the Arts in 1990.

10. Gao has on several occasions professed his determination to sever relations with China, with strong remarks like "China doesn't even appear in my dreams any more" when I interviewed him in 1998. However, in an interview conducted in January 2000, he sounded less categorical: "After I finished the writing of *Soul Mountain*, I wanted to say good-bye to China. Never to face it again, I want to start my life anew. But I wrote *August Snow* after that. The play, which is about Chinese Chan Buddhism, has not been staged. And then I wrote *One Man's Bible*. I thought I am through with my China complex. But it reemerged. Now I'm not so sure. Who knows? The dying embers may flare up again" (Gao 2001c:78).

11. In his discussion of experimentalism in Chinese theater of the 1980s, Zhao does acknowledge the significance of theatrical form when he observes that "the 'subversiveness' of experimentation in form" was recognized by the Chinese authorities in the early 1980s (2000:35). When it comes to Gao's theater, however, Zhao chooses to highlight its message rather than its form.

12. In his book, Zhao uses the transliterated form *"xieyi"* in an illuminating section mapping out conceptions of *xieyi* as discussed by various dramatists especially in the 1980s (2000:57–62). A term borrowed from the description of traditional Chinese ink painting (often translated as "freehand brushwork" in this context), *"xieyi"* was first used by the veteran Chinese dramatist Huang Zuolin (1962) to describe the nonrealist, suggestive nature of Chinese theater in contrast to the

realist representation of modern Western theater. To date, scholars have not come up with a generally acceptable English translation of *"xieyi."* I will discuss the concept of *xieyi* and its translation in more detail in chapter 1.

13. *Gongan*, literally meaning "public proposal," is more commonly known in its Japanese-derived form "koan." A *gongan* is a superficially nonsensical, paradoxical question that cannot be understood through the processes of logic; its solution requires a higher attainment of spiritual intuition. Originating in eleventh-century China, *gongan* practice was introduced to Japan as part of Chan in the thirteenth century.

14. Gilbert C. F. Fong's translation (Gao 1999a) is generally used for quotations in this book from Gao's later plays *(The Other Shore, Between Life and Death, Dialogue and Rebuttal, Nocturnal Wanderer, Weekend Quartet)* and staging suggestions for these plays by the playwright.

Chapter 1 Searching for Alternative Aesthetics

1. In 1953, Stanislavsky's system was officially canonized during a forum organized by the National Association of Drama Workers. It was pronounced that the system accords with the "performance science of materialistic dialectics" and is the "performance theory of realism." After that, Soviet specialists of Stanislavsky's system of directing and acting were invited to deliver speeches, conduct workshops, and assist in the staging of performances. Books by and on Stanislavsky were also in line for publication. This escalation of the reception of Stanislavsky was the result of amity between China and the Soviet Union and the need to transform Chinese theater from its wartime makeshift state to a peacetime standard theater (Sun 1987:141). The systematic and comprehensive introduction eliminated other schools of drama and made Stanislavsky's system the orthodoxy before the Cultural Revolution. The influence of the system went beyond that of spoken drama. During the peak of the Stanislavsky system in the 1950s, artists of *xiqu* (for a discussion of this term, see note 2) also discussed adopting the system to reform and improve their artistic representation.

2. There are a few terms relating to traditional Chinese theater the English translations of which have been rather confusing and need to be clarified before further discussion. By "traditional Chinese theater," I am referring collectively to Chinese theater in traditional forms, which exists in the past and the present. The Chinese term is *"Zhongguo chuantong xiju* (or *juchang),"* which includes traditional *xiqu* and primitive theater such as *nuoxi* (exorcist performance). The term *"xiqu,"* for which I use the transliterated form throughout this book, refers to refined theatrical performance, though often translated as "opera" or "music-drama," and includes genres such as *jingju* (Peking opera), *chuanju* (Sichuan opera), *minju* (Fujian opera), and so forth. As *xiqu* has gone through various stages of renovation—for example, in the 1950s and 1960s, it borrowed the socialist realist

method of representing characters, and in the 1980s it incorporated the spirit of modernism—and remained active on the Chinese stage, the notion of modern *xiqu* is different from traditional *xiqu*.

3. Most critics and historians regard Huang as the first dramatist to introduce Brecht into China. In fact, as early as in 1927, when Brecht just began to emerge in Europe, his works were already mentioned in an article by Zhao Jingshen (1902–1985) on German theater. In 1941, excerpts from Brecht's *Fear and Misery of the Third Reich* were published in *Jiefang ribao* (Lin Kehuan 1999b:68). Arguably, these earlier mentions of Brecht did not have much effect and thus were insignificant as compared to Huang's speech.

4. The debate began in 1983 as *Xiju yishu*, a journal published by Shanghai Academy of Drama, called for discussion of *xieyi* and dramatic concepts in general. Almost all major Chinese drama journals, such as *Xiju bao, Xiju, Juben,* and *Xiju jie*, had established special sections for the discussion. Important articles in the debate are also collected in two volumes titled *Xijuguan zhengming ji* (A collection of essays on the debate of dramatic concepts) published in 1986 and 1988, respectively (Zhongguo xiju chubanshe 1986 and 1988).

5. Being one of the "four great *dan* (female role)" performers during the Republican period, Mei Lanfang was the best-known actor of traditional Chinese theater in the international arena. This was probably because he toured frequently and widely to Japan and Western countries in Europe and America (Mackerras 1975:60). It was during Mei's Moscow visit in 1935 that Brecht first experienced his performance and found confirmation for his idea of the alienation effect (see below).

6. Heteroglossia, a key concept of the Russian critic M. M. Bakhtin, refers to the conflict between "centripetal" and "centrifugal," "official" and "unofficial" discourses within the same national language. The Russian term, *"raznorechie,"* literally means "different-speech-ness." For a more detailed discussion of the concept, see Morson and Emerson 1990:139–142.

7. In fact, the first post–Cultural Revolution play Huang directed was *Xin Changzheng jiaoxiangqu* (The symphony of the new Long March) in 1978. The play was a celebration of a new route for China's development, the so-called Four Modernizations (Sige xiandaihua). With this production, Huang returned to his experimental integration of elements from traditional Chinese theater, such as the acting and setting of *jingju*, and Brechtian techniques, namely the alienation effect, into spoken drama (Hsia 1987:153–154). But it was the production of *Galileo* in 1979 that elicited an overwhelming response and sparked a profound interest in Brecht among Chinese dramatists (see below).

8. Between the decision to stage *Mother Courage* and its actual production, there was only three month's time to prepare. The translated script was ready only one month before and, in the meantime, Huang had to struggle to adapt the script for staging and to get his team familiarized with Brechtian concepts (Hsia 1982:50–51).

9. One of the adjustments, unlinked to the play per se, was to adapt it to keep the performance time within three hours so that the audience would be able to catch the last bus home (Hsia 1982:60). Huang had taken care of all aspects to ensure the success of the production.

10. "Neoromanticism" *(xin langman zhuyi)* is a term used by the Chinese to include Western literary schools such as symbolism, expressionism, aestheticism, and futurism, which are, in Chinese terminological context, equated with modernism *(xiandai pai)*.

11. Realist playwrights Henrik Ibsen and George Bernard Shaw were the most widely known in the May Fourth era. The works of other realist dramatists such as the British John Galsworthy, the Norwegian Bjørnstjerne Bjørnson, the German Gerhart Hauptmann, and the Russian Anton Chekov were also translated and published. Some of the dramatists of other schools who were introduced in the early twentieth century were the Irish Oscar Wilde (especially his symbolist play *Salomé*), the Belgian Maurice Maeterlinck, the Russian Leonid Andreev, the Swede August Strindberg, the American Eugene O'Neill, and the Italian Filippo Marinetti. See Tian Benxiang et al. 1996:109–120.

12. What Williams meant by "naturalism" here is sometimes called "realism." One usage of "realism," according to Williams, is "to describe a method or an attitude in art and literature—at first an exceptional accuracy of representation, later a commitment to describing real events and showing things as they actually exist." However, realism in this sense is often faulted for excluding "inner reality" and replaced by the term "naturalism" (Williams 1988:259–261).

13. Both of the English words in parentheses are used by Huang in his article.

14. While this usage of different terms is practiced in mainland China, the practice in Taiwan until fairly recently was to adopt the single term *"xieshi zhuyi"* for both the formal and ideological aspects of realism. However, with the increased cultural interaction with the mainland since the late 1980s and the emergence of Marxist literary criticism, the use of *"xianshi zhuyi"* in Taiwan has become more common.

15. These points were stated in the first article of a series of seven published in *Suibi* from 1982 to 1983. The series was later collected in Gao 1988b, excluding this article (for the latter, see Gao 1982b:70–76). The series, according to Gao, was written to "make way for those of my plays that are perceived as unlike plays" (Gao 1988b:1). Before he presents his ideas on drama, in this first article, he clearly lays out the targets that he wants to subvert.

16. This passage was left out when the article originally containing it was collected in Gao 1988b. Although it might not seem relevant to the discussion of dramatic concepts (perhaps the reason for dropping it), it is telling with regard to the difficulties Gao and his contemporaries were facing when they tried to emphasize the renovation of forms in the early 1980s.

17. Interestingly, some Chinese critics have emphasized the fact that Brecht

did not have a good understanding of Chinese theater. As Brecht was unable to explore Chinese theater thoroughly, Ding Yangzhong argues, "it is normal that some of his views appear inappropriate and impractical" (1982:32). Adopting a postcolonialist approach, Min Tian suggests that Brecht misconceived the A-effect of Chinese acting, thereby "reducing them [the techniques of Chinese acting] to a set of quotable 'outer signs' at the expense of the onstage creation of the performer which gives them flesh and blood and saves them from becoming a rigid set of clichés and stereotypes" (Tian 1997:218). These arguments only serve to reiterate that misunderstanding has contributed to transcultural communication.

18. These are in fact also some of the major components in Gao's own dramaturgy. Among them, suppositionality, which will be further discussed in chapter 3, was widely debated among Chinese dramatists in the 1980s with respect to their search for new possibilities in representation within the theatrical space.

Chapter 2 Exploration in Action

1. These plays were published in Chinese literary journals and, with the exception of *The Other Shore*, have been collected in *Gao Xingjian xiju ji* (A collection of plays by Gao Xingjian) (1985a). *Alarm Signal* was published in *Shiyue* 5 (1982), *The Bus Stop* in *Shiyue* 3 (1983), *Wild Man* in *Shiyue* 2 (1985), and *The Other Shore* in *Shiyue* 5 (1986). In my discussion below, all citations will be taken from the collected edition, Gao 1985a, and all translations are mine. The three plays were republished in Taipei in 2001 (Gao 2001b, 2001a, 2001d) with very minor changes except for one instance, which I will discuss in note 9.

2. In 1981 Gao wrote a series of articles on modernism later published as *Xiandai xiaoshuo jiqiao chutan* (An introduction of modernist techniques in fiction). While many writers, such as Ba Jin and Liu Xinwu, and Feng Muxian of the Chinese Association of Writers positively received it, He Jingzhi of the Central Propaganda Department denounced it as reactionary and an act of capitalist liberalization. The real target of attack, according to Gao, was Wang Meng, who was rising with the reform faction of Hu Yaobang in power (Gao 1996a:158–161). Gao became a scapegoat in a power struggle at a higher level.

3. As the most reputable theater in China, the Beijing People's Art Theatre has the autonomy to approve its own productions. According to Gao, the members of the theater's censorship committee are open with regard to political issues but conservative in their artistic views (Gao 1998a).

4. Gao collected these songs and dances during his journey to the Yangtze region between 1983 and 1984. They had been preserved in the rural areas and were performed as rituals. The centerpiece, *Song of the Dark*, is an oral epic narrating myths of creation and other primitive legends. It survived the Cultural Revolution, during which many folk arts disappeared with the persecution of folk artists. In the early 1980s, several incomplete versions of *Song of the Dark* were

discovered by the historian Hu Chongjun (Gao 1985a:273–274; Gao 1988b: 175–176).

5. In his self-exile to southwest China in 1983 and 1984, Gao's primary plan was to collect materials for the writing of *Soul Mountain. Wild Man*, according to Gao, was a by-product of that journey (Gao 1988b:175). After he returned to Beijing in November 1984, he completed the play in ten days.

6. In the collected edition (Gao 1985a) and the latest Taiwanese edition (Gao 2001a), all multivocal parts are rearranged to display precisely how the utterances are overlapped, staggered, or connected. The layout gives a clearer picture of the way they are supposed to be presented on stage. This layout is evidence of Gao's awareness of theatricality as a playwright. His idea of theatricality will be discussed in the next chapter.

7. For example, when Gao talks about his experimentation with multivocality, he gives the following example in *The Bus Stop:* "Among the seven vocal parts, a main melody is established with the alternate succession of three vocal parts, the other four progress in parallel forming a polyphony in accompaniment" (Gao 1988b:126). It is apparent that the term "polyphony" in this context refers more to structure than to motif.

8. The video recordings of *Alarm Signal* and *Wild Man* are of the original production by the Beijing People's Art Theatre, which I obtained directly from the theater's library. There was no video recording of *The Bus Stop*. The reason could be that it was only staged for thirteen performances or that political attacks were expected.

9. The latest Taiwanese edition of *Wild Man* (Gao 2001b) contains some revisions to the previous printed edition (Gao 1985a). With respect to this quotation, the following revisions were made: (1) The phrase "is brightly lit" was deleted. (2) The word "bright" in "resembling the boy's bright dream" was deleted. (3) The phrase "Amidst the loud and boisterous music" was changed to "As the music fades away." (4) The word "happiness" in "in a cry of happiness" was deleted. (5) The entire passage from "In a carnivalesque atmosphere" onward was deleted (Gao 2001b:157–158). I first saw these revisions handwritten on Gao's personal copy, which he generously allowed me to photocopy. Apparently, Gao made the revisions to more closely reflect the actual performance. The significance of the disparity between the dramatic and performance texts is discussed below.

Chapter 3 Space and Suppositionality

1. In an interview, Gao said he directed three plays in China (Wu 1995). Apparently, he was referring to plays that actually name Lin Zhaohua as director. Gao has also stated explicitly that Lin and he conducted workshops during the rehearsal of *The Other Shore*, which stopped abruptly after a month (Gao 1996a: 223).

2. *Shanhaijing* (The classic of mountains and seas), written between the fourth and second centuries B.C., is an ancient record of Chinese geographical features and mythologies.

3. The aspirations of Gao and Lin were not realized, as the "Anti–Bourgeois Liberalization Campaign" escalated in 1986. Chinese experimental theater, however, continued to progress even in the unfavorable political atmosphere of the late 1980s. As compared to Gao's experimentation, experimental theater of the 1990s has moved from dependence on dramatic texts toward emphasis on performances. Furthermore, most of the performances are not open to the public. Practitioners and audiences are mainly college students (for example, from the Central Academy of Drama [Zhongyang xiju xueyuan] and the Beijing Academy of Film Studies [Beijing dianying xueyuan]), and some professional theater artists. Lin Zhaohua has been working closely with the Performance Studio (Yanju gongzuoshi). Young directors such as Meng Jinghui of the Exposed Drama Society (Chuanbang jushe) and Mou Sen of the Drama Workshop (Xiju chejian) are also important figures who have produced provocative experimental works. Wu Weimin (1998) and Lin Kehuan (2000) provide some details on the experimental theater activism of the 1990s, while Salter (1996) did an interview with Mou Sen. As experimental theater in China has always been marginalized, literature about it is scarce. Among Chinese materials, *Xianfeng xiju dang'an* (Avant-garde theater records), edited by Meng Jinghui (2000), provides important documentation of the Chinese avant-garde theater movement of the 1990s. There is also a special issue on "experimental theater" of *Jinri xianfeng* (Avant-garde today), a book-magazine devoted to the discussion of avant-garde arts in China (vol. 7 [1999]).

4. In his Theatre-Studio, established in 1913, Meyerhold referred to actors of Chinese traveling companies who performed without any stage conventions but remained attractive to the audience (the article was written in 1914). In another article written in 1916, Meyerhold listed "stage and acting conventions in the Japanese and Chinese theatres" as a subject for discussion in a training program for actors (1998:147, 154).

5. This line describing the entrance of the Plaster Seller is missing from the later book edition (Gao 1995a) and also from Gilbert Fong's translation (Gao 1999a). It is here quoted from the text first published in *Shiyue* 5 (1985):246.

6. When I asked Gao whether his idea of polyphony had been influenced by Bakhtin, he said, "The translation of Bakhtin's work appeared in China very late. . . . I don't agree with him. What he says is only complicated *(fuza)*, not polyphony *(fudiao)*" (Gao 1998a).

7. David Hawkes translates this couplet as "Truth becomes fiction when the fiction's true; Real becomes not-real where the unreal's real" (1973:55). Although Hawkes' translation of *Honglou meng* is well received, I do not use his version. In this case, he has condensed the meaning of the couplet and only translated the first line.

8. The characters in *xiqu* are normally categorized into several role types. In *jingju*, these are *sheng* (male), *dan* (female), *jing* (painted face), and *chou* (clown).

9. In Gao's plays, besides creating a carnivalesque mood, the *chou* is also employed as a dramatic character, especially for its well-roundedness in training and flexibility in acting. A good example is *Between Life and Death*. Among the three characters in the list, there is a clown *(chou)* playing various roles, including Man, Ghost, and Old Man.

10. There were representations of the real and the unreal in fictional writings before the appearance of *The Dream of the Red Chamber*, many of them using the dream as a mediator between the two worlds. Such works include Shen Jiji's *Zhen zhong ji* (A dream in the pillow) of the Tang dynasty and, later, Tang Xianzu's famous *Mudan ting* (The peony pavilion) of the Ming dynasty.

11. Many later scholars have presented illuminating discussions about the complex relations of the real and the unreal in *The Dream of the Red Chamber*. For example, see Yu Yingshi 1978 and Anthony C. Yu 1997. I will not go into detail, as my primary concern is to borrow the fundamental idea of the real and the unreal in *The Dream of the Red Chamber* for the analysis of Gao's unique employment of suppositionality.

12. A hat for informal wear, the *jin* is usually worn by the *sheng jue* (male role) in *jingju*. The action of putting on the hat in this instance signifies that the actor is entering the role of Zhuang Zhou.

Chapter 4 Performance in Alienated Voices

1. Augusto Boal is a Brazilian playwright, director, and theater activist strongly influenced by Brecht. Politically inclined, Boal's Forum Theater aims at provoking the spectators' concern for the protagonist's predicament. The spectators are invited to interrupt the play and express their opinion by taking up the role of the protagonist. They are thus transformed into active participants, which Boal calls "spect-actors," of the ongoing drama. For a description of his early experiments in South America, see Boal 1979.

2. In the original Chinese text, Gao uses "*nin*"—a respectful version of the pronoun "*ni*" (you)—when the Sleepwalker addresses another character and "*ni*" as the protagonist's self-referring pronoun. Such a distinction is not observed in Gilbert Fong's English translation, as he uses "you" for both "*ni*" and "*nin*." In the above excerpts, there is little problem identifying whether the "you" refers to the speaker himself or the party he is addressing. However, in other instances, one of which I discuss later, such a distinction is vital to the reading of the text. I therefore use italics for those respectful second-person pronouns *(nin)* that refer to the addressee.

3. This line is missing from the English translation. It is quoted and translated from Gao 1995b:66.

4. Gilbert Fong's translation of this line is "She's just realized that she's the one lonely in the whole wide world, not the other people, whose loneliness she has been observing" (Gao 1999a:59). I have used my own translation for this line. In the Chinese text, except for the first one, the pronoun "she" does not appear again, thus providing the statement with a cold and detached tone that enhances the sense of solitude.

5. "Reification" has a strong sociological connotation that, notably in Marx's theory, refers to the depersonalization of labor as workers are subjected to the capitalist industrialization and perceived as quantifiable commodities (Torrance 1977:294–295). I am using the term in a more general sense, meaning "the mental conversion of a person or abstract concept into a thing" *(OED)*.

6. That is, Zhuang Zhou in *The Nether City*, although the story is based on a *jingju* title that has little relevance to the philosophies of Daoism.

7. Gilbert Fong translates the first line of this speech by the Sleepwalker as "A word is a word," leaving out the phrase "you say" in the original Chinese version. Although whether the phrase "you say" is kept is not as important here as in other instances in my discussion, I have reinstalled it in brackets, quoting from Gao 1995e:113.

Conclusion

1. These articles were first serialized in *Suibi* in 1980 and then published as a book, *Xiandai xiaoshuo jiqiao chutan* (Gao 1981). Many Chinese writers and critics remember this series together with the production of *Alarm Signal* as the two most significant and influential events in Gao's career as a writer.

2. The essays in this series were later collected as *Dui yizhong xiandai xiju de zhuiqiu* (Gao 1988b), except for the first article, "Tong yiwei guanzhong tan xi" (Gao 1982b).

3. In fact, *The Story of Shanhaijing* remains Gao's only unstaged major play. The play was originally written for the Beijing People's Art Theatre. After the Tiananmen Incident in 1989, the production of Gao's plays was banned in China (Gao 1996a:244).

4. *August Snow* premiered in Taipei in December 2002 with Gao as the director. Although the cast was made up mainly of *jingju* performers, the production could hardly be categorized as a *xiqu*, traditional or modern. A hybrid of East and West, the performance of *August Snow* included artistic elements from various sources, including a choir resembling the chorus of ancient Greek theater, *jingju* performers who speak in the vernacular rather than using conventional stylized vocal expression, the accompaniment of a Western symphony orchestra throughout the entire performance, and physical movements of the ensemble performers that appear to be modern dance. In fact, the original label "modern *xiqu*" (which appeared in the printed edition of *August Snow* [Gao 2000a]) was replaced by

"geju" in the program of the performance. The term *"geju,"* literally song-theater, is a conventionally accepted translation of "opera." In this case, the adoption of *"geju"* to describe *August Snow* is apparently an informed choice by the playwright to posit the play closer to the Western genre than the Chinese one.

5. Although *Fleeing* is said to be based on the Tiananmen Incident, Gao has intentionally decontextualized his dramatic representation. As such, he steers his play away from specific incidents related to China and gives it a more universal appearance. In this case, Tiananmen Square is referred to as "the square."

Glossary

Anhui 安徽
Ba Jin 巴金
Ba yisheng jiaogei dang 把一生交給黨
Bai Hua 白樺
Bamian hongqi yingfeng piao
　　八面紅旗迎風飄
Bayue xue 八月雪
Beijing dianying xueyuan
　　北京電影學院
benzhi 本質
Bi'an 彼岸
bianlian 變臉
biaoyan de sanchongxing
　　表演的三重性
bingtang hulu shi 冰糖葫蘆式
Bubu jin'gen Mao Zhuxi
　　步步緊跟毛主席
Cao Xueqin 曹雪芹
Cao Yu 曹禺
caoshu 草書
Chaguan 茶館
Chan 禪
chang 場
Chen Yi 陳毅
Chen Yi chushan 陳毅出山
Chen Yi shizhang 陳毅市長
Chen Yong 陳顒
Chen Zidu 陳子度
Chezhan 車站
Chiyou 蚩尤

chou 丑
Chu 楚
Chuanbang jushe 穿幫劇社
chuanju 川劇
chuanshen dayi 傳神達意
da 打
Da pi guan 大劈棺
dan 旦
dawo 大我
Deng Zhiyi 鄧止怡
diaoshuxing 雕塑性
difang baowei zhongyang
　　地方包圍中央
Dijun 帝俊
Ding Yishan 丁一山
Dongjin! Dongjin! 東進！東進！
Duihua yu fanjie 對話與反詰
duo shengbu 多聲部
duo shengbu xiandai shishi ju
　　多聲部現代史詩劇
fei wenren wenhua 非文人文化
fei zhen 非真
Feng Muxian 馮牧先
Fengyue baojian 風月寶鑑
fudiao 複調
fuza 複雜
Gai Jiaotian 蓋叫天
gaige wenxue 改革文學
Gan 贛
Gan Yang 甘陽

Ganzhou 贛州

Gao Xingjian 高行健

geju 歌劇

geming de langman zhuyi
革命的浪漫主義

geming de xianshi zhuyi
革命的現實主義

Geren de shengyin 個人的聲音

Geri huanghua 隔日黃花

gongan 公案

Gou'er ye niepan 狗兒爺涅槃

guangming de weiba 光明的尾巴

Guangxi 廣西

Guanyin 觀音

guifanxing 規範性

Gushi xinbian 故事新編

Guo Moruo 郭沫若

guofang xiju 國防戲劇

guojia de xiandai shenhua
國家的現代神話

Guoke 過客

Hai'ou jushe 海鷗劇社

Han Shaogong 韓少功

Hanye de xingchen 寒夜的星辰

Hao liao ge 好了歌

He Jingzhi 賀敬之

hei bai wuchang 黑白無常

Hei'an zhuan 黑暗傳

Heilongjiang 黑龍江

Heizi 黑子

Honglou meng 紅樓夢

Hongren 宏忍

Hu Chongjun 胡崇峻

Hu Yaobang 胡耀邦

huaben xiaoshuo 話本小說

Huacheng 花城

huaju 話劇

Huang Zuolin 黃佐臨

huangdan ju 荒誕劇

Huangdi 黃帝

Hubei 湖北

Huineng 慧能

jia 假

Jia Hongyuan 賈鴻源

Jia Rui 賈瑞

jia zuo zhen shi zhen yi jia, wu wei
you chu you huan wu
假作真時真亦假，無為
有處有還無

jiadingxing 假定性

Jiang Qing 江青

Jiangsu 江蘇

Jiangxi 江西

jiayu cunyan 假語村言

jie gu yu jin 借古寓今

Jiefang ribao 解放日報

Jiliu yongjin 急流勇進

jin 巾

jing 淨

jingbai 京白

Jinghua yetan 京華夜談

jingju 京劇

Jingzhou 荊州

Jinri xianfeng 今日先鋒

ju 劇

Juben 劇本

juchang 劇場

juchang jiadingxing 劇場假定性

juchangxing 劇場性

jue 角

Juedui xinhao 絕對信號

kaichangbai 開場白

kaishu 楷書

Kang Mei yuan Chao dahuobao
抗美援朝大活報

Kouwen siwang 叩問死亡

kuangcao 狂草

langsong 朗誦

Lao She 老舍

Laozi 老子

leng de wenxue 冷的文學

li 里

Li Yu 李漁

liangdu xichao 兩度西潮

Lianhe bao 聯合報
Lin Kehuan 林克歡
Lin Liankun 林連崑
Lin Zhaohua 林兆華
Lingshan 靈山
Liu Gongquan 柳公權
Liu Huiyuan 劉會遠
Liu Jinyun 劉錦雲
Liu Xie 劉勰
Liu Xinwu 劉心武
Liu Zaifu 劉再復
liuchangxing 流暢性
Lu Min 盧敏
Lu Xun 魯迅
Ma Zhongjun 馬中駿
Mei Lanfang 梅蘭芳
Meiyou zhuyi 沒有主義
Meng Jinghui 孟京輝
mianqiang 勉強
miaohui 廟會
Mifeng 蜜蜂
Mingcheng 冥城
minju 閩劇
minzu 民族
minzu hua 民族化
Mou Sen 牟森
mu yecha 母夜叉
Mudan ting 牡丹亭
ni 你
nian 念
nin 您
nuo 儺
Ouyang Yuqian 歐陽予倩
Pan Gu 盤古
Pan Jinlian 潘金蓮
pangbai 旁白
Pei shi jiemei 陪十姐妹
peng 鵬
pingtan 評彈
puluo xiju 普羅戲劇
Qu Xinhua 瞿新華
Sangshuping jishi 桑樹坪紀事

Sanguo yanyi 三國演義
Sha Yexin 沙葉新
shanghen wenxue 傷痕文學
Shanhaijing 山海經
Shanhaijing zhuan 山海經傳
shen 神
Shen Congwen 沈從文
Shen Jiji 沈既濟
shenfen 身份
sheng 生
shenghuo shuqing xiju 生活抒情喜劇
Shengsi jie 生死界
Shennongjia 神農架
shensi 神似
shensuoxing 伸縮性
Shentu 神荼
shi ("artistically created conception")
    詩
shi (history) 史
shi (real) 實
Shi Chao 史超
shishiju 史詩劇
shiyan xiju 實驗戲劇
shiyan yanchu 實驗演出
Shiyue 十月
Shuguang 曙光
shuochang yiren 說唱藝人
shuoshu ren 說書人
Sige xiandaihua 四個現代化
Song Rongzi 宋榮子
Suibi 隨筆
Suo Yunping 所雲平
taiji 太極
Taizhou 泰州
Tang Xianzu 湯顯祖
tansuo 探索
tansuo xiju 探索戲劇
Taowang 逃亡
Tian Han 田漢
Tiananmen 天安門
tuoxie de chanwu 妥協的產物
Wang Jide 王驥德

Wang Meng 王蒙
wanquan de xiju 完全的戲劇
Wei Minglun 魏明倫
weilai de xiju 未來的戲劇
Wenhua da taolun 文化大討論
Wenhua re 文化熱
Wenxin diaolong 文心雕龍
Wucainiao 五彩鳥
wushu 武術
Wuwai you reliu 屋外有熱流
xi 戲
Xia Yan 夏衍
xiandai de dongfang xiju
　　　現代的東方戲劇
xiandai ju 現代劇
xiandai pai 現代派
xiandai yishi 現代意識
xianfeng xiju 先鋒戲劇
xiangsheng 相聲
xianshi zhuyi 現實主義
xiao juchang 小劇場
Xiaohao 小號
xiaoyao you 逍遙遊
xieshi 寫實
xieshi zhuyi 寫實主義
xieyi 寫意
Xiju 戲劇
Xiju bao 戲劇報
Xiju chejian 戲劇車間
Xiju jie 戲劇界
xiju shiyan 戲劇實驗
Xiju yishu 戲劇藝術
xijuxing 戲劇性
Ximao 細毛
Xin Changzheng jiaoxiangqu
　　　新長征交響曲
xin langman zhuyi 新浪漫主義
Xin shiqi 新時期
xin xianshi zhuyi 新現實主義
xinchao xiju 新潮戲劇
xing 形
xingshu 行書

xinju 新劇
xinli chang 心理場
xiqu 戲曲
Xixiang ji 西廂記
xu 虛
Xu Weisen 許渭森
Xuanxue 玄學
xuejiu 學鳩
Xungen re 尋根熱
xushiju 敘事劇
xushuxing 敘述性
Yan Zhenqing 顏真卿
Yandi 炎帝
Yang Jian 楊健
Yanju gongzuoshi 演劇工作室
yanyi 演義
Yazhou zhoukan 亞洲週刊
Yeren 野人
Yeyou shen 夜遊神
yi 一
Yige ren de shengjing 一個人的聖經
youyi 遊藝
Yu Shizhi 于是之
Yu wusheng chu 於無聲處
Yulei 鬱壘
Yun Zongying 鄆宗瀛
Yunnan 雲南
yuyan de yishu 語言的藝術
Zeng Bo 曾伯
zhang 章
Zhao Changkang 趙長康
Zhao Jingshen 趙景深
Zhao Menghu 趙孟頫
zheli ju 哲理劇
zhen 真
Zhen Shiyin 甄士隱
Zhen zhong ji 枕中記
zhenshi yinqu 真事隱去
Zhongguo chuantong xiju
　　　中國傳統戲劇
Zhongguo qingjie 中國情結
Zhongwen zuojia 中文作家

zhongxing yanyuan　中性演員
Zhongyang xiju xueyuan
　　中央戲劇學院
zhongyuan　中原
Zhou Xinfang　周信芳
Zhou Zuoren　周作人
Zhoumo sichongzou　週末四重奏
Zhu Xiaoping　朱曉平

Zhuang Zhou　莊周
Zhuangzi　莊子
Zhuangzi　莊子
zibao jiamen　自報家門
ziran　自然
Zong Fuxian　宗福先
zonghexing　綜合性
zuo　作

Bibliography

Works by Gao Xingjian

Gao Xingjian 高行健. 1981. *Xiandai xiaoshuo jiqiao chutan* 現代小説技巧初探 (An introduction to the modern techniques of fiction). Guangzhou: Huacheng chubanshe.

———. 1982a. *Alarm Signal*. Video recording of the production by the Beijing People's Art Theatre.

———. 1982b. "Tong yiwei guanzhong tan xi" 同一位觀眾談戲 (A conversation with an audience on drama). *Suibi* 隨筆 23:70–76.

———. 1983a. "The Bus-stop (Excerpt)." Translated by Geremie Barmé. *Renditions* 19/20:379–386.

———. 1983b. "Lun xijuguan" 論戲劇觀 (On the concepts of drama). *Xijujie* 戲劇界 1:27–34.

———. 1983c. "Tan jiadingxing" 談假定性 (On suppositionality). *Suibi* 隨筆 29:96–103.

———. 1983d. "Tan xijuxing" 談戲劇性 (On dramaticality). *Suibi* 隨筆 26:116–123.

———. 1985a. *Gao Xingjian xiju ji* 高行健戲劇集 (A collection of plays by Gao Xingjian). Beijing: Qunzhong chubanshe.

———. 1985b. *Wild Man*. Video recording of the production by the Beijing People's Art Theatre.

———. 1988a. "Chidao le de xiandai zhuyi yu dangjin Zhongguo wenxue" 遲到了的現代主義與當今中國文學 (Belated modernism and today's Chinese literature). *Wenxue pinglun* 文學評論 3:11–76.

———. 1988b. *Dui yizhong xiandai xiju de zhuiqiu* 對一種現代戲劇的追求 (In pursuit of modern drama). Beijing: Zhongguo xiju chubanshe.

———. 1990a. *Lingshan* 靈山 (Soul mountain). Taipei: Lianjing.

———. 1990b. "Wild Man." Translated by Bruno Roubicek. *Asian Theatre Journal* 2 (Fall): 195–249.

———. 1992. "Xiju yishu gexinjia Lin Zhaohua" 戲劇藝術革新家林兆華 (Lin

Zhaohua: innovator in the dramatic arts). In Lin Kehuan, ed., *Lin Zhaohua daoyan yishu*, 1–5.

———. 1993. Shanhaijing *zhuan* 山海經傳 (The story of Shanhaijing [*The Classic of Mountains and Seas*]). Hong Kong: Tiandi tushu.

———. 1994a. "Dangdai xifang yishu wang hechu qu?" 當代西方藝術往何處去? (Where are contemporary Western arts heading?). *Ershiyi shiji* 二十一世紀 22:5–13.

———. 1994b. "Xiju: rouhe xifang yu Zhongguo de changshi" 戲劇：揉合西方與中國的嘗試 (Drama: an attempt to integrate Western and Chinese). *Ershiyi shiji* 二十一世紀 21:62–64.

———. 1995a. *Bi'an* 彼岸 (The other shore). Taipei: Dijiao chubanshe.

———. 1995b. *Duihua yu fanjie* 對話與反詰 (Dialogue and rebuttal). Taipei: Dijiao chubanshe.

———. 1995c. *Mingcheng* 冥城 (The nether city). Taipei: Dijiao chubanshe.

———. 1995d. Shanhaijing *zhuan* 山海經傳 (The story of Shanhaijing [*The Classic of Mountains and Seas*]). Taipei: Dijiao chubanshe.

———. 1995e. *Shengsi jie* 生死界 (Between life and death). Taipei: Dijiao chubanshe.

———. 1995f. *Taowang* 逃亡 (Fleeing). Taipei: Dijiao chubanshe.

———. 1996a. *Meiyou zhuyi* 沒有主義 (No ism). Hong Kong: Tiandi tushu.

———. 1996b. *Zhoumo sichongzou* 週末四重奏 (Weekend quartet). Hong Kong: Xin shiji chubanshe.

———. 1997. "Weishenme xiezuo" 為什麼寫作 (Why do I write?). In Wanzhi 萬之, ed., *Goutong: miandui shijie de Zhongguo wenxue* 溝通：面對世界的中國文學 (Breaking the barriers: Chinese literature facing the world), 96–103. Stockholm: Olof Palme International Center.

———. 1998a. Interviews by Sy Ren Quah. Paris, May 2 and 3.

———. 1998b. "Xiandai hanyu yu wenxue xiezuo" 現代漢語與文學寫作 (Modern Chinese language and literary writing). *Xianggang xiju xuekan* 香港戲劇學刊 1:147–159.

———. 1999a. *The Other Shore: Plays by Gao Xingjian*. Translated by Gilbert C. F. Fong. Hong Kong: Chinese University Press.

———. 1999b. *Yige ren de shengjing* 一個人的聖經 (One man's bible). Taipei: Lianjing.

———. 2000a. *Bayue xue* 八月雪 (August snow). Taipei: Lianjing.

———. 2000b. "The Case for Literature." English translation by Mabel Lee. *http://www.nobel.se/literature/laureates/2000/gao-lecture.html*.

———. 2000c. *Soul Mountain*. Translated by Mabel Lee. Sydney: HarperCollins.

———. 2001a. *Chezhan* 車站 (The bus stop). Taipei: Lianjing.

——— 2001b. *Juedui xinhao* 絕對信號 (Alarm signal). Taipei: Lianjing.

———. 2001c. *Wenxue de liyou* 文學的理由 (The case for literature). Hong Kong: Mingbao.

———. 2001d. *Yeren* 野人 (Wild man). Taipei: Lianjing.
———. 2002. *One Man's Bible.* Translated by Mabel Lee. Sydney: HarperCollins.

Works by Other Authors

Artaud, Antonin. 1993. *The Theatre and Its Double.* Translated by Victor Corti. London: Calder.
Bakhtin, M. M. 1981. *The Dialogic Imagination.* Edited and translated by Michael Holquist; translated by Caryl Emerson. Austin: University of Texas Press.
———. 1984. *Rabelais and His World.* Translated by Helene Iswolsky. Bloomington: Indiana University Press.
Bal, Mieke. 1997. *Narratology: Introduction to the Theory of Narrative.* 2d edition. Translated by Christine Van Boheemen. Toronto: University of Toronto Press.
Banu, Georges. 1986. "Mei Lanfang: A Case against and a Model for the Occidental Stage." Translated by Ella L. Wiswell and June V. Gibson. *Asian Theatre Journal* 3 (2): 153–178.
Barmé, Geremie. 1983a. "Chinese Drama: To Be or Not to Be." *Australian Journal of Chinese Affairs* 10:139–145.
———. 1983b. "A Touch of the Absurd—Introducing Gao Xingjian and His Play *The Bus-stop.*" *Renditions* 19/20:373–377.
Beckett, Samuel. 1971. *Waiting for Godot.* London: Faber and Faber.
———. 1990. *The Complete Dramatic Works.* London: Faber and Faber.
Beijing renmin yishu juyuan 北京人民藝術劇院, ed. 1985. Juedui xinhao *de yishu tansuo* 《絕對信號》的藝術探索 (Artistic exploration of *Alarm Signal*). Beijing: Zhongguo xiju chubanshe.
Benjamin, Walter. 1983. *Understanding Brecht.* Translated by Anna Bostock. London: Verso.
Berman, Marshall. 1983. *All That Is Solid Melts into Air: The Experience of Modernity.* London: Verso.
Bharucha, Rustom. 2000. *The Politics of Cultural Practice: Thinking through Theatre in an Age of Globalization.* London: Athlone Press.
Boal, Augusto. 1979. *Theatre of the Oppressed.* Translated by Charles A. McBride and Maria-Odilia Leal McBride. London: Pluto Press.
Brecht, Bertolt. 1974. *Brecht on Theatre: The Development of an Aesthetic.* 2d edition. Edited and translated by John Willett. London: Methuen.
———. 1980. "On the Formalistic Character of the Theory of Realism." In Taylor, ed., *Aesthetics and Politics,* 70–76.
Brook, Peter. 1990. *The Empty Space.* London: Penguin.
Brustein, Robert. 1991. *The Theatre of Revolt: Studies in Modern Drama from Ibsen to Genet.* Chicago: Elephant Paperback.
Chen Long 陳龍. 1995. "Xianshi zhuyi: Xinshiqi xiju tansuo de guisudi" 現實主

義：新時期戲劇探索的歸宿地 (Realism: the destination of New Era drama exploration). *Yishu baijia* 藝術百家 4:14–19.

Chen, Xiaomei. 1995. *Occidentalism: A Theory of Counter-Discourse in Post-Mao China*. New York: Oxford University Press.

Chen Xiaoming. 1996. "The Disappearance of Truth: From Realism to Modernism." In Chung, ed., *In the Party Spirit*, 158–165.

Chen Yong. 1982. "The Beijing Production of *Life of Galileo*." In Tatlow and Wong, eds., *Brecht and East Asian Theatre*, 88–95.

Chow, Rey. 1991. *Woman and Chinese Modernity: The Politics of Reading between West and East*. Minneapolis: University of Minnesota Press.

Chung, Hilary, ed. 1996. *In the Party Spirit: Socialist Realism and Literary Practice in the Soviet Union, East Germany and China*. Amsterdam: Rodopi.

Cosdon, Mark. 1995. "'Introducing Occidentals to an Exotic Art': Mei Lanfang in New York." *Asian Theatre Journal* 12 (1): 175–189.

Coulson, Anthony. 1997. *Exiles and Migrants: Crossing Thresholds in European Culture and Society*. Brighton: Sussex Academic Press.

Counsell, Colin. 1996. *Signs of Performance: An Introduction to Twentieth-Century Theatre*. London: Routledge.

Culler, Johnathan. 1983. *On Deconstruction: Theory and Criticism after Structuralism*. London: Routledge.

De Bary, Wm. Theodore. 1970. "Individualism and Humanitarianism in Late Ming Thought." In de Bary, ed., *Self and Society in Ming Thought*, 145–248. New York: Columbia University Press.

Ding Luonan 丁羅男. 1991. "Tansuo xiju de jiazhi yu zouxiang" 探索戲劇的價值與走向 (The significance and direction of exploratory drama). *Xiju yishu* 戲劇藝術 1:4–6.

Ding Yangzhong 丁揚忠. 1982. "Brecht's Theatre and Chinese Drama." In Tatlow and Wong, eds., *Brecht and East Asian Theatre*, 28–45.

———. 1985. "Bulaixite he women de shidai" 布萊希特和我們的時代 (Brecht and our era). *Xiju xuexi* 戲劇學習 2:13–25.

Dobrez, L. A. C. 1986. *The Existential and Its Exits: Literary and Philosophical Perspectives on the Works of Beckett, Ionesco, Genet and Pinter*. London: Athlone Press.

Dolby, William. 1983. "Early Chinese Plays and Theater." In Mackerras, ed., *Chinese Theater*, 7–31.

Eagleton, Terry. 1990. *The Ideology of the Aesthetic*. Oxford: Basil Blackwell.

Esslin, Martin. 1984. *Brecht: A Choice of Evils*. 4th edition. London: Methuen.

———. 1991. *The Theatre of the Absurd*. 3d edition. London: Penguin.

Fang Zixun 方梓勳 (Gilbert Fong), ed. 2000. *Xin jiyuan de Huawen xiju* 新紀元的華文戲劇 (Chinese drama in the new era). Hong Kong: Xianggang xiju gongcheng, Xianggang xiju xiehui.

Fei, Faye Chunfang. 1991. "Huang Zuolin: China's Man of the Theatre." Ph.D. dissertation, City University of New York.

Fludernik, Monika. 1994. "Introduction: Second-Person Narrative and Related Issues." *Style* 28 (3): 281–311.

Friedman, Edward. 1994. "Reconstructing China's National Identity: A Southern Alternative to Mao-Era Anti-Imperialist Nationalism." *Journal of Asian Studies* 53 (1): 67–91.

Gan Yang 甘陽. 1989. "Bashi niandai wenhua taolun de jige wenti" 八十年代文化討論的幾個問題 (A few questions on the cultural discussion of the eighties). In Gan Yang, ed., *Zhongguo dangdai wenhua yishi* 中國當代文化意識 (Cultural consciousness of contemporary China), 1–35. Hong Kong: Sanlian shudian.

Gao Mingluan 高鳴鸞. 1992. "Tansuo huaju xinlun" 探索話劇新論 (A new discussion on exploratory drama). *Xiju* 戲劇 4:86–91.

Gao Wensheng 高文升 et al., eds. 1990. *Zhongguo dangdai xiju wenxueshi* 中國當代戲劇文學史 (A history of contemporary Chinese dramatic literature). Guangxi: Renmin chubanshe.

Ge Yihong 葛一虹. 1990. *Zhongguo huaju tongshi* 中國話劇通史 (A comprehensive history of Chinese spoken drama). Beijing: Wenhua yishu chubanshe.

Goldman, Merle, ed. 1987. *China's Intellectuals and the State: In Search of a New Relationship.* Cambridge, Mass.: Harvard University.

Goldman, Merle, and Timothy Cheek. 1987. "Uncertain Change." In Goldman, ed., *China's Intellectuals and the State*, 1–20.

Grotowski, Jerzy. 1969. *Towards a Poor Theatre.* Edited by Eugenio Barba. London: Methuen.

Hamrin, Carol Lee. 1987. "Conclusion: New Trends under Deng Xiaoping and His Successors." In Goldman, ed., *China's Intellectuals and the State*, 275–304.

Han Shaogong 韓少功. 1985. "Wenxue de 'gen'" 文學的 "根" (The "roots" of literature). *Zuojia* 作家 4:2–5.

Hawkes, David, trans. 1973. *The Story of the Stone: A Chinese Novel by Cao Xueqin in Five Volumes.* London: Penguin.

He Wen. 1983. "Postscript: On Seeing the Play *The Bus-stop*." Translated by Chan Sin-wai. *Renditions* 19/20:387–392.

Herman, Vimala. 1998. *Dramatic Discourse: Dialogue as Interaction in Plays.* London: Routledge.

Hsia, Adrian. 1982. "The Reception of Bertolt Brecht in China and Its Impact on Chinese Drama." In Tatlow and Wong, eds., *Brecht and East Asian Theatre*, 46–64.

———. 1987. "Huang Zuolin's Ideal of Drama and Bertolt Brecht." In Tung and Mackerras, eds., *Drama in the People's Republic of China*, 151–162.

Hsia, C. T. 1971. "Obsession with China: The Moral Burden of Modern Chinese Literature." In Hsia, *A History of Modern Chinese Fiction*, 533–554. 2d edition. New Haven: Yale University Press.

Hu Miaosheng 胡妙勝. 1988. "Zhongguo chuantong xiqu wutai yu xiandai xifang wutai sheji" 中國傳統戲曲舞台與現代西方舞台設計 (The design of the Chinese traditional *xiqu* stage and the modern Western stage). In Xia and Lu, eds., *Bijiao xiju lunwen ji*, 66–97.

Hu Xingliang 胡星亮. 1995. *Ershi shiji Zhongguo xiju sichao* 二十世紀中國戲劇思潮 (Ideological trends in Chinese drama of the twentieth century). Jiangsu: Jiangsu wenyi chubanshe.

Hu Yaoheng 胡耀恆. 1995. *Bainian gengyun de fengshou* 百年耕耘的豐收 (The harvest of a hundred year's cultivation). Taipei: Dijiao chubanshe.

Huang Lihua 黃麗華. 1988. "Gao Xingjian xiju shikong lun" 高行健戲劇時空論 (The temporal and spatial dimensions of Gao Xingjian's drama). *Xiju yishu* 戲劇藝術 1:42–48.

Huang Meixu 黃美序. 2000. "Shitan Gao Xingjian xiju zhong de seng dao renwu" 試探高行健戲劇中的僧道人物 (A preliminary discussion on the Buddhist and Daoist characters in Gao Xingjian's plays). In Fang, ed., *Xin jiyuan de Huawen xiju*, 296–309.

[Huang] Zuolin 黃佐臨. 1962. "Mantan 'xiju guan'" 漫談 "戲劇觀" (A brief talk on the concepts of drama). *Renmin ribao* 人民日報, April 25, 5.

———. 1982. "Mei Lanfang, Sitannisilafusiji, Bulaixite xijuguan bijiao" 梅蘭芳、斯坦尼斯拉夫斯基、布萊希特戲劇觀比較 (A comparison of the dramatic concepts of Mei Lanfang, Stanislavsky, and Brecht). *Baihuazhou* 百花州 1:163–169, 45.

———. 1983. "Huang Zuolin yu Meiguo liuxuesheng de tanhua" 黃佐臨與美國留學生的談話 (A conversation between Huang Zuolin and an American student). *Xiju yishu* 戲劇藝術 4:1–6.

———. 1988. "Zhongguoshi de shishiju" 中國式的史詩劇 (Chinese-style epic theater). In Zhongguo xiju chubanshe, ed., *Xijuguan zhengming ji 2*, 1–8.

Innes, Christopher. 1993. *Avant Garde Theatre (1892–1992)*. London: Routledge.

Intrater, Roseline. 1988. *An Eye for an "I": Attrition of the Self in the Existential Novel*. New York: Peter Lang.

Jia Hongyuan 賈鴻源 and Ma Zhongjun 馬中駿. 1980. "Xie *Wuwai you reliu* de tansuo yu sikao" 寫《屋外有熱流》的探索與思考 (Exploration and reflection on *Hot Spring Outside*). *Juben* 劇本 6:90–92.

Johnstone, Keith. 1989. *Impro: Improvisation and the Theatre*. London: Methuen.

Kalb, Jonathan. 1994. "The Mediated Quixote: The Radio and Television Plays, and *Film*." In Pilling, ed., *The Cambridge Companion to Beckett*, 124–144.

Kennedy, Andrew K. 1989. *Samuel Beckett*. Cambridge: Cambridge University Press.

Kinkley, Jeffrey C. 1987. *The Odyssey of Shen Congwen*. Stanford: Stanford University Press.

Lee, Leo Ou-Fan (Li Oufan 李歐梵). 1983. "The Quest for Modernity, 1895–1927." In John K. Fairbank, ed., *The Cambridge History of China*, vol. 12: *Republican China 1912–1949, Part I*, 451–504. Cambridge: Cambridge University Press.

———. 1987. *Voices from the Iron House: A Study of Lu Xun*. Bloomington: Indiana University Press.

———. 1996. *Xiandaixing de zhuiqiu* 現代性的追求 (In search of modernity). Taipei: Maitian.

Lee, Mabel. 1996. "Personal Freedom in Twentieth-Century China: Reclaiming the Self in Yang Lian's *Yi* and Gao Xingjian's *Lingshan*." In Mabel Lee and Michael Wilding, eds., *History, Literature and Society: Essays in Honour of S. N. Mukherjee*, 133–155. Sydney: Sydney Association for Studies in Society and Culture.

———. 1998. "Gao Xingjian's Dialogue with Two Dead Poets from Shaoxing: Xu Wei and Lu Xun." In Raoul D. Findeisen and Robert H. Gassmann, eds., *Autumn Floods: Essays in Honour of Marián Gálik*, 401–414. Bern: Lang.

Lin Kehuan 林克歡. 1983. "Zaixian xinli xingxiang de dadan changshi" 再現心理形象的大膽嘗試 (A bold attempt to re-present interior images). *Hebei xiju* 河北戲劇, August, 24–29.

———. 1999a. Interview by Sy Ren Quah. Beijing, May 7.

———. 1999b. "Yuan jujie yong baochi ziwo fanxing de nengli" 願劇界永保持自我反省的能力 (Maintain the reflective ability in theater circles). In Lin Kehuan, *Jiewen yu xixi* 詰問與嬉戲 (Retort and play), 67–70. Hong Kong: Guoji yanyi pinglunjia xiehui.

———. 2000. "Huangdan yu pintie: jiushi niandai Zhongguo neidi de shiyan xiju" 荒誕與拼貼：九十年代中國內地的實驗戲劇 (Absurdity and collage: mainland Chinese experimental theater of the nineties). In Fang, ed., *Xin jiyuan de Huawen xiju*, 235–242.

———, ed. 1992. *Lin Zhaohua daoyan yishu* 林兆華導演藝術 (The art of directing of Lin Zhaohua). Harbin: Beifang wenyi chubanshe.

Lin Zhaohua 林兆華. 1989. "Kenhuang" 墾荒 (Cultivating the wasteland). In Xu, ed., *Gao Xingjian xiju yanjiu*, 231–251.

Liu, Lydia H. 1995. *Translingual Practice: Literature, National Culture, and Translated Modernity—China, 1900–1937*. Stanford: Stanford University Press.

Liu Zaifu 劉再復. 1985 and 1986. "Lun wenxue de zhutixing" 論文學的主體性 (On the subjectivity of literature). *Wenxue pinglun* 文學評論 1985 (6): 11–26 and 1986 (1): 3–19.

———. 1993. "Shanhaijing zhuan xu" 《山海經傳》序 (An introduction to *The Story of Shanhaijing*). In Gao, *Shanhaijing zhuan*, 1–10.

———. 1999. "Bainian Nuobei'er wenxuejiang he Zhongguo zuojia de quexi" 百
年諾貝爾文學獎和中國作家的缺席 (A hundred years of the Nobel Prize in
Literature and the absence of Chinese writers). *Lianhe wenxue* 聯合文學
(Unitas) 171:44–77.

———. 2000. *Lun Gao Xingjian zhuangtai* 論高行健狀態 (On the state of Gao
Xingjian). Hong Kong: Mingbao.

Lodén, Torbjörn. 1993. "World Literature with Chinese Characteristics: On a
Novel by Gao Xingjian." *Stockholm Journal of East Asian Studies* 4:17–39.

Lovell, Julia. 2002a. "China's Search for a Nobel Prize in Literature: Literature,
and National and Cultural Identity in Twentieth-Century China." Ph.D.
dissertation, University of Cambridge.

———. 2002b. "Gao Xingjian, the Nobel Prize, and Chinese Intellectuals: Notes
on the Aftermath of the Nobel Prize 2000." *Modern Chinese Literature and
Culture* 14 (2): 1–50.

Lu Min 盧敏. 1988. "Gao Xingjian juzuo lun" 高行健劇作論 (On Gao Xingjian's
dramatic works). *Xiju* 戲劇 4:36–45.

———. 1999. Interview by Sy Ren Quah. Beijing, May 6.

Lu Xun. 1981. "Ah Chang yu *Shanhaijing*" 阿長與山海經 (Ah Chang and *The
Classic of Mountains and Seas*). In *Lu Xun quanji* 魯迅全集 (Complete works
of Lu Xun), vol. 2, 243–250. Beijing: Renmin wenxue chubanshe.

Luk, Yun-tong, ed. 1990. *Studies in Chinese-Western Comparative Drama*. Hong
Kong: Chinese University Press.

Ma Sen. 1989. "The Theater of the Absurd in Mainland China: Gao Xingjian's
The Bus Stop." *Issues and Studies* 25 (8): 138–148.

———. 1991. *Zhongguo xiandai xiju de liangdu xichao* 中國現代戲劇的兩度西潮
(The two Western tides in modern Chinese drama). Taipei: Wenhua
shenghuo xinzhi.

Ma Wenqi 麻文琦. 1994. *Shuiyue jinghua: houxiandai zhuyi yu dangdai xiju* 水月鏡
花：後現代主義與當代戲劇 (Illusory images: postmodernism and contemporary drama). Beijing: Zhongguo shehui chubanshe.

Ma Zhongjun 馬中駿, Jia Hongyuan 賈鴻源, and Qu Xinhua 瞿新華. 1980.
"Wuwai you reliu" 屋外有熱流 (Hot spring outside). *Juben* 劇本 6.

Mackerras, Colin. 1975. *The Chinese Theatre in Modern Times: From 1840 to the
Present Day*. London: Thames and Hudson.

———, ed. 1983. *Chinese Theater: From Its Origin to the Present Day*. Honolulu:
University of Hawai'i Press.

Mackerras, Colin, and Elizabeth Wichmann. 1983. "Introduction." In Mackerras,
ed., *Chinese Theater*, 1–6.

Marranca, Bonnue, and Gautam Kasgupta, eds. 1991. *Interculturalism and Per
formance*. New York. PAJ.

McDougall, Bonnie S., and Kam Louie. 1997. *The Literature of China in the Twentieth Century*. London: Hurst.

Meng Jinghui 孟京輝. 2000. *Xianfeng xiju dang'an* 先鋒戲劇檔案 (Avant-garde theater records). Beijing: Zuojia chubanshe.

Meyerhold, Vsevolod. 1998. *Meyerhold on Theatre*. Revised edition. Edited and translated by Edward Braun. London: Methuen.

Mitter, Shomit. 1992. *Systems of Rehearsal: Stanislavsky, Brecht, Grotowski and Brook*. London: Routledge.

Morris, Pam, ed. 1994. *The Bakhtin Reader: Selected Writings of Bakhtin, Medvedev and Voloshinov*. London: Arnold.

Morson, Gary Saul, and Caryl Emerson. 1990. *Mikhail Bakhtin: Creation of a Prosaics*. Stanford: Stanford University Press.

Ouyang Yuqian 歐陽予倩. 1990. "Guanyu jicheng chuantong he yanjiu Sishi tixi" 關於繼承傳統和研究斯氏體系 (On inheriting traditions and studying Stanislavsky's system). In Ouyang Yuqian, *Ouyang Yuqian quanji*, 歐陽予倩 全集 (The complete works of Ouyang Yuqian), vol. 4, 363–371. Shanghai: Shanghai wenyi chubanshe.

Owen, Stephen. 1992. *Readings in Chinese Literary Thought*. Cambridge, Mass.: Harvard University.

Pavis, Patrice. 1996. "Introduction: Towards a Theory of Interculturalism in Theatre?" In Patrice Pavis, ed., *The Intercultural Performance Reader*, 1–21. London: Routledge.

Pilling, John, ed. 1994. *The Cambridge Companion to Beckett*. Cambridge: Cambridge University Press.

Pronko, Leonard Cabell. 1967. *Theater East and West: Perspectives Towards a Total Theater*. Berkeley: University of California Press.

Quah, Sy Ren. 2000. "Searching for Alternative Aesthetics in the Chinese Theatre: The Odyssey of Huang Zuolin and Gao Xingjian." *Asian Culture* 24:44–66.

———. 2001. "Space and Suppositionality in Gao Xingjian's Theatre." In Kwok-kan Tam, ed., *Soul of Chaos: Critical Perspectives on Gao Xingjian*, 157–199. Hong Kong: Chinese University Press.

———. 2002a. "Exploration in Action: Gao Xingjian's Theatre in the Context of 1980s China." *Asian Culture* 26:80–103.

———. 2002b. "Gao Xingjian: The Playwright as an Intellectual." *Nantah Journal of Chinese Language and Culture* 5 (1): 201–242.

———. 2002c. "Performance in Alienated Voices: Mode of Narrative in Gao Xingjian's Theater." *Modern Chinese Literature and Culture* 14 (2): 51–98.

Roubicek, Bruno. 1990. "*Wild Man*: A Contemporary Chinese Spoken Drama." *Asian Theatre Journal* 7 (2): 184–191.

Salter, Denis. 1996. "China's Theatre of Dissent: A Conversation with Mou Sen and Wu Wenguang." *Asian Theatre Journal* 13 (2): 218–228.

Schmidt, Paul, ed. 1981. *Meyerhold at Work*. Translated by Paul Schmidt, Ilya Levin, and Vern McGee. Manchester: Carcanet New Press.

Scott, A. C. 1983. "The Performance of Classical Theater." In Mackerras, ed., *Chinese Theater*, 118–144.

Sha Yexin 沙葉新. 1981. *Chen Yi shizhang* 陳毅市長 (Mayor Chen Yi). Beijing: Zhongguo xiju chubanshe.

Spolin, Viola. 1973. *Improvisation for the Theatre: A Handbook of Teaching and Directing Techniques.* London: Pitman.

Stanislavsky, Konstantin. 1967. *Stanislavsky on the Art of the Stage.* 2d edition. Translated by David Magarshack. London: Faber and Faber.

Sun, William Huizhu. 1987. "Mei Lanfang, Stanislavsky and Brecht on China's Stage and Their Aesthetic Significance." In Tung and Mackerras, eds., *Drama in the People's Republic of China*, 137–150.

Sweeney, Kevin W. 1996. "Competing Theories of Identity in Kafka's *The Metamorphosis*." In Franz Kafka, *The Metamorphosis*, translated and edited by Stanley Corngold. New York: Norton.

Tam, Kwok-kan (Tan Guogen 譚國根). 1990. "Drama of Dilemma: Waiting as Form and Motif in *The Bus-stop* and *Waiting for Godot*." In Luk, ed., *Studies in Chinese-Western Comparative Drama*, 23–45.

———. 2000. "Zhongguo huajushi shang de sanzhong huayu yu jutan xingshi chuangxin" 中國話劇史上的三種話語與劇壇形式創新 (Three discourses and innovations of dramatic form in the history of Chinese spoken drama). In Tan, *Zhuti jiangou zhengzhi yu xiandai Zhongguo wenxue* 主體建構政治與現代中國文學 (The politics of subject construction in modern Chinese literature), 135–148. Hong Kong: Niujin daxue.

———, ed. 2001. *Soul of Chaos: Critical Perspective on Gao Xingjian.* Hong Kong: Chinese University Press.

Tatlow, Antony, and Wong, Tak-wai, eds. 1982. *Brecht and East Asian Theatre: The Proceedings of a Conference on Brecht in East Asian Theatre.* Hong Kong: Hong Kong University Press.

Tay, William. 1990. "Avant-Garde Theatre in Post-Mao China: *The Bus-Stop* by Gao Xingjian." In Howard Goldblatt, ed., *Worlds Apart: Recent Chinese Writing and Its Audiences*, 111–118. New York: Sharpe.

Taylor, Ronald, ed. 1980. *Aesthetics and Politics.* London: Verso.

Tian Benxiang 田本相. 1988. "Xianshi zhuyi de huichao he shanbian" 現實主義的回潮和嬗變 (Resurgence and transformation of realism). *Juben* 劇本 8:39–41.

———, ed. 1998 *Huawen xi hui* 華文戲薈 (Meetings of Chinese drama). Beijing: Zhongguo xiju chubanshe.

Tian Benxiang et al., eds. 1996. *Xinshiqi xiju shulun* 新時期戲劇述論 (Discussions on New Era drama). Beijing: Wenhua yishu chubanshe.

Tian, Min 1997. "'Alienation-Effect' for Whom?—Brecht's (Mis)interpretation of the Classical Chinese Theatre." *Asian Theatre Journal* 14 (2): 200–222.

Tian Xuxiu 田旭修. 1988. *Duoshengbu de juchang* 多聲部的劇場 (Multivocal theater). Hebei: Huashan wenyi chubanshe.

Tong Daoming 童道明. 1981. "Meiyehede de gongxian" 梅耶荷德的貢獻 (The contributions of Meyerhold). *Wenyi yanjiu* 文藝研究 5:78–91.

Torrance, John. 1977. *Estrangement, Alienation and Exploitation: A Sociological Approach to Historical Materialism*. London: Macmillan.

———. 1981. "Alienation and Estrangement as Elements of Social Structure." In R. Felix Geyer and David Schweitzer, eds., *Alienation: Problems of Meaning, Theory and Method*, 68–96. London: Routledge and Kegan Paul.

Tung, Constantine. 1987. "Tradition and Experience of the Drama of the People's Republic of China." In Tung and Mackerras, eds., *Drama in the People's Republic of China*, 1–27.

Tung, Constantine, and Colin Mackerras, eds. 1987. *Drama in the People's Republic of China*. Albany: State University of New York Press.

Wang, David Der-wei. 1992. *Fictional Realism in Twentieth-Century China: Mao Dun, Lao She, Shen Congwen*. New York: Columbia University Press.

———. 1997. *Fin-de-Siècle Splendor: Repressed Modernities of Late Qing Fiction, 1849–1911*. Stanford: Stanford University Press.

Wang, Jing. 1996. *High Culture Fever: Politics, Aesthetics, and Ideology in Deng's China*. Berkeley: University of California Press.

Wang Xiaoying 王曉鷹. 1995. *Xiju yanchu zhong de jiadingxing* 戲劇演出中的假定性 (Suppositionality in drama performance). Beijing: Zhongguo xiju chubanshe.

Wang Xinmin 王新民. 1997. *Zhongguo dangdai xiju shigang* 中國當代戲劇史綱 (A brief history of contemporary Chinese drama). Beijing: Shehui kexue wenxian chubanshe.

Willett, John. 1977. *The Theatre of Bertolt Brecht: A Study from Eight Aspects*. Revised edition. London: Eyre Methuen.

———. 1998. *Brecht in Context: Comparative Approaches*. Revised edition. London: Methuen.

Willett, John, and Ralph Manheim, eds. 1983. *Bertolt Brecht Collected Plays, 4iii*. London: Methuen.

Williams, Raymond. 1988. *Keywords—a Vocabulary of Culture and Society*. Revised edition. London: Fontana Press.

———. 1993. *Drama from Ibsen to Brecht*. London: Hogarth.

Wu Wanru 吳婉茹. 1995. "Zhaoxun xinzhong de lingshan" 找尋心中的靈山 (Searching for the spirit mountain in his heart). *Zhongyang ribao* 中央日報 (Taipei), December 22–23.

Wu Weimin 吳衛民. 1998. "Lun dangdai Zhongguo wutai de 'xianfeng xiju'" 論當代中國舞台的 "先鋒戲劇" (On "avant-garde theater" of the contemporary Chinese stage). In Tian, ed., *Huawen xi hui*, 78–102.

Xia Xieshi 夏寫時 and Lu Runtang 陸潤棠, eds. 1988. *Bijiao xiju lunwen ji* 比較戲

劇論文集 (Essays on comparative drama). Beijing: Zhongguo xiju chuban-she.

Xu Guorong 許國榮, ed. 1989. *Gao Xingjian xiju yanjiu* 高行健戲劇研究 (A study of Gao Xingjian's plays). Beijing: Zhongguo xiju chubanshe.

Yan, Haiping. 2001. "Theatrical Impulse and Posthumanism: Gao Xingjian's 'Another Kind of Drama.'" *World Literature Today* 75 (1): 21–29.

Yang, Lan. 1996. "'Socialist Realism' versus 'Revolutionary Realism plus Revolutionary Romanticism.'" In Chung, ed., *In the Party Spirit*, 88–105.

Yao Wenfang 姚文放. 1997. *Zhongguo xiju meixue de wenhua chanshi* 中國戲劇美學的文化闡釋 (The cultural interpretation of Chinese dramatic aesthetics). Beijing: Zhongguo renmin daxue chubanshe.

Ye Tingfang 葉廷芳. 1989. "Yishu tanxian de 'jiantoubing'" 藝術探險的 "尖頭兵" (A pioneer in artistic exploration). In Xu, ed., *Gao Xingjian xiju yanjiu*, 1–22.

Yip, Terry Siu-han. 2001. "A Chronology of Gao Xingjian." In Tam, ed., *Soul of Chaos*, 311–339.

Yu, Anthony C. 1997. *Reading the Stone: Desire and the Making of Fiction in Dream of the Red Chamber*. Princeton: Princeton University Press.

Yu Pingbo 俞平伯. 1988. *Yu Pingbo lun Hongloumeng* 俞平伯論紅樓夢 (Yu Pingbo on *Dream of the Red Chamber*). Shanghai and Hong Kong: Shanghai guji chubanshe, Sanlian shudian.

Yu Shangyuan 余上沅. 1986. "Jiuxi pingjia" 舊戲評價 (Evaluation of traditional drama). In Yu, *Yu Shangyuan xiju lunwen ji* 余上沅戲劇論文集 (A collection of critical essays on drama by Yu Shangyuan), 150–155. Hubei: Changjiang wenyi chubanshe.

Yu Yingshi 余英時. 1978. Hongloumeng *de liangge shijie* 紅樓夢的兩個世界 (The two worlds of *Dream of the Red Chamber*). Taipei: Lianjing.

Zhang Jiong 張炯 et al., eds. 1990. *Xin Zhongguo huaju wenxue gaiguan* 新中國話劇文學概觀 (An overview of new China's spoken dramatic literature). Beijing: Zhongguo xiju chubanshe.

Zhang, Xudong. 1997. *Chinese Modernism in the Era of Reforms: Cultural Fever, Avant-Garde Fiction, and the New Chinese Cinema*. Durham: Duke University Press.

Zhang Yi 張毅. 1986. "Lun Gao Xingjian xiju de meixue tansuo" 論高行健戲劇的美學探索 (On the aesthetic exploration of Gao Xingjian's drama). *Xiju* 戲劇 4:65–75.

Zhao Yiheng 趙毅衡 (Henry Y. H. Zhao). 1999. *Jianli yizhong xiandai Chan ju: Gao Xingjian yu Zhongguo shiyan xiju* 建立一種現代禪劇：高行健與中國實驗戲劇 (Creating a modern Zen theater: Gao Xingjian and Chinese experimental theater). Taipei. Erya chubanshe.

———. 2000. *Towards a Modern Zen Theatre: Gao Xingjian and Chinese Theatre Experimentalism*. London: School of Oriental and African Studies.

Zhen Yanci 甄艷慈. 1993 and 1994. "Dangdai xiju de xin zouxiang—Gao Xing-jian, Ma Sen duitanlu" 當代戲劇的新走向——高行健、馬森對談錄 (The new direction of contemporary drama—a dialogue between Gao Xingjian and Ma Sen). *Mingbao yuekan* 明報月刊, December 1993, 98–101; November 1994, 98–101.

Zheng Baoyin 鄭寶寅. 1990. *Chuantong wenhua yu gudian xiqu* 傳統文化與古典戲曲 (Traditional culture and ancient *xiqu*). Hubei: Hubei jiaoyu chubanshe.

Zhongguo xiju chubanshe 中國戲劇出版社, ed. 1986. *Xijuguan zhengming ji 1* 戲劇觀爭鳴集一 (A collection of essays on the debate of dramatic concepts, vol. 1). Beijing: Zhongguo xiju chubanshe.

———. 1988. *Xijuguan zhengming ji 2* 戲劇觀爭鳴集二 (A collection of essays on the debate of dramatic concepts, vol. 2). Beijing: Zhongguo xiju chubanshe.

Zhou Jie 周捷. 1990. "Cong *Zhongguo meng* kan xieyi xiju de shenmei texing" 從《中國夢》看寫意戲劇的審美特性 (Observing the aesthetic characteristics of *xieyi* drama in *China Dream*). *Huaju* 話劇 5:8–16.

Zhou Zuoren 周作人. 1989a. "Hanyi *Gushiji shendaijuan* yinyan" 漢譯《古事紀：神代卷》引言 (Preface to the Chinese translation of *Kojiki*). In Zhou, *Tan long ji* 談龍集 (On the dragon), 49–54. Hunan: Yuelu shushe.

———. 1989b. "Samanjiao de lijiao sixiang" 薩滿教的禮教思想 (The moral teachings of shamanism). In Zhou, *Tan hu ji* 談虎集 (On the tiger), 200–202. Hunan: Yuelu shushe.

Zhuangzi 莊子. 1983. Zhuangzi *jinzhu jinyi* 莊子今註今譯 (A modern annotated and translated edition of *Zhuangzi*). Translated and annotated by Chen Guying 陳鼓應. Beijing: Zhonghua shuju.

Zou, Jiping. 1994. "Gao Xingjian and Chinese Experimental Theatre." Ph.D. dissertation, University of Illinois at Urbana-Champaign.

Index

absurdity, 19, 58, 65, 67–68, 119–120, 165; situational, 84–85, 87. *See also* Theater of the Absurd

aesthetics, alternative, 168; in post–Cultural Revolution era, 39, 41, 45, 53, 55, 57–59; in pre–Cultural Revolution era, 25–28

alienation, 11, 22, 69, 76, 115, 137, 139, 184; definition of, 146; as state of existence, 141, 143, 145–156, 158, 162

alienation effect: in Brechtian theater, 16, 31, 33, 45, 50, 104, 137, 192nn.5, 7; in Chinese theater, 49–50

Artaud, Antonin, 32, 47–48, 51–52, 71–72, 93–95, 167

avant-garde drama (theater), 56, 61, 63, 85

Ba Jin, 8, 194n.2

Beckett, Samuel, 2, 19, 40, 61, 67, 72, 77, 79, 93, 130, 167. Works: *Cascando*, 68; *Play*, 78, 80; *Waiting for Godot*, 7–8, 16, 62, 64–65, 67; *Words and Music*, 68

Beijing Academy of Film Studies, 196n.3

Beijing Central Academy of Drama, 163–164

Beijing People's Art Theatre, 1, 6, 8–11, 61, 62, 94, 96, 163, 194n.3, 195n.8, 198n.3

Boal, Augusto, 132, 197n.1

Brecht, Bertolt, 6, 8, 16, 51, 58, 70, 72–73, 77, 94, 130, 137, 169, 197n.1; appropriation of, 42–44; and Chinese theater, 49–50,

192n.5; in Gao Xingjian's discussion, 45–46; in Huang Zuolin's discussion, 28–32, ideological aspect, 110, 132, 134; influence of, on Gao Xingjian, 131–133; reception of (pre–Cultural Revolution), 25–36, 192n.3; reception of (post–Cultural Revolution), 36–41, 193n.17. Works: "Alienation Effects in Chinese Acting," 49; *Fear and Misery of the Third Reich*, 43, 192n.3; *The Good Person of Szechwan*, 6, 29, 132; *Life of Galileo*, 29, 36–39, 42, 192n.7, 193n.9; *Mother Courage and Her Children*, 28, 34–37, 192n.8; "A Short Organum for the Theater," 29

Brook, Peter, 93–94, 103

Buddhism. *See* Chan Buddhism

Cao Yu, 9

capacity(ies): of actor, 95, 97, 104, 112, 125–126, 128–129, 131–133, 166; of character, 42, 135–136, 142, 156

carnival, 38; and clown, 115–117, 119; in Gao's theater, 18, 104, 114–115, 118–123; and folk theater, 116–117; laughter, 117–119

carnivalesque, 18, 88, 95, 114–115, 122–123, 197n.9

Central Academy of Drama, 196n.3

Chan Buddhism, 3–4, 10, 19–20, 74, 77, 174, 182, 189n.4, 190n.10, 191n.13

Chekov, Anton, 6, 27, 193n.11

Chinese Communist Party, 4, 33

Chineseness, 12, 16, 186; alternative, 168–174

total theater, 10, 47–48, 51–53, 71–72, 95–104, 166
traditional Chinese theater, 5, 10, 28–32, 45–54, 57, 95, 114, 133, 167, 171, 190n.7, 191n.2, 192nn.5, 7. See also *jingju* and *xiqu*
transcultural, 26, 186, 194n.17; theater, 13–22, 168
tripartite of performance, 133
truth, 124–125, 127–129, 130, 134–135, 138–139, 147, 151. *See also* real *and* unreal

unreal, 37, 108–110, 114, 120, 123–129, 197n.11. *See also* suppositionality
utterance, meaning of. *See* words, meaning of

Vakhtangov, Evgeny, 6, 27
voice. *See* narrative mode

Wang Jide, 108
Wenxin diaolong (Liu Xie), 70–71

Where There is Silence (Zhong Fuxian), 56
words, meaning of, 160–162

Xia Yan, 8
xieshi, 30, 44. *See also* realism
xieyi, 19, 29–30, 33, 42–44, 51, 53, 71, 95, 106, 109, 167, 190nn.7, 12, 192n.4. *See also* suppositionality
xiqu, 69–71, 74, 77, 96, 102, 105, 108–109, 113–114, 116–117, 121–123, 133, 171, 173–174, 190n.7, 191nn.1, 2, 197n.8, 198n.4
Xu Weisen, 110

Yu Shangyuan, 29
Yu Shizhi, 8

Zhao Jingshen, 192n.3
Zhou Xinfang, 70
Zhou Zuoren, 171
Zhuangzi, 74, 157–159, 168

About the Author

Sy Ren Quah attended National Taiwan University (B.A.), National University of Singapore (M.A.), and the University of Cambridge (M. Phil., Ph.D). He is presently assistant professor of Chinese literature at Nanyang Technological University, Singapore.

Production Notes for QUAH / GAO XINGJIAN AND TRANSCULTURAL
CHINESE THEATER

Designed by the University of Hawai'i Press Production Staff
with text in Giovanni and display text in Amber

Composition by Josie Herr in QuarkXPress

Printing and binding by The Maple-Vail Book Manufacturing Group

Printed on 60# Sebago Eggshell, 420 ppi